THE INTENTIONAL REMNANT

Marilyn N. Anderes

The Intentional Remnant

Copyright 2020 Marilyn N Anderes
Cover Design: Larry Stuart

First Printing. August 2020

ISBN: 978-1-7350113-0-1

Printed in the United States of America
www.LivingGodsLongings.com
PO Box 72 Oakland, MD 21550

Table of Contents

Dedication

This work is dedicated to the pastors in our lives and their wives. They have led the way by word and example in being those who stand in the gap for Jesus in our present culture. They joyfully remain on the front lines being God's intentional remnant with love and biblical determination. My husband and I are grateful for these men and women and the outposts of Truth and Grace they have created through their surrender to God.

Ivan and Cindy Ackerman
Mark and Lisa Anderes
George and Carol Anderson
Mike and Sharrie Badolato
Kevin and Michelle Baker
Arnold and Ares Bracy
Greg and Ruth Burgner
Joe and Naomi Byler
Tony and Pam Capps
Tim and Cindy Carson
Dave and Cathy Dent
Larry and Anne Dyson
Joe and Amy Heinrichs
Greg and Jeni Laible
Mark and Dee Lehmann
Matthew and Brandi Lehmann
Tim and Amy Maxson
Jason and Charity Rose
Lew and Nancy Schrumm
Andy and Tracie Searles
Dennis and Faye Short
Jorge and Sarah de Solorzano

Marilyn Anderes

Ron and Wanda Sommers
Greg and Mary Kay St. Cyr
Frank and Stephanie Taylor
Joey and Katie Tomassoni
Tim Webster
Barbara Wilson
Dr. Mark and Joy Wootton

Preface

The first words of the Bible declare that where there is darkness, emptiness and formlessness, God intervenes. *"In the beginning God created the heavens and the earth. Now the earth <u>was</u> formless and empty and darkness was over the surface of the deep, and the Spirit of God was hovering over the waters."* (Genesis 1:1-2 NIV) The formlessness was touched and order came. Chaos was dispelled. The evening was separated from the morning, the dry land from water, the heavens from the earth. The emptiness was caressed and the earth was filled with vegetation, animals, birds that fly, sea creatures and people——male and female people. The darkness was overcome with just a word. *"Let there be light!"*

As human history marched forward, man chose formlessness, emptiness and darkness over the order, the fullness and the light God offered. God judged. And, always a remnant remained and grew by His masterful touch. When the flood came on the land, Noah and his family stood tall and strong. When Sodom and Gomorrah were destroyed by fire, Lot and his family were the called-out ones. With Joseph in the lead, Jacob's family went into Egypt and came out a mighty nation. When thousands bowed the knee to Baal, Elijah led those who did not. Always a remnant.

The definition of "remnant" is a "small, remaining quantity of something"; "a small, surviving group." In the scriptures, the term "remnant" is used in the context of both judgment and salvation. One of the best pictures of God's idea of His remnant is painted by the prophet Isaiah. As he chronicles his call from God to go to a people with calloused hearts, closed eyes, and stopped-up ears in Isaiah 6, he ends with the following words. *"Though the terebinth and oak leave stumps when they are cut down, so the holy seed will be the stump in the land."* (Isaiah 6:13) Isaiah expands the picture when he declares further that those who escape cultural compromise and perversion shall *"take root downward and bear fruit upward."* (Isaiah 37:31) while the unfaithful will know root rot, dust for blossoms and no mention of fruit. (See Isaiah 5:24.)

A stump! Stark. Ugly to some. Plain. It looks dead. And, yet … new growth springs up. The Spirit of God hovers and life appears. As the prophet Ezekiel proclaims: *"I will put My Spirit in you and you shall live!"* (Ezekiel 37:14) A mighty right arm touches and beauty arises. It is the intentional move of God when there is form-lessness, emptiness and darkness.

We are living in such a time. Darkness swirls around us. The choices of the people in our land march daily further from the light. There is emptiness and hollowness of soul and little order, purpose and form. But, once again, the Most High God is raising up a remnant; a small, remaining quantity of people who know Him and His ways and want to make Him known. To many they look dead. To some they are ugly. They are in stark contrast to the glitzy crookedness and perversion of the culture. These are the sur-vivors and the hand of the Creator is on them. A thing of beauty is in the making.

The best illustration I can think of is what has been created at the home of Charles and Betty Lewis in Hanover, Maryland. A large tree was felled on their country acreage. It left a large 9' ugly stump. It looked dead. There was nothing attractive about it. But then the hand of a commissioned chainsaw artist intentionally transformed the remaining stump of the once stately tree into a thing of beauty. There He was! Jesus holding His sheep.

You and I have a choice. As Peter said to the scattered church, we can either *"be carried along by the Holy Spirit"* (2 Peter 1:21 NIV) or we can *"be carried away by the error of the lawless."* (2 Peter 3:17 NIV) It's time to step into the gap; this huge chasm between God and the culture. It's time to be salt and light. It's time to sur-render to the touch of the Master Craftsman's Hand. The holy seed WILL become the stump in the land. The intentional remnant at

churches of fully-devoted followers of Jesus can be part of what God uses to turn our country around.

The culture will not change until the church changes, and the church will not change until individual hearts change. My heart and your heart. We must be sheep intentionally following the Good Shepherd; humbling ourselves, praying, seeking His face, turning from our wicked ways and watching with great anticipation for God to hear, forgive and heal our land. (See 2 Chronicles 7:14) And, if, as some say, *"it is too late for revival,"* we must still intentionally follow the Shepherd, humble ourselves, pray, seek His face and turn from our wicked ways. It needs to be our desire to be fashioned by the Master's Hand into His faithful, intentional remnant. No matter what!

This book explores a vision from the prophet Ezekiel and the call on the life of the prophet Isaiah intended to clarify our eyesight; to help us know what it means to be God's remnant today. We are *"the holy seed"*—*"the stump in the land"*—and I believe God has an expectation that we will grow and bear fruit even in adversity. In the Ezekiel vision we can see the pre-shadowing of Jesus and the mark He places on the foreheads of those who *"sigh and cry over all the abominations"* that are done in the land.

The remainder of the book is devoted to determining what those abominations may be today in our land and how we—choosing to say "Yes!" to be God's remnant—can live His way intentionally. This purposeful, surrendered endeavor to live God's way in the midst of darkness, emptiness and chaotic formlessness serves to inform a *"perverse and dark"* culture that there is a better way.

This book is a call to awareness, an invitation to be part of God's remnant and a call to prayer. The culture will not change until the church changes and the church will not change until individual hearts change. The Spirit of God is still hovering. So, come, my friend. Put your hand in His. A transformation is in the making. Who knows. God just may hear, forgive and heal our land.

CHAPTER ONE –
"THE MAN WITH THE INKHORN"

God's Remnant is Intentional in Living His Way In This Dark Culture

> "The culture will not change until the church changes, and
> the church will not change until individual hearts change.
> My heart and your heart."
> —Marilyn N. Anderes—

These are exciting times in which to live! In Acts 17:26 NIV, in the middle of Paul's apologetic at Mars Hill, he asserts that *"From one man He made all the nations, that they should inhabit the whole earth; and He marked out their appointed times in history and the boundaries of their lands."* That means that you and I were chosen by Him to live where we live at this moment in history. I think it's because God knew *when* in time and space that you and I would have the most potential for bringing glory to His name——if we surrendered to Him. The decade of 2020 in the USA promises to be a dark time, spiraling further into post-Judeo/Christian thinking by the second. The nation has turned its back on God and the results are realized every day—even a global pandemic. But God is at work, raising up a remnant who will bow their knee to Him, confess His name, and live His precepts. Mere complaining about how things are going in the culture is not sufficient. God is raising up an army. The dry bones are coming to life. And, He wants to enlist YOU.

In his book, "Radical," David Platt recounts the story of the

SS United States. In the late 1940's the U.S. Navy commissioned William Francis Gibbs to build the largest, fastest troop carrier ever made. It was to be able to sail anywhere in the world within ten days and to carry 15,000 troops. The only thing is, it never served in that capacity. It sat on stand-by during the Cuban missile crisis in 1962, but otherwise it never sailed under its original intent. Instead, it became a luxury liner for presidents, heads of state and celebrities, fully fitted with air-conditioned staterooms, heated, luxurious pools, elevators, and several restaurants and bars. Consider Platt's own words.

"Things look radically different on a luxury liner than they do on a troop carrier. The faces of soldiers preparing for battle and those of patrons enjoying their bonbons are radically different. The conservation of resources on a troop carrier contrasts sharply with the opulence that characterizes the luxury liner. And the pace at which the troop carrier moves is by necessity much faster than that of a luxury liner. After all, the troop carrier has an urgent task to accomplish; the luxury liner, on the other hand, is free to casually enjoy the trip.

"When I think about the history of the SS United States, I wonder if she has something to teach us about the history of the church. The church, like the SS United States, has been designed for battle. The purpose of the church is to mobilize a people to accomplish a mission. Yet we seem to have turned the church as a troop carrier into the church as a luxury liner. We seem to have organized ourselves, not to engage in battle for the souls of peoples around the world, but to indulge ourselves in the peaceful comforts of the world."[1]

The culture will not change until the church changes, and the church will not change until individual hearts change. My heart and your heart.

At this juncture it is worth repeating the assertions in the Preface of this book. (I am sure there are some of you who never read such introductions.) The first words of the Bible tell us that

"In the beginning, God created the heavens and the earth." Genesis marches on with the exposure of three things that were true BEFORE God touched anything. Genesis 1:1-2 (NIV) tells us: *"Now the earth WAS formless, and empty* (some versions say *"void"*), *darkness was over the surface of the deep, and the Spirit of God was hovering over the waters."* Formlessness. Emptiness. Darkness. And then God touched it and the chaos was dispelled. Differentiations were made. The heavens were separated from the earth. The waters from the land. Male from female. There was no confusion. Order prevailed. Next the emptiness was caressed and the land was filled with vegetation, animals, birds, sea creatures and people. And, with a word the darkness was dispelled. *"Let there be light!"* The problem was that as the history of man moved forward, mankind chose the formless purposelessness, the emptiness and the darkness over what God was offering. And, God did two things. He judged because He is a righteous God. And, He raised up a remnant, because He is a merciful, reconciling, restorative God.

When the flood came upon the earth because man was evil in his choices, Noah and his family were raised up. When Sodom and Gomorrah were leveled by fire, God used Lot and his family to carry His banner. Joseph was sold into slavery in Egypt but Jacob's family came out a mighty nation under the leadership of Moses. When thousands bowed the knee to the Baals, Elijah led those who would not. Always a remnant. Forever a small, surviving group through which God could work His wonders of salvation.

Isaiah was one such faithful man sent into the culture to warn, to speak truth, to offer a return to the intentions of God's heart——purpose and order, fullness, and light. He was told to go to a nation that had eyes that did not perceive and ears that did not listen and understand; a nation with a calloused heart. Wait a minute! That sounds like our culture today. God rounds out His call to the prophet with a word picture of what the remnant would look like. Isaiah 6:13 NIV says: *"And though a tenth remains in the land, it will again be laid waste. But as the terebinth and oak leave stumps when they are cut down, so the holy seed will be the stump in the land."*

When I first read that, I wasn't too sure I wanted to be called "a stump." Stumps look useless; the sort of thing you want to dig out and grind up. But, God is saying, it may look dead and useless and stark in contrast to a glitzy, perverse culture, but He will create new growth. A small shoot can become an effective remnant in the hands of our Skilled Craftsman.

A Strange Vision

All of this focus on being God's remnant came to my attention during a time of fasting and prayer. My heart had been grieved for some time over the state of the nation. The evening news compounded my fears and my disgust. In a daily quiet time, I started reading the book of Ezekiel. When I came to Chapter Nine, my heart was riveted. What on earth was God saying? Was He speaking it just to me or was I to share what I was reading and understanding? I could not get away from the words on the page. God persisted in His prodding. *"Read it again. Savor it. Don't leave it until you understand what I am saying to you. Memorize it. Study it. Meditate on it!"*

I will share Ezekiel 9 (NKJV) with you, accompanied by comment. Verse one declares the following. *"Then He called out in my hearing with a loud voice, saying, 'Let those who have charge over the city draw near, each with a deadly weapon in his hand.'"*

In Matthew 28:18 Jesus declared: *"All authority has been given to Me in heaven and on earth."* In Luke 10:19 we are told *"Behold, I give you the authority to trample on serpents and scorpions, and over all the power of the enemy, and nothing shall by any means hurt you."* (NKJV) Jesus is the ONLY ONE who could give us such authority. Make no mistake. The formlessness (chaos), emptiness and darkness that envelops our world is not from God. It is the work of the enemy. We are told we have authority over ALL the power of the enemy. That means that a God-moment is upon us. Either we will receive that authority and become God's intentional remnant in a wayward culture, or we will not. When you finish reading these words, some of you will go into the schools you have been assigned to, either as a teacher or a student. YOU have authority in that place to live God's way; to draw near to Him. Some of you will remain in your homes and parent your children. YOU have authority from Him to be the intentional remnant in your place of residence. Some of you will return to your workplace. Again, YOU have authority to be God's man or God's woman in that place; carrying a "deadly weapon" with you. What is your deadly weapon? Your prayer and your praise of Him!

Ezekiel 9:2 continues the narrative. *"And suddenly six men came from the direction of the upper gate, which faces north, each with a battle-ax in his hand. One man among them was clothed with linen and had a writer's inkhorn at his side. They went in and stood beside the bronze altar."* We will discuss the "man with the inkhorn" later, but I want us to turn our attention to "the bronze altar." God the Father was speaking and the six men that responded to His call went into the temple and stood next to the bronze altar. That altar was located at the threshold of the temple where sacrifices were made. It is significant in the light of verse three.

Ezekiel 9:3 goes on. *"Now the glory of the God of Israel had gone up from the cherub, where it had been, to the threshold of the temple. And He called to the man clothed with linen, who had a writer's inkhorn at his side."* Why did the glory of God move? The cherub were over the mercy seat, which was located in the Holy of Holies in the center of the temple; where the presence of the Most High God resided. It departed from that place and moved to the threshold of the temple where the faithful ones He was calling out were to meet with Him. We discover in the context of this chapter—in the reading of Ezekiel 8—that God's glory left the place where His presence had been because the temple was being defiled. Ezekiel 8:9 reports that there were *"wicked abominations"* going on inside the temple, with some of the elders worshiping *"creeping things, abominable beasts, and idols."* The women were weeping for other gods. And, Ezekiel 8:16 reveals that *"about seventy-five men with their backs toward the temple of the Lord and their faces toward the east, were worshiping the sun toward the east."* And they had the nerve to declare: *"The Lord does not see us, the Lord has forsaken the land."* (Ezekiel 8:12)

God continues in Ezekiel 9:4 to give directions to the one clothed with linen, who had a writer's inkhorn at his side. He said to him, *"Go through the midst of the city, through the midst of Jerusalem, and put a mark on the foreheads of the men who sigh and cry over all the abominations that are done within it."* What does it mean to "sigh and cry?" I believe God is looking, even now in our culture, for those who will sigh and groan over the things He sighs and groans over. He is seeking those who will cry out to Him for help, and who will cry a message of truth to anyone who will listen.

Directions are given to the other five men in Ezekiel 9:5-6. *"To the others He said in my hearing, 'Go after him through the city and kill; do not let your eye spare, nor have any pity. Utterly slay old and young men, maidens and little children and women; but do not come near anyone on whom is the mark; and begin at My sanctuary.' So they began with the elders who were before the temple."* 1 Peter 4:17 echoes this truth in the declaration that *"judgement begins at the house of God."* The culture will not change until the church changes, and the church will not change until individual hearts change. My heart and your heart. These verses leave us with a choice. We will either be those with the mark on our foreheads or experience spiritual death.

Ezekiel 9:7 compounds the gravity of the situation. The Lord gives a strong command. *"Defile the temple; and fill the courts with the slain. Go out!' And they went out and killed in the city."* This was a desperate command. God's own Law, in Leviticus 21:11 NIV, says: *"He must not enter a place where there is a dead body. He must not make himself unclean, even for his father or mother".* Even in

Orthodox Jewish temples today, it is forbidden to have a dead body on the premises, even for family funerals. So, why would God say such a thing? I believe He was saying, in effect, "You have already defiled the temple so go ahead, and do it up royally." Oh, how the heart of God must have been grieved and the Spirit quenched. But, in His sorrow, He is raising up a remnant. Hope is on the horizon.

Ezekiel 9:8 records Ezekiel's response. *"So it was, that while they were killing them, I was left alone; and I fell on my face and cried out, and said, 'Ah, Lord God! Will You destroy all the remnant of Israel in pouring out Your fury on Jerusalem?'"* You cannot miss the anguish of heart that the prophet was experiencing. "Ah, Lord God", indeed! God's response was quick in coming. Ezekiel 9:9 says: *"Then He said to me, 'The iniquity of the house of Israel and Judah is exceedingly great, and the land is full of bloodshed, and the city full of perversity; for they say, 'The Lord has forsaken the land, and the Lord does not see.'"* Our land is also full of bloodshed. Mass shootings are reported with alarming regularity. And, the cities are full of perversity. The biggest of our cities are rife with homeless wanderers littering city centers with needles, human feces and drugs. Make no mistake. God has NOT forsaken the land. The land has forsaken God. And, God does indeed SEE.

Ezekiel 9:10 records God's intention. *"And as for Me also, My eye will neither spare, nor will I have pity, but I will recompense their deeds on their own head."* Verse eleven rounds out the vision with the following words. *"Just then, the man clothed with linen, who had the inkhorn at his side, reported back and said, 'I have done as You commanded me.'"*

The big question is: Who is this guy? Most scholars agree that the man clothed with linen, sporting an inkhorn, was a pre-shadowing of Jesus. Our Messiah is known as Prophet, Priest and King. In the days of Ezekiel, only the prophets wore the writer's inkhorn at their sides. It was usually a ram's horn turned upside down and filled with ink and writing instruments to record on papyrus the words spoken by their God. Only priests were clothed with linen.

This man was like all the other men called out, but unlike them. And, he was totally obedient. It was this One who put the writing on the foreheads of the faithful remnant God was calling as His own. That would coincide with what the Book of the Revelation reveals. Revelation 22:4 NKJV says: *"They shall see His face, and His name shall be on their foreheads."* The record is speaking of God's servants. God's own. His intentional remnant.

God is making a similar call today. I believe He is appealing to His own. "Be aware. I am calling forth My remnant. I am looking for anyone willing to pray and seek My face for the nation." Are you one He is looking for?

The Need Made Clear

Paul wept before the church at Philippi. He says the following in Philippians 3:18-19 NIV. *"For, as I have often told you before and now tell you again even with tears, many live as enemies of the cross of Christ. Their destiny is destruction, their god is their stomach, and their glory is in their shame. Their mind is set on earthly things."* The apostle mentions four pieces of evidence that would identify one as "an enemy of the cross."

1. Their destiny is destruction. Anyone who turns their back on God is headed for a dark future. The outlook (destiny) is not a pretty one.

2. Their god is their stomach. This refers to all things temporal. Things go into the stomach and go out of the stomach. In and out. In and out. It is not eternal. It is passing.

3. Their glory is in their shame. In our culture today we are no longer just to accept LGBTQ rhetoric. We are now to celebrate it with Gay Pride Parades festooned with rainbow colors. Please don't misunderstand me. I am not *against* anyone caught in this lifestyle. I am, however, *for*

their freedom; for them to know a blessed life. I can either "love" them as the politically correct say I must, or I can love them well, as God says I must.

4. <u>Their mind is on earthly things</u>. In Matthew 6:10, as part of the model prayer Jesus taught, we are told to pray: *Your kingdom come. Your will be done. On earth as it is in heaven."* But, for those with an earthly mindset, the litany is turned upside down. "My kingdom come. My will be done. In heaven as it is on earth."

But Paul doesn't end with these words. Philippians 3:20-21 goes on to say: *"BUT our citizenship is in heaven. And we eagerly await a Savior from there, the Lord Jesus Christ, who, by the power that enables Him to bring everything under His control, will transform our lowly bodies so that they will be like His glorious body."*

Paul also reminds us of the perils of the end of the age when he writes to Timothy in 2 Timothy 3:1-5 NKJV. *"But know this, that in the last days perilous times will come."* Paul's warning includes an extensive list of the ills that will plague men and women in the last days. The accounting continues as follows: *"Men will be lovers of themselves,*

> *lovers of money,*
> *boasters,*
> *proud,*
> *blasphemers,*
> *disobedient to parents,*
> *unthankful, unholy, unloving, unforgiving,*
> *slanderers,*
> *without self-control,*
> *brutal,*
> *despisers of good,*
> *traitors,*
> *headstrong,*

haughty,
lovers of pleasure rather than lovers of God,
having a form of godliness but denying its power."

Paul's advice about folks like this was to the point. *"And from such people turn away!"*

The list is an eerie picture of today's society. We must take note.

Choices

With such evidence staring us in the face, we must make choices. Here are a few options to consider. Will we choose to embrace the cross or become an enemy of the cross? Will we be *"carried along by the Holy Spirit"* (2 Peter 1:21 NIV) or will we be *"carried away by the error of the lawless?"* (2 Peter 3:17 NIV) Will we stand in the gap or ignore the chasm? (See Ezekiel 22:30 NKJV.) Will we be salt and light or will we be bland and hide ourselves under a basket? (See Matthew 5:13-16.) Will we be troop carrier Christians or luxury liner Christians? Will we be God's intentional remnant with His mark on our foreheads or will we know certain spiritual death?

Isaiah made the right choice. When God said: *"Whom shall I send, and who will go for Us?"*, (Isaiah 6:8 NKJV), Isaiah's response was: *"Here am I. Send me."*

I am wondering what your response might be.

What God's Intentional Remnant Looks Like

It's only fair that before you sign on, you know what's at stake. Using an acrostic of the word **R-E-M-N-A-N-T,** I will tell you what at least some of the character qualities of His chosen remnant are.

R – God's Remnant is REPENTANT. 2 Chronicles 7:14 NKJV spells out our part of the equation for national health and God's response. *"If My people who are called by My name will humble themselves and pray and seek My face, and turn from their wicked ways, then I will hear from heaven, and will forgive their sin and heal* *their land."* Our four directives are: 1. Pray. 2. Humble Ourselves. 3. Seek His Face. And, 4. Turn from our wicked ways. The word repentant means "to turn around and go a better way." The culture won't change until the church changes and the church won't change until individual hearts change. Mine. And yours. If we do that—and it's a BIG if—then God will hear, forgive and heal.

E – God's Remnant ENGAGES with the Culture. In Jesus' High Priestly prayer in John 17, we discover that He wants us to rub shoulders with the world. But He doesn't want us to look like the world, but to be different. Set apart. He wants us to be "in the world," but "not of the world." "Sent In," but, "Set Apart." John 17:15-18 is clear. *"My prayer is not that You take them out of the world, but that You protect them from the evil one. They are not of the world, even as I am not of it. Sanctify them by the truth; Your word is truth. As You sent Me into the world, I have sent them into the world."*

There are only four choices with Jesus' directive to be in the world, but not of it. 1. We can choose not to rub shoulders with the world and keep our distance, but it would reveal a heart desire for safety and comfort. We may disdain the world's ways, but it also appears that we disdain the world's people. We have the answer for the culture, but we are not available to share it. Our theme song would be "Onward Christian Soldiers" as we head for the Sunday potluck. 2. We could choose to cavort with the world AND be of it also. That reveals a clear heart desire for pleasure. We would then love the world's people, but also love their ways. We know the answer for societal ills, but we're so watered down, we become ineffective. The theme song of such Christians is "Trust and Obey for there's no other way", sung while at the pub or in a lottery line. 3. We can also choose to be out of the world, but of it. That is total disobedience. Our heart aim with this choice is personal peace and affluence and we find ourselves disdaining the world's people while loving their ways. These Christians, too, have the answer for a needy culture, but they are so busy collecting blessings from God, they have no time to work with God. Their theme song is "I'd

Rather Have Jesus Than Anything" as they drive past the speed limit in their new BMW. 4. The only totally obedient response is to do what Jesus said; be in the world but not of it. The aim of these obedient ones is to exalt God; to glorify His name. They have the answer and they share it with credibility and relevance. They sing all three of the aforementioned hymns—and mean it. And, their impact is immeasurable.

M – God's Remnant Carries A MESSAGE of Truth. 2 Corinthians 5:18-20 NKJV proclaims the desire of God's heart. *"Now all things are of God, who has reconciled us to Himself through Jesus Christ, and has given us the ministry of reconciliation, that is, that God was in Christ reconciling the world to Himself, not imputing their trespasses to them, and has committed to us the word of reconciliation. Now then, we are ambassadors for Christ, as though God were pleading through us: we implore you on Christ's behalf, be reconciled to God."*

When we "sigh and cry", we agree with God about His message. We become His ambassadors; part of His diplomatic corp. We have opportunity to speak so clearly on His behalf that it would be as if He Himself were making the appeal. And, as the old cliché goes, if necessary we can use words.

N – God's Remnant Has NO Fear. Psalm 27:1 NKJV – *"The Lord is my light and my salvation; whom shall I fear? The Lord is the strength of my heart; of whom shall I be afraid?"* – 2 Timothy 1:7 NKJV – *"For God has not given us a spirit of fear; but of power and of love and of a sound mind."* Philippians 1:27-28 NIV – *"Whatever happens, conduct yourselves in a manner worthy of the gospel of Christ. Then, whether I come and see you or only hear about you in my absence, I will know that you stand firm in one Spirit, striving together as one for the faith of the gospel without being frightened in any way by those who oppose you. This is a sign to them that they will be destroyed, but that you will be saved——and that by God."*

"Perfect love casts out fear." (See 1 John 4:18.) Perfect love has a name. It is Jesus. When He is with us, there is no fear. And, when

we host His presence, there is no fear. Opposition makes no difference to us. We become like Nehemiah in the rebuilding of the wall. Sanballat and Tobiah were able adversaries, but Nehemiah's response to their persistent taunts was *"I am doing a great work, so that I cannot come down."* (See Nehemiah 6:3.)

A – God's Remnant is ALL IN! Deuteronomy 4:29 NKJV – *"But from there you will seek the Lord your God, and you will find Him if you seek Him with all your heart and with all your soul."* And, Mark 12:30 NKJV – *"And you shall love the Lord your God with all your heart, with all your soul, with all your mind, and with all your strength."*

You've heard it said before. You're either all in or you're not in at all. God is looking for 150 per-centers. There needs to be a passion to be the one He is looking for who will represent Him well. No turning back!

N – God's Remnant Has NO IMPURITY! Philippians 2:15-16 NIV – *"...that you may become blameless and pure, 'children of God without fault in a warped and crooked generation.' Then you will shine among them like stars in the sky as you hold out the word of life."* 1 Peter 2:11-12 NIV – *"Dear friends, I urge you, as foreigners and exiles, to abstain from sinful desires, which wage war against your soul. Live such good lives among the pagans that, though they accuse of doing wrong, they may see your good deeds and glorify God on the day He visits us."*

We must look different than the culture around us. No stain. No wrinkle. No smudges to spoil a clear picture of Christlikeness.

T – God's Remnant TRUSTS Him! In ALL ways at ALL times in EVERY circumstance. How do we do that? We keep our eyes on Him, the author and perfecter of our faith. When we trust in ourselves, we become anxious because we know we are not sufficient for the task. When we complain and moan and focus on the problems of the culture around us, it causes anger. But, when we keep our eyes on Jesus, we become assured and we lean on His guidance.

Proverbs 3:5-6 NKJV – *"Trust in the Lord with all your heart, and lean not on your own understanding; in all your ways acknowledge Him, and He shall direct your paths."* Hebrews 11:6 NKJV – *"But without faith it is impossible to please Him, for he who comes to God must believe that He is, and that He is a rewarder of those who diligently seek Him."*

Conclusion

The definition of "intentional" is "done on purpose" or "deliberate." Some of the listed synonyms are things like "calculated," "planned," "willful," and "premeditated."

To you, the reader, I appeal. The truth is: *"the Spirit of God is hovering"* over us——just like at the beginning of time. The Father is asking, *"Who will go for Us? Whom shall I send?"* As His intentional remnant you will need to obey——on purpose. Your actions and words will need to be deliberate, calculated, willful, planned. Premeditated!

Missionary to Moslems, Dick Brogden, says "We must not be afraid to try, to cry or to die!"[2] He knows of what he speaks. People are martyred in his part of the world. Regularly. He leads a ministry called "LIVE DEAD!" We, too, must heed his warning. Revelation 12:11 NIV states: *"And they overcame him* (the enemy) *by the blood of the Lamb and by the word of their testimony, and they did not love their lives to the death."* We can TRY to be the intentional remnant because of the blood of the Lamb. We can CRY the truth by the word of our own testimony and we need not be afraid to DIE if we love Him more than our very lives.

This echoes Paul's testimony in Galatians 2:20. NKJV *"I have been crucified with Christ; it is no longer I who live, but Christ lives in me; and the life which I now live in the flesh I live by faith in the Son of God, who loved me and gave Himself for me."*

In his classic work, "The Imitation of Christ", Thomas a Kempis made this observation. "Jesus today has many who love his heavenly kingdom but few who carry his cross; many who yearn for comfort, few who long for distress. Plenty of people he finds to share his banquet, few to share his fast. Everyone desires to take part in his rejoicing, but few are willing to suffer anything for his sake. There are many that follow Jesus as far as the breaking of the bread, few as far as drinking the cup of suffering; many that revere his miracles, few that follow him in the indignity of his cross."[3]

We give our all when we choose to be troop carrier Christians, no longer luxury liner believers and when we embrace the cross (crucified—held by the nails, not Velcro). Then, we are NOT enemies of the cross. We enlist in His army when we stand in the gap, not ignore the chasm and when we are carried along by the Holy Spirit, not carried away by the error of the lawless. We need to long for His mark on our foreheads.

Covid-19 is not such a distant memory in our hearts and minds. Psalm 91:6 has been true. The pestilence that lurked in the darkness showed its destruction at the height of the day. Deaths were up and the Dow was down. One morning in the midst of the crisis God woke me with these thoughts on my heart and mind. The message was clear and pointed. The thoughts were as follows:

"My church has succumbed to a deadly virus and they have been on ventilators far too long. I want you to live! You have to get off the ventilators to live the abundant life I planned for you all along. Instead of demanding that more ventilators be produced, or borrowing as many as you can get from other areas, you need to get off of life support and truly live. What are your ventilators? They are: entertainment practices, business models, psychology, feel good places where everybody knows your name, celebrity attention and appearance-driven meetings; in other words, country clubs. If you get off of these ventilators and breathe fresh air, you will leave your sickbed and walk free. Allow My Holy Spirit to breathe air into your lungs. Allow My Word to give you life. Come to Me for life!"

God's Intentional Remnant is made up of the front-line folks that help others live and truly live, allowing God to be their very breath. Will you say: *"Here am I. Send me?"*

Prayer Points To Consider

1. Repentance and Mercy for us

   a. As A Nation
   b. As the Church of Jesus Christ
   c. As Individuals

2. God's Grace to be *"Carried along by the Holy Spirit"* and NOT *"Carried away by the error of the lawless."*

3. Show us how to "Sigh and Cry" Your Truth, O God

4. However the Spirit leads

CHAPTER TWO – "HERE AM I. SEND ME!"

God's Remnant is Responsive to the Call of God

> "What is our role? First, it is not to abandon the earth to chaos and evil.
> Jesus told us to 'do business until I come.'
> Jesus' followers should be the most energetic in the civic sphere—the best doctors, lawyers, artists, athletes, scientists, mothers, fathers, politicians and civil servants.
> We live and act as signs of the coming kingdom, but we do so with clear-eyed realism that we swim against the tide of humanity and that the world is only going to get worse.
> This makes our kingdom living all the more noticeable, and all the more poignant.
> Yes, the world is self-destructing, but the King is coming."[4]
> —Dick Brogden—

The heart's desire of many who call themselves followers of Christ is that the land they live in and love would know revival; a return to the fear of God and the care of man devoid of any thought of self. The intentional remnant can be used of God; a tool to aid in bringing revival. British writer, Selwyn Hughes, affirms that there are three unmistakable characteristics of true revival. They are: 1. "A palpable sense of God's Presence. 2. A deep desire to be rid of all known sin. And, 3. A powerful impact on the outside community."[5] The Welsh revival of 1904 and 1905 is cited as an example.

It had a profound impact on Britain, Scandinavia and the rest of Europe. Prayer and the reading of scripture led the way and the result was packed churches and a transformation of the spiritual landscape of a whole continent.

The prophet Isaiah gives credit to *"the zeal of the Lord"* for such movements. In Isaiah 37:31-32 NASB it is reported: *"The surviving remnant of the house of Judah will again take root downward and bear fruit upward. For out of Jerusalem will go forth a remnant and out of Mount Zion survivors. The zeal of the Lord of hosts will perform this."* Though there are raised up people who follow God's bidding, it is the Lord of hosts Himself who stirs in the hearts of those He knows will respond to His call. Psalm 22:30-31 NKJV echoes Isaiah's pronouncement. *"A posterity shall serve Him. It will be recounted of the Lord to the next generation. They will come and declare His righteousness to a people who will be born, that He has done this."*

Once again, to refresh your memory, the definition of a "remnant" is a "small remaining quantity of something; a surviving group." The term "remnant" is consistently used in the Bible both in the contexts of judgment and salvation. God judges wayward peoples, but He mercifully raises up a surviving group to help in the redemption and restoration of those same peoples. Noah and his family served in that capacity during The Flood. The fires of Sodom and Gomorrah saw Lot and his family step up to the plate. Joseph led the way for Jacob's family to survive in Egypt and eventually be led to the Promised Land by Moses. Elijah led those who did not bow their knees to the Baals. Always a remnant. Always by God's design. The prophet Jeremiah tells of God's heart intention. *"'But I will gather the remnant of My flock out of all countries where I have driven them and bring them back to their folds; and they shall be fruitful and increase. I will set up shepherds over them who will feed them; and they shall fear no more, nor be dismayed, nor shall they be lacking,' says the Lord."* (Jeremiah 23:3-4 NKJV)

Those verses bring great comfort; even to us who grieve—sigh and cry—over what we see in our land at the beginning of the twenty-first century. God is about the work of gathering. With Him in the lead, there is fruitfulness promised; leaders who will feed, no more fear and dismay. And, no lack. I don't know about you, but I long for that in our land in the present time.

So, how does God see this remnant? What picture does He raise? As was mentioned in the last chapter, this remnant looks like a stump. I know. Not very appealing. But, the picture is hopeful. An illustration may be helpful. One summer not long ago my husband and I traveled with friends to Yellowstone National Park. It was close to the time when wildfires had devastated much of the acreage. It was disillusioning to see the blackened landscape. One charred tree after another. Nothing growing. And then, we saw it. Hidden in the rubble was a tiny clump of wild flowers, reaching toward the sun with kaleidoscope colors and boldly declaring: "We are here and we will not be defeated!" It is the best picture of hope I have ever witnessed. That's what a sprouting stump is. HOPE! This remnant heeds the words of Paul to the Roman church. *"May the God of hope fill you with all joy and peace as you trust in him, so that you may overflow with hope by the power of the Holy Spirit."* (Romans 15:13 NIV) What does the overflow look like? 1 Peter 3:15-16 NIV gives directions. *"But in your hearts revere Christ as Lord. Always be prepared to give an answer to everyone who asks you to give the reason for the hope that you have. But do this with gentleness and respect, keeping a clear conscience, so that those who speak maliciously against your good behavior in Christ may be ashamed of their slander."* That is God's intentional remnant at work; His sprouting stump.

The Call of the Remnant

Two messages come from the mouth of our Savior that define our call as God's remnant. 1. *"Do business until I come!"* (Luke 19:13) and 2. *"Watch and pray!"* (Luke 21:34-36)

1. "Do Business Until I Come!" – Luke 19:11-27

This directive is in the context of the parable of the minas (or talents). You know the story well. Ten servants were given one mina each with instructions to put them to work to yield more. When the nobleman giving the minas doled them out, his word to the servants was *"Do business till I come."* (Luke 19:13) In the Kingdom of God multiplication is expected. Unfortunately, in the current church climate, the result is more often division.

An accounting was made when the master returned. The first servant reported that his mina had yielded ten more. He was commended. *"Well done, good servant, because you were faithful in a very little, have authority over ten cities."* (Luke 19:17) The second servant earned five more minas and again a commendation came with authority given over five cities. The third servant operated out of fear. He still had the one mina, but there was no increase. The nobleman condemned this one, calling him *"a wicked servant."* (Luke 19:22) He instructed the bystanders to take the one mina from the man and give it to the man who had earned ten more, saying these words. *"To everyone who has will be given; and from him who does not have, even what he has will be taken away from him. But bring here those enemies of mine, who did not want me to reign over them, and slay them before me."* (Luke 19:26-27)

This is eerily akin to what is presented in Ezekiel 9. As God's remnant, we can either desire His reign over us and take charge over the city, multiplying God's presence by our words and deeds in the everyday things of life, OR we can be slayed before Him; ones with the mark on our foreheads OR know certain spiritual death.

What does it mean to practically "do business until I come?" The prophet Jeremiah gives us a clue. In a letter that he dictated from the heart of God to the elders carried off into Babylonian exile, he gave the following directions. *"Thus says the Lord of hosts, the God of Israel, to all who were carried away captive, whom I have caused to be carried away from Jerusalem to Babylon: Build houses and dwell in them, plant gardens and eat their fruit. Take wives and beget sons and daughters, and take wives for your sons and give your daughters to husbands, so that they may bear sons and daughters—that you may be increased there, and not diminished. And see the peace of the city where I have caused you to be carried away captive, and pray to the Lord for it; for in its peace you will have peace."* (Jeremiah 29:4-7 NKJV)

Jeremiah finished his letter with words familiar to all of us. In Jeremiah 29:11-14a NKJV he said: *"For I know the thoughts that I think toward you, says the Lord, thoughts of peace and not of evil, to give you a future and a hope. Then you will call upon Me and go out and pray to Me, and I will listen to you. And you will seek Me and find Me, when you search for Me with all your heart. I will be found by you...."*

Our job, then, is to live our lives into however many generations God allows in the midst of a wayward culture. We are to take charge and live His way. In The Message, Eugene Peterson, renders God's intention for His remnant this way. *"So here's what I want you to do, God helping you: Take your everyday, ordinary life——your sleeping, eating, going-to-work, and walking-around life——and place it before God as an offering. Embracing what God does for you is the best thing you can do for Him. Don't become so well-adjusted to your culture that you fit into it without even thinking. Instead, fix your attention on God. You'll be changed from the inside out. Readily recognize what He wants from you, and quickly respond to it. Unlike the culture around you, always dragging you down to its level of immaturity, God brings the best out of you, develops well-formed maturity in you."* (Romans 12:1-2)

2. "Watch and Pray." – Luke 21:34-36

The context of this chapter written by Dr. Luke is the end of the age. Jesus predicted the destruction of the Temple and spoke of *"wars"* and *"earthquakes, famine and pestilences."* (Luke 21:9-11 NKJV) Persecution was foretold and the stern warning: *"you will be hated by all for My name's sake."* (Luke 21:17) He continued to speak of the destruction of Jerusalem and the coming of the Son of Man, and then underscored the importance of watching.

"But take heed to yourselves, lest your hearts be weighed down with carousing, drunkenness, and cares of this life, and that Day come on you unexpectedly. For it will come as a snare on all those who dwell on the face of the whole earth. Watch therefore and pray always that you may be counted worthy to escape all these things that will come to pass, and to stand before the Son of Man." (Luke 21:34-36 NKJV)

Our God is pleading for our awareness. And, our heart-felt prayers. Can we do less? Peter sums up the essence of the message in his first letter to the scattered church. *"Live such good lives among the pagans that, though they accuse you of doing wrong, they may see your good deeds and glorify God on the day He visits us."* (1 Peter 2:12 NIV)

Ten Things Learned About the Remnant from Isaiah 6

The call on Isaiah's life is recorded in chapter six of the prophet's writings. It contains, among other things, insight on exactly what God's intentional remnant is like in character and action.

Isaiah 6:1-13 NIV

[1] *"In the year that King Uzziah died, I saw the Lord, high and exalted, seated on a throne; and the train of His robe filled the temple.* [2] *Above Him were seraphim, each with six wings: With two wings they covered their faces, with two they covered their feet, and with two they were flying.* [3] *And they were calling to one another: 'Holy, Holy, Holy is the Lord Almighty; the whole earth is full of His glory.'"* [4] *"At the sound of their voices the doorposts and thresholds shook and the temple was*

filled with smoke. [5] *'Woe to me!' I cried. 'I am ruined! For I am a man of unclean lips, and I live among a people of unclean lips, and my eyes have seen the King, the Lord Almighty.'* [6] *Then one of the seraphim flew to me with a live coal in his hand, which he had taken with tongs from the altar.* [7] *With it he touched my mouth and said, 'See, this has touched your lips; your guilt is taken away and your sin atoned for.'"* [8] *"Then I heard the voice of the Lord saying, 'Whom shall I send? And who will go for us?' And I said, 'Here am I. Send me!'* [9] *He said, 'Go and tell this people: 'Be ever hearing, but never understanding; be ever seeing, but never perceiving.* [10] *Make the heart of this people calloused; make their ears dull and close their eyes. Otherwise they might see with their eyes, hear with their ears, understand with their hearts, and turn and be healed.'* [11] *"Then I said, 'For how long, Lord?' And He answered: 'Until the cities lie ruined and without inhabitant, until the houses are left deserted and the fields ruined and ravaged,* [12] *until the Lord has sent everyone far away and the land is utterly forsaken.* [13] *And though a tenth remains in the land, it will again be laid waste. But as the terebinth and oak leave stumps when they are cut down, so the holy seed will be the stump in the land.'"*

1. God's Remnant understands the truth about thrones and those who sit on them. – Isaiah 6:1

Isaiah 6:1 begins with a time check. We are told that Isaiah received his call from God *"in the year that King Uzziah died."* The plot thickens when we discover *how* Uzziah lost his throne and eventually his life. The story is recorded in 2 Chronicles 26. Uzziah is listed as a good king, one who *"did what was right in the sight of the Lord."* (v.4) But, verse five of the account offers a pre-shadowing of trouble. It says: *"as long as he sought the Lord, God made him prosper."* It leads the reader to believe by inference that perhaps there was a time when he did not seek the Lord. As the account moves on, verse sixteen highlights just such an incident. Pride won the day in Uzziah's heart. *"But when he was strong his heart was lifted up, to his destruction, for he transgressed against the Lord his God by entering the temple of the Lord to burn incense on the altar of incense."* The priest, Azariah, ran after him with dire warnings. "Get out!" "You are transgressing!" But Uzziah became furious and would not listen to him. The result? Leprosy broke out on his forehead. He certainly did not have *God's* mark on his forehead. And, the leprosy remained until his death because there was no repentance.

Uzziah was no longer on the throne. But, Isaiah knew that God was still on the throne. There are many verses in scripture that remind us of that fact. Psalm 47:7-8 NKJV – *"God is king over all the earth. Sing praises with understanding. God reigns over the nations; God sits on His holy throne."* Psalm 97:1-2 NKJV – *"The Lord reigns; let the earth rejoice; let the multitude of isles be glad. Clouds and darkness surround Him. Righteousness and justice are the foundation of His throne."* Psalm 145:13 NIV – *"Your kingdom is an everlasting kingdom and Your dominion endures throughout all generations."*

It is true for us today, too. It makes no difference who is in charge of the nations; who is on the thrones of global dominions, because God is on His throne and He is *"high and exalted."*

One interesting fact concerns the words *"the train of His robe filled the temple."* Scholars have revealed that in Old Testament times when a king of any region won a victory, he would confiscate the train of the opposing king's robe and attach it to his own. The king with the longest robe had the most triumphs. Our God's train *"filled the temple."* That's quite long! The battles are His and He is the Victor!

2. God's Remnant includes people of humility. – Isaiah 6:2

Verse two of Isaiah 6 mentions seraphim with six wings. These angelic beings sported six wings and the scripture tells us that *"with two wings they covered their faces, with two they covered their feet, and with two they were flying."* Covering their faces, they felt they were not worthy to look on the Lord. Covering their feet caused them to bow. And, flying indicated obedience to the will of God. In each case, the actions actively implied humility of heart.

God's remnant needs to be humble as well. Once again, it is Peter who informs us. 1 Peter 5:5-6 NIV declares: *"All of you, clothe yourselves with humility toward one another, because, 'God opposes the proud but shows favor to the humble.'"*

Jeremiah shows us one practical way we can do that. In Jeremiah 15:19 NASB states: *"If you extract the precious from the worthless, you will become My spokesman. They for their part may turn to you, but as for you, you must not turn to them."* It is easy to be critical of the waywardness of the culture around us, but God is clear. His spokesman, His remnant, will be the one that in humility chooses to focus on the precious, not the worthless. We may turn to God's ways, not the ways of the culture. We must live in such a way that people in the culture around us would want to turn to God for answers.

3. God's Remnant has senses that are alive to the presence of God. – Isaiah 6:1, 3-4

In these verses describing Isaiah's call to service it is apparent that all of his senses were alive to the living God. He <u>saw</u> the Lord. He <u>heard</u> the seraphim calling to one another. He <u>felt</u> the doorposts and thresholds shake. He <u>smelled</u> the smoke as it filled the temple. It begs the question in my heart. When is the last time, Marilyn, that you saw the Lord or heard His voice or felt His presence or even smelled Him in a room? And, for that matter, what about you, the reader?

There are some among you who would agree that we can see, hear and even feel the presence of God, but smelling His presence is a foreign concept. I offer you this account to help you know that the sweet fragrance of the Lord is evident to those who will choose to be aware of it. The true story is told of a young girl, now about seven or eight years old. She was sitting with her mother at her brother's baseball game. It was a refreshing evening with a promise of showers in the air. A breath of air floated by and with it came an unmistakable odor; different than the usual. To that, the young girl said to her mother: *"Mommy, do you smell that?"* She seemed unusually excited. You see, this young girl had an amazing story of restoration to tell. When she was born she had multiple challenging physical defects including a neurological disorder that rendered it painful even for the infant to be held. The medical community reported with certainty. *"She will never walk or talk. She will not understand much and you most likely will need to institutionalize her."* But a miracle occurred. The youngster did walk ...... and talk ...... and understand. In fact, she was as normal as any other child her age. Back to the baseball game. The little girl began to insist. *"Mommy, Mommy, do you smell that?"* Her mother responded that often coming rain smells a bit peculiar. But the youngster persisted. *"No, Mommy. It smells like Him when He holds you close!"* I need no further convincing. What about you?

The psalmist writes of those who make idols and trust in them. In Psalm 115:4-8 NKJV it is said: *"The idols are silver and gold, the work of men's hands. They have mouths, but they do not speak; eyes they have, but they do not see; they have ears, but they do not hear; noses they have, but they do not smell; they have hands, but they do not handle; feet they have, but they do not walk; nor do they mutter through their throat. Those who make them are like them; so is everyone who trusts in them."*

Our culture is unaware of the presence of God. May that never be said of those who identify themselves as called by His name.

4. God's Remnant Understands His Transcendent Holiness and they See and Confess their own Unholiness and the Waywardness of the Nation they live in. – Isa. 6:3, 5

The seraphim called it as they saw it. *"Holy, holy, holy!"* (Verse 3)

Why three times? I believe it is for the Father, the Son and the Holy Spirit. They further declared: *"The whole earth is full of His glory."*

Isaiah's response was sure and swift. In light of the holiness of God he was aware of his own unholiness and the impurity of the people around him. *"'Woe to me!' I cried. 'I am ruined! For I am a man of unclean lips and I live among a people of unclean lips, and my eyes have seen the King, the Lord Almighty.'"* (Verse 5) This is a confession of wondrous proportions.

With any conviction of sin by the Holy Spirit, we have two choices. We can either confess it—agree with God—or try to cover it up. Isaiah was on the brink of a monumental challenge, a God-sized mission, and he needed to be clean before this holy God. The same is true of you and me.

1 John 1:5-10 The Message makes it clear. *"This, in essence, is the message we heard from Christ and are passing on to you: God is light, pure light; there's not a trace of darkness in him. If we claim that we experience a shared life with him and continue to stumble around in the dark, we're obviously lying through our teeth——we're not living what we claim. But if we walk in the light, God himself being the light, we also experience a shared life with one another, as the sacrificed blood of Jesus, God's Son, purges all our sin. If we claim that we're free of sin, we're only fooling ourselves. A claim like that is errant nonsense. On the other hand, if we admit our sins——make a clean breast of them——he won't let us down; he'll be true to himself. He'll forgive our sins and purge us of all wrongdoing. If we claim that we've never sinned, we out-and-out contradict God——make a liar out of him. A claim like that only shows off our ignorance of God."*

5. <u>God's Remnant Receives God's Touch and is Purified.</u> <u>– Isaiah 6:6-7</u>

Immediately after Isaiah confessed his sin God sent one of the seraphim to him with *"a live coal in his hand."* This purifying agent came directly from the altar in the temple. Isaiah reported: *"With it he touched my mouth and said, 'See, this has touched your lips; your guilt is taken away and your sin atoned for.'"* This divine action is historical. Always before in God's dealings with His people, He required them to approach Him with an atoning sacrifice. This is the first time the Holy God reached toward man with the intention of purification. He kept His word. If you confess, I will forgive and cleanse. Indeed!

Malachi 3:2-3 NKJV reports: *"But who can endure the day of His coming? And who can stand when He appears? For He is like a refiner's fire and a launderer's soap. He will sit as a refiner and a purifier of silver; He will purify the sons of Levi, and purge them as gold and silver, that they may offer to the Lord an offering of righteousness."* Undoubtedly, you know the truth of purification. When a silversmith purifies his metal for whatever utensil he is creating, he knows it is at the state of perfection—true purification—when he can see his own image in the molten liquid. It is true of us as well. We are purified completely when the Father sees the image of His Son in our lives. Christlikeness.

This transformation is a delight to our God. When one of our grandsons was born, I was given the unspeakable gift of being present at his debut. When this little guy came forth, all I could think of was that he looked just like his father—our son—when he was born. I squealed with joy. Jumped up and down. Had a hard time containing myself. It wasn't until days later that God spoke to my heart saying, *"Now you know the delight I experience when you look like My Son!"*

6. God's Remnant Hears God's Voice and has a Willing Heart to Serve in His Mission. – Isaiah 6:8-9

What is interesting to me is that Isaiah only heard God's voice *after* he confessed his sin. He lived the will of His Father in heaven. That sounds like Christlikeness. Isaiah 53:10 NIV says about the Messiah Jesus: *"The will of the Lord will prosper in His hand."*

When we confess, we come near to God. In our nearness, we find Him rubbing off on us. Our priority is to be with Him with nothing in the way of a clear relationship. That sounds like the intention of Jesus' heart for His disciples in Mark 3:13-15: *"And He went up on the mountain and called to Him those He Himself wanted. And they came to Him. Then He appointed twelve, that they might be with Him and that He might send them out to preach, and to have power to heal sicknesses and to cast out demons."*

God's Remnant are ones who are called out. And, the priority of the mission is to *"be with Him."* First and foremost. Then, we sigh and cry—as Ezekiel's vision directed—as we are *"sent out to preach and heal and to take authority over darkness."*

7. God's Remnant Understands that the Culture Around Them is Full of People Who Have Dull Eyes, Closed Ears and Calloused Hearts. – Isaiah 6:9-10

No surprise! The culture doesn't get it. Their eyes do not see the wonders of God all around them and the voices of the world are much louder and numerous than the Almighty's whispers to them. The apostle Paul reminded the Roman church that there was no excuse for not seeing and hearing Him. *"For since the creation of the world God's invisible qualities——his eternal power and divine nature——have been clearly seen, being understood from what has been made, so that people are without excuse."* (Romans 1:20 NIV) Did you get that? His "invisible qualities" are "clearly seen." That's astounding. People are indeed without excuse. Paul knew what he was talking about. When the light from heaven flashed around him at his conversion on the Damascus Road (See Acts 9:1-22), he was physically blinded for three days. After that time, God sent a disciple named Ananias to restore his sight. Why? In a testimony recorded in Acts 26:16-18 Paul tells exactly what Jesus spoke to him on that road that day. *"I am sending you to them to open their eyes."* The apostle's eyes were opened so he could be used by God to open other peoples' eyes.

But, the truth remains. In the culture there are dull eyes, stopped-up ears and hardened hearts. We encounter it everywhere. Jesus echoes Isaiah's words in Matthew 13:13-15a NIV. *"This is why I speak to them in parables: 'Though seeing, they do not see; though hearing, they do not hear or understand.' In them is fulfilled the prophesy of Isaiah; 'You will be ever hearing but never understanding; you will be ever seeing but never perceiving. For this people's heart has become calloused; they hardly hear with their ears, and they have closed their eyes.'"*

Jesus goes on in His discourse. *"BUT blessed are YOUR EYES because they see, and YOUR EARS because they hear."* (Matthew 13:16 NIV) Responsibility is attached to seeing eyes and hearing ears. We must tell what we have seen and heard. We must live what we have observed and understood. God's remnant will be intentional in this matter.

8. God's Remnant Knows that the Father Has Longings for these Same People. – Isaiah 6:10

He wants them to see, to hear, to understand, to turn and to be healed. Peter reminded the scattered, persecuted church of this matter. In 2 Peter 3:9 NIV he said: *"The Lord is not slow in keeping his promise, as some understand slowness. Instead he is patient with you, not wanting anyone to perish, but everyone to come to repentance."* The turning around, so essential for healing, is the repentance Peter speaks of.

9. God's Remnant Perseveres. – Isaiah 6:11-12

Isaiah asked a pertinent question. *"For how long, Lord?"* This is akin to David's query in Psalm 6:3 NIV. *"My soul is in deep anguish. How long, Lord, how long?"* What is really astounding is the question

God Himself asks in Psalm 4:2 NIV. *"How long will you people turn my glory into shame? How long will you love delusions and seek false gods?"*

We all want to know "how long?" How long can we stand the barrage of ungodly tongues and unrighteous actions? How long can we endure the persecutions of those who say that ones who speak the truth of God's Word are filled with hate-speech? How long? To be intentional is to persevere. Jeremiah lobbied for staying power with these words. *"If you have run with the footmen, and they have wearied you, then how can you contend with the horses? And if in the land of peace, in which you trusted, they wearied you, then how will you do in the floodplain of the Jordan?"* (Jeremiah 12:5 NKJV)

A comforting word comes through Paul in 2 Thessalonians 3:5. *"God direct your hearts into the love of God and the perseverance of Christ."* The love we need to accomplish this mission is not ours. It belongs to God. The perseverance we need to hang in with the battle is not ours. It belongs to Christ. Our job is to surrender to Him; to stay close; and see these qualities in the overflow of our words and actions.

10. God's Remnant are Agents of Hope. – Isaiah 6:13

"The holy seed (that's you and me) *WILL BE the stump in the land."* The prophet Habakkuk, living in a time and place of cultural demise, teaches us lessons of hope. Habakkuk asked questions. It's permissible to ask God questions in this journey. He said: *"O Lord, how long shall I cry?"* (Habakkuk 1:2 NKJV) Sound familiar? *"Why do You show me iniquity and cause me to see trouble?"* (1:3) *"Why do You look on those who deal treacherously, and hold Your tongue when the wicked devours a person more righteous than he?"* (1:13)

Habakkuk watched. *"I will stand my watch, and set myself on the rampart, and watch to see what He will say to me, and what I will answer when I am corrected."* (3:2)

Habakkuk prayed. (He sighed.) (2:1) *"Revive Your work in the midst of the years! In the midst of the years make it known; in wrath remember mercy."*

Habakkuk proclaimed. (He cried out.) *"Though the fig tree may not blossom, nor fruit be on the vines; though the labor of the olive may fail, and the fields yield no food; though the flock may be cut off from the fold, and there be no herd in the stalls——yet will I rejoice in the Lord, I will joy in the God of my salvation. The Lord God is my strength; He will make my feet like deer's feet, and He will make me walk on my high hills."* (3:17-19)

British writer, Selwyn Hughes makes this assertion. "If, like Habakkuk, we would make the name and the glory of God, rather than world events, the prime focus of our praying, we would come closer to the biblical pattern and be more likely to see His glory revealed."[6] We, too, can be ready for the fray with the same posture as this seasoned prophet.

What the Unfaithful Looks Like

Most people in the church are familiar with the prayer Jesus taught us to pray. It is recorded in Matthew 6:9-13. *"In this manner, therefore, pray: Our Father in heaven, hallowed be Your name. Your kingdom come. Your will be done on earth as it is in heaven. Give us this day our daily bread. And forgive us our debts, as we forgive our debtors. And do not lead us into temptation, but deliver us from the evil one. For Yours is the kingdom and the power and the glory forever. Amen."* (NKJV)

However, the unfaithful among us——those who will not choose to be a part of God's intentional remnant——are the opposite of the Father's wishes as expressed in the manner Jesus taught us to pray. First, God is not their real Father. Second, holiness is not prized. Third, their own kingdom is exalted and clashes with His. Fourth, their own will and way is elevated. Fifth, they are self-sufficient people who will provide their own daily bread, thank you very much. Sixth, they are unforgiving. Seventh, they are not resistant to temptation. And, eighth, they do not bow to God's power and glory.

Contrasts

Stark contrasts are evident between the unfaithful and the true remnant of God. The Unfaithful have closed eyes, dull ears and calloused hearts. God's Remnant, on the other hand, has all their senses alive. The Unfaithful knows root rot and their blossoms are but dust. The Remnant takes root downward and bears fruit upward. The Unfaithful are mere fading flowers, but the Remnant is a diadem of beauty. The Unfaithful are full of compromise, while the Remnant is "Not For Sale!" They do not give in to the ungodly requests of the culture around them. The Unfaithful plows wickedness and reaps iniquity while the Remnant sows righteousness and reaps mercy. The Unfaithful are exposed as being hungry, thirsty, ashamed and sorrowful. God's Intentional Remnant eats, drinks, rejoices and sings for joy of heart. In chart form it would look like the following.

The Unfaithful	Scripture	God's Remnant
Calloused Hearts, Closed Hearts, Dull Ears	Isaiah 6:1, 3-4, 9-10	All Senses Alive
Root Rot Blossoms = Dust	Isaiah 5:24; 37:31; Hosea 9:6; 2 Kings 19:30-31	Takes Root Downward Bears Fruit Upward
A Fading Flower	Isaiah 28:1,4,6	A Diadem of Beauty
Full of Compromise	1 Kings 21	"Not For Sale!"
Plowed Wickedness; Reaped Iniquity	Hosea 10:13; Hosea 10:12	Sowed Righteousness; Reaped Mercy
Hungry, Thirsty, Ashamed, Sorrowful	Isaiah 65:13-14	Eats, Drinks, Rejoices, Sings for Joy of Heart

Conclusion

God's questions pierce my heart. *"Whom shall I send? And who will go for us?"* Isaiah's answer prods me. It stirs my motivation and makes ME want to say *"Here am I. Send me!"* I want to be faithful with the mina He places in my hand and I long to hear His words. *"Well done, good servant. You were faithful."* So, I choose to *"do business until He comes."* I am opting for watching and praying. I ask for His grace to keep my eyes and ears open, my heart soft and my resolve strong. I am counting on His storehouse of perseverance and looking to the Holy Spirit to help me keep short accounts with Him; to confess when I need to. I long to live His purpose in my own generation.

And, I am praying that you do too.

Prayer Points To Consider

1. Lord God, show me if I am truly a part of Your Remnant or The Unfaithful.

2. Reveal if I am a Bearer of Hope or Despair.

3. Make my senses alive to Your Presence. Help me welcome Your touch, Your voice and Your mission.

4. Show me how to persevere.

5. Consider praying the prayers of personal and national confession of Daniel and Nehemiah. (Daniel 9:4-19; Nehemiah 1:5-11)

6. As the Holy Spirit leads.

CHAPTER THREE –
A MESSAGE OF TRUTH

God's Remnant Delivers an Intentional Message of Truth In Word and Deed

> "The art of preaching is to somehow or other get around our third-person defenses and compel a second-person recognition, which enables a first-person response."[7]
> —Eugene Peterson—

The very best messages are those that are life-born; things we observe and act on in real time coupled with a true understanding of who God is. These messages are birthed in awareness of conditions; they are events that we participate in and respond to. The message comes *to* us and continues *through* us. It is what the intentional remnant needs to be ready to articulate to anyone who will listen.

The message of truth for any culture is that there is a God and you and I are not Him. But, we have need of Him. Jesus lived a sinless life, died in crucifixion, was buried, rose on the third day, ascended into heaven, appears to the sons of men and promises to return. That is the Gospel message. True truth.

Eugene Peterson goes on to say after his introductory quote that the prophet Nathan was a perfect example of one speaking true truth. He was the messenger God sent to David after his affair with Bathsheba saying *"You are the man!"* No more playing around with being disgusted with the man in the parable that Nathan offered. NO. You need to be aware and recognize that not only are you capable of the same vile thing, YOU are the very culprit. Defenses are demolished. Recognition is apparent. And, a response of repentance is necessary. When God's remnant articulates His message in the culture around them, they need to bow to God's rescuing grace so that defenses melt, recognition occurs and a positive, humble response is forth-coming. It won't happen if we wag a bony finger of guilt. It won't happen with vitriol. It can occur with truth spoken in love, and, better yet, lived out before the watching world.

Such a message of truth can be observed in Acts 17:16-34. It is the account of Paul and his mission in Athens. The record is as follows in the New International Version.

16. "While Paul was waiting for them in Athens, he was greatly distressed to see that the city was full of idols. 17. So he reasoned in the synagogue with both Jews and God-fearing Greeks, as well as in the marketplace day by day with those who happened to be there. 18. A group of Epicurean and Stoic philosophers began to debate with him. Some of them asked, 'What is this babbler trying to say?' Others remarked, 'He seems to be advocating foreign gods.' They said this because Paul was preaching the good news about Jesus and the resurrection. 19. Then they took him and brought him to a meeting of the Areopagus, where they said to him, 'May we know what this new teaching is that you are presenting? 20. You are bringing some strange ideas to our ears, and we would like to know what they mean.' 21. (All the Athenians and the foreigners who lived there spent their time doing nothing but talking about and listening to the latest ideas.)
22. Paul then stood up in the meeting of the Areopagus and said: 'People of Athens! I see that in every way you are very religious. 23. For as I walked around and looked carefully at your objects of worship, I even found an altar with this inscription: TO AN UNKNOWN GOD. So you are ignorant of the very

thing you worship—and this is what I am going to proclaim to you.

24. 'The God who made the world and everything in it is the Lord of heaven and earth and does not live in temples built by human hands. 25. And he is not served by human hands, as if he needed anything. Rather, he himself gives everyone life and breath and everything else. 26. From one man he made all the nations, that they should inhabit the whole earth; and he marked out their appointed times in history and the boundaries of their lands. 27. God did this so that they would seek him and perhaps reach out for him and find him, though he is not far from any one of us. 28. 'For in him we live and move and have our being.' As some of your own poets have said, 'We are his offspring.'

29. 'Therefore since we are God's offspring, we should not think that the divine being is like gold or silver or stone—an image made by human design and skill. 30. In the past God overlooked such ignorance, but now he commands all people everywhere to repent. 31. For he has set a day when he will judge the world with justice by the man he has appointed. He has given proof of this to everyone by raising him from the dead.'

32. When they heard about the resurrection of the dead, some of them sneered, but others said, 'We want to hear you again on this subject.' 33. At that, Paul left the Council. 34. Some of the people became followers of Paul and believed. Among them was Dionysius, a member of the Areopagus, also a woman named Damaris, and a number of others."

Paul's Observations

Paul was acutely aware of conditions operating in that culture. The exact words for his notice were: *"He was greatly distressed to see...."* (Verse 16 in the NIV) The NKJV says *"his spirit was provoked within him."* In verse 22 Paul confesses *"I see that in every way you are very religious."* The NKJV uses the word *"perceive".* God was making Paul aware of the state of affairs around him. And, God is making us aware in our day as well.

While Paul was in Athens, he was alert to three glaring conditions operating in that culture. 1. The city was full of idols. 2. The people there—residents and visitors alike—spent their time doing nothing but talking about and listening to the latest ideas. And, 3. He observed that the people were "very religious." They had even erected an altar to "an unknown god," just to be sure they had not offended any pagan deities.

While the cognizance of these things is quite amazing, an astounding parallel awareness comes to mind. These same three things are prevalent in our culture today in the twenty-first century.

Full of Idols. An idol is defined as "an image or representation of a god used as an object of worship." It is a "representation"; not the real thing. We were all created to worship, but not everyone worships the true God. When we worship, we bow down and serve that person or thing. The following list is a multitude of entities and philosophies that our culture bows to at present. Some of them are more prevalent than others.

> Comfort
> Convenience
> Individualism
> Entertainment/Pleasure
> "Science"
> Power/Control
> Acceptance
> Political Correctness
> Materialism
> Church Buildings/Programs
> Entitlement
> Psychology in Place of God
> Business Models in Place of God
> Victimhood

The Latest Ideas. There are always concepts that get attention—inside and outside of the church. One of the latest "church" efforts is what some are calling "Progressive Christianity." Though it sounds loving and follows a meek and mild Jesus, when the masks are off it seems to be, as some others have said, just a slower track to denying the faith. Isaiah 5:20-21 pronounces woes on such ones. *"Woe to those who call evil good and good evil, who put darkness for light and light for darkness, who put bitter for sweet and sweet for bitter. Woe to those who are wise in their own eyes and clever in their own sight."*

Another idea the church has concocted is "Seeker Sensitive Churches." That came out of the mega-church milieu and had as its focus "being big." Don't say or do anything that would offend; not even a proclamation of the true truth of the scriptures as they were written centuries ago. Speaking of sin is seen as uncomfortable and unnecessary. Today the name has been changed to the "Attractional Church Paradigm", but changing the name has not made it any less insidious. Folks adhering to such thinking would be the first to say they could not say or do anything that would offend the millennials. Have mercy on us!

Other things on this list would be Inclusiveness and Reparations and Erasing Disagreeable History, and fostering a Victim Mentality. We even have folks in this culture who feign being a victim for the attention it welcomes. Unfortunately, we spend lots of time talking about these things, and others I am sure you could identify, and listening to anyone who desires to harp on them.

A Religious Spirit. This has always been with us. Stephen defined it best in Acts 7:51-53 NIV when he exposed the Sanhedrin—the full assembly of the religious elders of Israel. He said: *"You stiff-necked people! Your hearts and ears are still uncircumcised. You are just like your ancestors: You always resist the Holy Spirit! Was there ever a prophet your ancestors did not persecute? They even killed those who predicted the coming of the Righteous One. And now you* *have betrayed and murdered him—you who have received the law that was given through angels but have not obeyed it."*

Oh my! The incriminating pieces of evidence are stacked high.

1. Stiff Necks. – An unwillingness to be soft and pliable.

2. Uncircumcised Hearts. – Not set apart for God's agenda.

3. Uncircumcised Ears. – Giving credence only to a self-agenda and listening to only what their itching ears want to hear.

4. Resistant to the Holy Spirit. – Interested in their own kingdom and dominion.

5. Given To Being Persecutors. – Punishing anyone who doesn't think the way they do.

6. Receive the Law but Do Not Obey It. – These are people who the prophet Isaiah called out long ago. *"The Lord says; 'These people come near to me with their mouth and honor me with their lips, but their hearts are far from me. Their worship of me is based on merely human rules they have been taught.'"* (Isaiah 29:13 NIV)

There are many in the culture today—in this post-Christian time—who would exhibit these pieces of evidence. And, sadly, there are many in the church who join them. What is scary is what is said will happen when anyone tries to put anything filled with the Holy Spirit to death. The scriptures report that *"Stephen was full of the Holy Spirit."* (Acts 6:5; 7:55) Stephen was martyred. Killed by stoning! (Acts 7:54-59) The religious leaders tried to snuff out anything aligned with the Holy Spirit because they were the epitome of a "religious spirit." Acts 8:1-3 NIV lists five things that will inevitably happen when anything filled with the Holy Spirit is killed.

1. Persecution. 2. Scattering of the true church. 3. Mourning. 4. Destruction. And, 5. Bondage.

"On that day a great _persecution_ broke out against the church in Jerusalem, and all except the apostles were _scattered_ throughout Judea and Samaria. Godly men buried Stephen and _mourned_ deeply for him. But Saul began to _destroy_ the church. Going from house to house, he dragged off men and women and put them in _prison_." (Emphases mine.) A religious spirit is deadly.

Paul's Response to his Observations

Immediately after Paul noticed the prevalence of idolatry in the Athenian culture, he started on God's mission. The record states in Acts 17:16 that he was _"greatly distressed"_ when he saw the problem at hand. The very next verse says: _"So he reasoned in the synagogue ... "_ He started his message of truth with the people of God because he knew that the culture will not change until the church changes, and he was counting on changing the minds of the Jews and God-fearing Greeks who were there. One at a time. But, he didn't end there. He also went to _"the marketplace."_ He spoke _"with those who happened to be there."_ And, who happened to be there? Some philosophers who ascribed to Stoic and Epicurean ideologies.

What is fascinating is that those ideologies are thriving today too. For Stoics, virtuous living is at a premium. For Epicureans, natural and necessary pleasure is the sought-after prize. Both of these philosophies try hard to avoid pain but they do it in differing ways. Stoics attempt to train their perception of what is happening to them and try to live according to nature. Epicureans treat pain indifferently and work at anxiety-free lives by living simply and cultivating strong relationships. We see it in our own culture persistently. One can purchase calming apps for your cell phone or engage in various meditation techniques. There is much talk of who has the higher moral ground, yet few folks look to the God— the King of kings—who created all things and is the author of all that is good and upright. They follow the precepts of those who lived in the time of the judges in Israel. *"In those days there was no king in Israel; everyone did what was right in his own eyes."* (Judges 21:25 NKJV)

Paul continued on from the marketplace and went willingly to the think-tank of the day—the Areopagus. This locale was also known as Mars Hill (literally called Ares Rock) and was the site of Paul's brilliant apologetic delivered before the aristocrats gathered there. It was in this place at the end of his discourse that Paul called *"all people everywhere to repent."* (Acts 17:30) The intellectuals there, who were talking about and listening to whatever idea would be presented next, said to Paul: *"We want to hear you again on this subject."* (Acts 17:32) Paul quickly exited the place. It is my belief that it was because he refused to turn this into a mere intellectual exercise. This was serious business.

As asserted earlier, Paul was working at removing defenses to allow recognition that would usher in a positive response to the true God these people were ignoring. The message delivered to the Romans by this same apostle was true of these men as well. *"Although they knew God, they did not glorify Him as God, nor were thankful, but became futile in their thoughts, and their foolish hearts were darkened."* (Romans 1:21 NKJV)

Responses to the Apostle

Part of the reason this section of scripture has caught my attention is because I identified with the multitude of responses to Paul's message of truth. He was called names. The philosophers named him a *"babbler."* (Acts 17:18) They also misunderstood what he said to them, perhaps intentionally. They reported: *"He seems to be advocating foreign gods."* (Acts 17:18) They were astonished that he actually believed in the resurrection and some of them *"sneered."* (Acts 17:32) But there were also those who believed. The account even names these men and women; Dionysius and Damaris and *"a number of others."* (Acts 17:34)

In delivering messages of truth, I, too, have been called names and have been misunderstood. People have sneered; sitting in the front rows at gatherings with arms folded and looks on their faces that blurted: *"Go ahead! Make my day."* What is the answer for such treatment? More love. Not a backing away from speaking a message of truth, but saying it with love and accompanying it with loving-kindness. The prophet Jeremiah delivered God's message about the Father's desire for those who would be His spokesmen. In Jeremiah 15:19 NASB God made it clear. *"If you extract the precious from the worthless, you will become My spokesman."* The NIV translation renders the same scripture: *"if you utter worthy, not worthless, words, you will be my spokesman."* The NKJV says: *"If you take out the precious from the vile, you shall be as My mouth."*

God's remnant operates for an audience of One. The only response we need to be concerned about is from the Father, the Son and the Holy Spirit. We do not want to do or say anything that will grieve or quench Him and His desires. The most loving, truthful message is to speak the truth plainly about who our God is and how much He is in love with all people. We need to be ambassadors of His longings for freedom of spirit, connection with Him, knowing that He loves us, desiring a purpose for all of us as the priesthood of believers and holiness of living. Our message needs to be one of reconciliation, so our ways need to exhibit a spirit of reconciliation.

Paul's Apologetic

Now we come to the best part of this whole account—Paul's message of truth to the Athenians. After Paul saw the altar with the inscription of *"TO AN UNKNOWN GOD"*, he made this statement. *"So you are ignorant of the very thing you worship—and this is what I am going to proclaim to you."* Today there are many in our culture who are "ignorant" of God. I led a group of young women—wives of NBA players—for a time and I was startled to hear one of them ask: *"Could you tell me what all the fuss is about Easter? I've always wanted to know what that is about."* She had lived in the United States all of her life, was in her early 30's, and had no clue that Easter was about the resurrection of the Son of God from the dead. Ignorance is defined as "lack of knowledge or information." Interesting with so much technology available. Part of the reason the culture around us is lacking knowledge of the Holy is because the church has not told them the truth.

In Acts 17:24-31 we are witness to perhaps the greatest apologetic ever uttered. In it Paul raises up nine things we can know for sure about the True God. They are as follows.

1. **He is the Creator of all.** – Acts 17:24 NIV – *"The God who made the world and everything in it."* The letter written to the Colossian church expands this truth *""He (Jesus) is the image of the invisible God, the first-born over all creation. For by Him all things were created that are in heaven and on earth, visible and invisible, whether thrones or dominions or principalities or powers. All things were created through Him and for Him."* (Colossians 1:15-16 NKJV)

2. **He is the Lord of all.** – Acts 17:24 NIV – *"He is the Lord of heaven and earth."* That means that He did not just make it all, wind it up, and walk away. He is deeply involved in its on-going good. That concept was foreign to the Stoics and Epicureans that frequented the Athenian marketplace.

3. **He is the First Cause of All Things.** – Acts 17:24-25 NIV – *"He does not live in temples built by human hands. And he is not served by human hands, as if he needed anything."* In our culture, the thinking is much more like that

of Nebuchadnezzar, king of old. In Daniel 4:30 NKJV we are told of the king's pompous words. *"Is not this great Babylon, that I have built for a royal dwelling by my mighty power and for the honor of my majesty?"* That's quite different than the truth spoken to the Romans about the Living God. *"For of Him and through Him and to Him are all things, to whom be glory forever. Amen."* (Romans 11:36 NKJV) Our culture, and even some Christians, are stuck with the notion that they are the first cause in all of life. It is <u>for</u> them and <u>through</u> them and <u>to</u> them that all exists and operates. Of course, then, all the glory goes to them. But, it is not so. *"He is before all things, and in Him all things consist."* (Colossians 1:17 NKJV)

4. **He is the Giver of Life.** – Acts 17:25 NIV – *"He Himself gives everyone life and breath and everything else."* Jesus told us in John 10:10 NKJV that *"He has come that they might have life, and that they may have it more abundantly."* Once again, the first cause.

5. **He is the Determiner of Times and Places.** – Acts 17:26 NIV – *"From one man he made all the nations, that they should inhabit the whole earth; and he marked out their appointed times in history and the boundaries of their lands."* We could have been on the planet in Jerusalem when Jesus walked the byways. We could have been in the USA during the Civil War. But, we are in fact in existence in <u>this</u> culture <u>at this time</u> in history because The Determiner willed it so. I think it's because He knows when we have the greatest potential for bringing Him glory and fulfilling His mission—IF we choose to live His way. The time is NOW. The philosophers in Athens seemed to assume that they were the captains of their own fate and the destinies they carved out were of their own making; free of pain, if possible. Not unlike today.

6. **He is the Approachable God.** – Acts 17:27 NIV – *"God did this* (determined our times and places) *so that they would seek him and perhaps reach out for him and find him, though he is not far from any one of us."* Our God is not a capricious god. He is neither uncaring nor far off. He longs for us to be near Him. The blood of Jesus paved the way. Ephesians 3:12 NIV tells us: *"In Him and through faith in Him we may approach God."* Hebrews 4:15-16 NKJV says: *"For we do not have a High Priest who cannot sympathize with our weaknesses, but was in all points tempted as we are, yet without sin. Let us therefore come boldly to the throne of grace, that we may obtain mercy and find grace to help in time of need."* God's favorite word is "COME!" He says it with arms open wide and a smile on His face. This generation needs to know, as the psalmist testified, that *"it is good for me to draw near to God."* (Ps. 73:28) Our culture needs to know; in fact, followers of Jesus need to be reminded, that our time of need is … … always. Acts 17:28a NIV makes it clear. *"For in him we live and move and have our being."*

7. **He is Our Father.** – Acts 17:28b NIV – *"As some of your own poets have said, 'We are his offspring.'"* Yes! He IS our Father. Our Abba. Our Daddy. And, He is everything that "Father" represents; being, name, connection, protection, provision, guidance, discipline, and direction. Think of it! We are His children. And if we are His children, we are His heirs. Heirs receive an inheritance. In 1 Peter 1:3-5 NKJV Peter speaks to the scattered church and reminds them of this inheritance. *"Blessed be the God and Father of our Lord Jesus Christ, who according to his abundant mercy has begotten us again to a living hope through the resurrection of Jesus Christ from the dead, to an inheritance incorruptible and undefiled and that does not fade away, reserved*

in heaven for you, who are kept by the power of God through faith for salvation ready to be revealed in the last time." What characterizes this inheritance? It is incorruptible, undefiled and unfading. And, wonder of wonders, it is kept in heaven for you and me while we are being kept for it—by the power of God. Hallelujah!

8. **He is the Judge and the Source of All Justice.** – Acts 17:29-31a NIV – *"Therefore since we are God's offspring, we should not think that the divine being is like gold or silver or stone—an image made by man's design and skill. In the past God overlooked such ignorance, but now he commands all people everywhere to repent. For he has set a day when he will judge the world with justice by the man he has appointed."* The Call is for us and for all in our culture who will listen to us. "REPENT!" I see no way to wiggle out of the words *"all people everywhere."* These idols that so capture attention will not save the day. We cannot wiggle away from the truth of Psalm 115:4-8 NKJV. *"Their idols are silver and gold, the work of men's hands. They have mouths, but they do not speak; eyes they have, but they do not see; they have ears, but they do not hear; noses they have, but they do not smell; they have hands, but they do not handle; feet they have, but they do not walk; nor do they mutter through their throat. Those who make them are like them; so is everyone who trusts in them."* Our message of truth must be clear and concise. He is the Judge. People and governments are judges only under His eye and will. True justice will only be served in His time, in His way. The rule of law is His.

9. **He is the Victor Over Death.** – Acts 17:31b NIV – *"He has given proof of this* (that He will judge the world) *to everyone by raising him from the dead."* The same power that brings dead things to life is the dynamite that has the capacity to judge all things. We live in a culture obsessed

with death but totally inadequate to deal with it because they do not know the One who overcomes death. *"O Death, where is your sting? O Hades, where is your victory?' The sting of death is sin, and the strength of sin is the law. But thanks be to God, who gives us the victory through our Lord Jesus Christ. Therefore, my beloved brethren, be steadfast, immovable, always abounding in the work of the Lord, knowing that your labor is not in vain in the Lord."* (1 Corinthians 15:55-58 NKJV) God's remnant must be intentional in showing them the hope that is in the Lord Jesus Christ.

Conclusion

To cement these words in practical reality I share with you a current situation. It could easily be a metaphor for Christians in our current culture. It concerns a young woman who is a Master Hairstylist. For many years she worked in an upscale metro hair salon, reaching the top skill level of her vocation in that place. In recent years she has witnessed a decline in the overall spirit of the place; the hiring of some questionable people and the lowering of standards of integrity with the management and ownership of the company. After many prayers over a considerable time, she made the decision to leave that salon and venture into a new company that allowed seasoned veterans like herself to start their own business.

The offer was incredible. She would have her own glassed-in cubicle, her own clientele and her own rules. The parent company owned only the site and offered supplies needed on contract. She decided to make the big jump. Things were going very well. She was making more money than before and the atmosphere could be as she dictated. Her cubicle was a place of laughter and safety. It was prayer central. Anyone desiring prayer would not be turned away. She even led people to Jesus in that place.

Then the unthinkable occurred. The old salon abruptly closed and some of the questionable operators came flocking to this new business venture. Now the new place is filled with people sporting multiple piercings, foul language and highly offensive tattoos. The spirit of the new location is beginning to sour. So, what should she do?

The easy thing to do would be to complain. She could distance herself from the less-than-desirable newcomers. She could flee. She could fight the bad behavior with words of condemnation, a pointing finger and malicious talk. OR, she could stay put and be part of God's intentional remnant. She could remain and show a better way, to speak and live a message of truth. The Message of Truth is Jesus Christ. She could be His hands and feet, His mouth, and His heart for these people and their clients.

It's not always easy. Somedays her heart doesn't follow what her head says would please God. But God is gaining ground through her. It's no mistake that her cubicle is the first to be seen when you walk into the salon. God set that up before the others joined in. It bursts with light and laughter, with truth and life. With prayer, defenses WILL come down. Recognition of need WILL arise. And faces WILL turn in positive response to the One who is the Creator, the Lord of all, the First Cause, the Giver of Life, the Determiner of Times and Places, the Approachable One, our Father, the Judge and the Victor over Death.

What a wonder!

Prayer Points To Consider

1. Ask God to show you what things to observe about the culture in which you live and move and have your being.

2. Pray that defenses would come down, an awareness of need would grow and a positive response to the King of kings and the Lord of lords would occur.

3. Ask God if any of the present-day idols or latest ideas have captured your heart. If they have, repent and ask God for help in eradicating them from your life.

4. Ask God if any of the pieces of evidence concerning a religious spirit are inherent in you. Again, repent, if there are any, and ask His help in surrender to His Holy Spirit.

5. Ask God to help you speak and act with clarity so that the watching world will know the character of the True God.

6. Ask God to help you be unoffended by name-calling, being misunderstood, and being sneered at. Ask Him to help you only care about what He thinks.

7. Enlist God's help in not complaining about conditions around you, or distancing yourself, or running away from the fray or pointing fingers. Ask Him to help you "extract the precious from the worthless."

8. As the Spirit leads.

CHAPTER FOUR –
TODAY'S ABOMINATIONS

God's Remnant Knows What
Grieves the Heart of God

> "To try to live life completely independent of God is like trying to drive a beautiful boat down a superhighway. That boat is a wonderful creation, loaded with amazing design details, but it was not built to run on a hard surface. If you try to run it on land, you will destroy the boat and you will go nowhere fast."[8]
> ——Paul David Tripp——

Because God desires for us to be close, when we choose to live independent of Him several things will inevitably happen. First, and most important, we grieve the heart of God. And, second, we will march ignorantly away from what pleases His heart. There is a name given to those things that God finds hateful, detestable and grievous. It is "abomination." It is like trying to steer a boat down a superhighway and it makes no sense.

The prophet Ezekiel's vision, spoken of in an earlier chapter, declared what the Lord said to the man clothed with linen who had a writer's inkhorn at his side. *"Go through the midst of the city, through the midst of Jerusalem, and put a mark on the foreheads of the men who sigh and cry over all the abominations that are done within it."* (Ezekiel 9:4 NKJV) We have already ascertained that this man—like other men, but unlike them—was none other than a pre-shadowing of our Jesus. And this Jesus has been clearly portrayed in Scripture as prophet, priest and king. The prophets, God's proclaiming messengers—faithful witnesses—carried inkhorns to record their messengers. The priests, God's mediating "bridges" between God and man, were the only ones who wore linen. Jesus is our High Priest. And He is the King of kings with authority over all things.

The mark that Jesus put on the foreheads of certain men was placed there because they were ones who were identified as *"sighing and crying"* over all the abominations occurring in the land. These marked men were the intentional remnant God was raising up to come alongside Him in bringing redemption and restoration to a wayward culture. So, the obvious question is: What were they sighing and crying about? Ezekiel, chapter eight, helps us to see the ways even the religious leaders were grieving God's heart. The more important question is: What are today's abominations about which we are to respond by living God's way and speaking when necessary?

To answer that question in my own heart, I spent months in prayer and fasting. "Show me, Lord, what are we to stand with You on right now? What is detestable to You in our culture? How could I, only one, make a difference?" God began to answer my query with scripture. In Luke 16:15 He spoke to the Pharisees and said to them: *"You are those who justify yourselves before men, but God knows your hearts. For what is highly esteemed among men is an abomination in the sight of God."* It forced me into a quest to discover what men and women esteem as contrasted with what God esteems. I found the following to be the essence of what defines an "abomination" to God. Read on to see what I mean.

ESTEEMED AMONG MEN	ESTEEMED IN GOD'S SIGHT
Pride and Swagger	Humility
Self-Promotion and Protection	Looking To the Interests of Others
Independence	Surrender/Dependence on God
Eating, Drinking, Being Merry	Being Hungry and Thirsty for God
Living Behind Masks	Confession and Vulnerability
Being In Charge	Being Under Authority
The Avoidance of Suffering	Sharing in Christ's Sufferings
Being Able To Articulate	Being Able To Listen
Outward Appearance	The Heart

The next thing God made clear to me was that if I chose to be a part of His intentional remnant, it would be costly. Once again, the scriptures were informative. Jeremiah was known to stand tall in his culture for God's ways and he was thrown into a cistern and his writings were burned. Micaiah was hated because he would not lie and speak what God had NOT told him to say. He exposed the lying spirit of the false prophets and for his effort, he was struck and imprisoned. Jesus, of course, was crucified in His perfect following of the Father's will. And, Paul, was beaten, imprisoned and eventually beheaded in his zeal to follow God's commands.

The following are the abominations raised up in our culture today. Surely there are more and they do not appear in any specific order. Some of them refer specifically to God's own people and some of them are rampant in the worldly culture swirling around us. They are:

1. Not Many of God's Own People Passionate To Spend Time With Him in Prayer
2. No Fear of God
3. Little Gratefulness
4. Little Attention to Absolute Truth
5. Little Regard for God's Word
6. A Lack of Responsible Shepherds

7. Little to No Purity
8. Upside-Down Thinking
9. An Unwillingness to Embrace Suffering
10. Little Regard for the Sanctity of Life
11. People Not Maintaining God's Unity
12. God's Own People Not Living in His Power

We will look briefly at each entry. The need to live God's way will be highlighted as well as examples of cultural and church abuse. And each "abomination" will be inspected in light of the truth that surrounds it. This chapter is only an introduction to each abomination. Each of the remaining twelve chapters will discuss each in length.

Not Many of God's Own People Passionate to Spend Time With Him in Prayer

God's remnant must spend extravagant time with Him in prayer. Without doing that we have little to nothing to offer the watching world. A good example of that was on 9/11 when our country was attacked by terrorists. Many people, unused to cathedrals, synagogues and local houses of worship flocked to these locations. Fear had a tight grip on the human heart. What was happening? How can we make sense of this? What help is available? The Covid-19 pandemic posed the same questions.

The problem with 9/11 was that God's church was impotent and people looking for help soon learned that many of those houses of worship were nothing more than "country clubs" with religious labels. As others have said before me, "They were looking for a Bakery where they might find the Bread of Life, but all they found was the faint smell of something baking that had no substance." The story is still out on the Covid-19 aftermath.

A contemporary Christian song implores the church "to live loud." But, before it can live loud in this culture of cacophony, they must first be still in prayer in a personal relationship with the

One who can transform all things—even the pray-er. Billy Graham is quoted as saying "To get nations back on their feet, we must first get down on our knees." No revival has ever occurred without a concert of prayer preceding it. Even one heart bowing to the Almighty.

No Fear of God

God's remnant must reverence Him. We need people who fear God; even in small ways. I learned just how absent the fear of God is in our culture while gathering research for this book. I usually start with on-line entries on any subject and then dig deeper as the need arises. When I checked the internet for "Fear of God", I found only one entry that discussed the fear of God I was looking for. All the rest—and there were over fifty more—were concerned with a clothing design line called, you guessed it, "Fear of God." The clothes are the genius of their creator Jerry Lorenzo and are of the grunge variety that appeals to young Hollywood big names and hopefuls. A downline is sold for regular folks at places like PacSun under the title "Fog."

I am here to tell anyone who will listen that the fear of the living God that I am talking about is not in the fog. It is real. And, when neglected, even in small ways—perhaps especially in small ways—it grieves the heart of the Most High. It necessitates the understanding that even though you may be able to trick people, you will never be able to con a watching God. He notices if you short change someone or speak a "white lie" or exceed the speed limit by ten miles per hour. He is not looking to wag a finger or scowl at you. He wants to transform your life from a self-center to a God-center and that grace deserves more respect and awe than that. The hymn-writer, John Newton, said in his "Amazing Grace" offering: "Twas grace that taught my heart to fear."

Pastor Adrian Rogers is credited with saying the following. "A child delights in what he has. A youth delights in what he does. An adult delights in who he is. The more mature you are, the more you desire to be something, not just have or do something. So, what do you desire today? To be someone known for the way they dress? Or the deals they close? Or the house they live in? Or one who fears God, is totally surrendered and utterly devoted to Him?"⁹

"The fear of the Lord is the beginning of wisdom." (Psalm 111:10)

Little Gratefulness

God's remnant needs to be intentional in gratefulness, not complaining. This is an identity issue. If life is all about you, then it will be apparent that not everything goes your way and you will be a complainer. But, if it is all about God, you will wonder at His daily blessings, far beyond your deserving, and you will have a grateful heart.

The culture we live in is steeped in entitlement. Once again, while doing research for this material, I read a secular book on the value of being grateful. One statement in particular in this volume astounded me. Though the author realized the value of gratefulness physically, mentally and emotionally, she confessed that she did not know who to thank. I have a suggestion for her.

This is not a new issue. Jesus asked a piercing question after ten lepers were healed, but only one returned to give thanks. *"Where are the nine?"* (Luke 17:17) Many scriptures give us a heads up that *"in the last days"* there will be a host of apparent difficulties and among them will be people who are *"unthankful."* (See 2 Timothy 3:1-5.)

G. K. Chesterton is credited with saying: "I would maintain that thanks are the highest form of thought, and that gratitude is happiness doubled with wonder."¹⁰

Little Attention to Absolute Truth

I recently saw a cartoon with two movies showing at a local theater. One offering was titled "An Inconvenient Truth." There was no one in the queue. The other movie was called "A Reassuring Lie". The waiting line for that flick was around the block.

God's remnant needs to hold to absolute truth as God defines it at all cost; not disagreeably, but speaking and living the truth in love. So-called "progressive" thinking is merely a slower track to denying the faith.

Two quotes are helpful at this juncture. Dr. Henry Cloud has said: "When Truth presents itself, the wise person sees the light, takes it in, and makes adjustments. The fool tries to adjust the Truth so he does not have to adjust to it."[11] And, C.S. Lewis has asserted: "There is no neutral ground in the universe; every square inch, every split-second, is claimed by God and counter-claimed by Satan."[12]

Our culture is big on doing what feels good and on embracing situational ethics. It is like the time of the judges of Israel. *"Everyone did what was right in his own eyes."* (Judges 21:25)

Little Regard for God's Holy, Inspired, Eternal Word

In an April, 2018 GQ Magazine article titled "Twenty-one Books You Don't Have To Read", the secular editors included the Holy Bible in their list of throw-aways. Concerning all the books mentioned, the editors spoke of them with the following words. "Some are racist and some are sexist, but most are just really, really boring. So we—a group of unboring writers—give you permission to strike these books from the canon."[13]

And, lest you think this problem lurks only in the culture outside of the church, I bring your attention to a Barna study of March 27, 2018. The question asked of church-goers included in the survey was: "Have you heard of the Great Commission?" The statistics that emerged are alarming. 6% said "I'm not sure." 25% reported "Yes, but I can't recall the exact meaning." 17% said "Yes, and it means…." 51% said "No!"

God told us His intention for His Word in Hebrews 4:12. *"For the word of God is living and powerful* (some versions say "active") *and sharper than any two-edged sword, piercing even to the division of soul and spirit, and of joints and marrow, and is a discerner ("judge"* in other translations) *of the thoughts and intents of the heart."* It is alive; NOT dead. It is powerfully active; NOT passive and impotent. It is sharp; NOT dull. It is piercing; NOT bull-dozing. And it is a discerning judge of thoughts and actions; NOT benign. It is worthy of attention and heeding. God's remnant should be the first to take it seriously.

A Lack of Responsible Shepherds

In John 10:1 NKJV Jesus says: *"Most assuredly, I say to you, he who does not enter the sheepfold by the door, but climbs up some other way, the same is a thief and a robber."* That same word in The Message says: *"Let me set this before you as plainly as I can. If a person climbs over or through the fence of a sheep pen instead of going through the gate, you know he's up to no good—a sheep rustler!"* Later in the same chapter Jesus identified Himself as "The Gate." (John 10:7-9) In other words, if any leader tries to approach the sheep by any other means than Jesus, he is considered a sheep-rustler. Sheep-rustlers are thieves. In the Middle Ages their motivation was poverty, but in the present age, where they are still in operation, what keeps them on the move is greed.

Peter made it clear in his letter to the scattered church that no flock belongs to its leader; the under-shepherd. It is owned by God Himself. He paid the price for it. 1 Peter 5:2 commands *"Shepherd the flock of God which is among you."* And He is looking for willing servant leaders who don't lord it over their flock but serve as shining examples. Unfortunately, there are many leaders in the church today who do not live up to those expectations. God's remnant needs to be intentional about being shepherds who care for the flock and certainly are ones who do not lead God's people astray.

One example of abuse in this arena was showcased in an interview in a Seattle newspaper of a pastor in the Presbyterian Church USA. The clergyman had served his flock for several decades and was now embarking on retirement. The reporter's question was simple. "What is the most significant contribution you have made in your many years as minister at this church?" The man's reply was astounding. "I took a little Bible-believing congregation and turned it into a multi-faith community. The greatest moment in my personal spirituality was the moment I discovered that Jesus is not God, not Savior; not even an historical individual; but the concept of love." If you are like me, my response was utter amazement. Mouth open, but nothing to say. I thought to myself upon reading this that I would die for the cause of Christ, but would never die for a "concept of love."

John Ortberg has said: "God has entrusted us with His most precious treasure——people. He asks us to shepherd and mold them into strong disciples, with brave faith and good character."[14] I don't think the man mentioned above qualified.

Little or No Purity
God's remnant needs to intentionally pursue holy living allowing the Refiner's Fire to purify them. Missionary Dick Brogden has said: "We are not the Christ; we are not even mini-Christs. We are not the Word of God. We are the stationary on which He writes, and as such, we need to be clean, pure, holy and true. Nothing must detract from the handwriting of God."[15] His statement motivates me to ask myself: "What smudges does my life create in His penmanship?"

Cultural lack of purity is not difficult to find. We have witnessed sexual improprieties in government, media, academia, entertainment and sports. Abuse issues have been brought front and center with the #MeToo movement. There is a pornography epidemic in this country and it is not just with the secularists among us. Ecclesiastical pedophilia is rampant especially among priests in the Catholic Church. There are more and more couples living together before marriage; even Christians, who see nothing wrong with that social dynamic.

But, God has declared that His people need to be set apart for His personal use. The process is called sanctification. It is hard to curb appetites and our senses are the first to be tempted. Remember the Sunday School song you sang as a youngster? "Be careful little eyes what you see. Be careful little eyes what you see. For the Father up above is looking down in love, so be careful little eyes what you see." The tune goes on to mention what little hands touch, little ears hear, and little mouths taste. The senses are a prime target for the enemy because he knows that God made the senses so that we might use them to worship Him.

Hebrews 12:16 in the Message gives an apt command. *"Watch out for the ESAU SYNDROME: Trading away God's lifelong gift in order to satisfy a short-term appetite."*

Upside-Down Thinking
Isaiah 55:8-9 NIV declares a bold truth. *"'For my thoughts are not your thoughts, neither are your ways my ways,' declares the Lord. 'As the heavens are higher than the earth, so are my ways higher than your ways and my thoughts than your thoughts.'"* That makes sense! The God who made all things (even our minds) knows better than we do. In 1 Corinthians 1:25 Paul proclaimed: *"The foolishness of God is wiser than human wisdom."* James agreed with Paul. *"The wisdom that is from above is first pure, then peaceable, gentle, willing to yield, full of mercy and good fruits; without partiality and without hypocrisy."* (James 3:17 NKJV) James contrasts God's wisdom with the wisdom *"that does not descend from above."* Its notable qualities are quite different. Among them are *"bitter envy, self-seeking, confusion and evil."* (James 3:14-16 NKJV) James is quick to remind his readers that if you lack wisdom, you can ask God for it. (See James 1:5) God's remnant is intentional about asking for His wisdom and not assuming that their own path is straight.

Ravi Zacharias has said that today "we are living in a time when people are thinking with their feelings."[16] Facts seem to have been tossed to the wind. Years ago CRU, formerly known as Campus Crusade for Christ, offered a tract on the orthodox view of the proper order of Facts, Faith and Feelings. They used the illustration of a train. The engine represented FACTS and by facts they were referring to the promises of God. The fuel car for the train was FAITH and that meant the trusting of God's Word. The caboose represented FEELINGS; gifts from God and not to be discounted, but not what should run things. Today, things have been turned upside down. The engine—that which runs and steers the train—is FEELINGS. The fuel car—that which feeds the feelings—is PERSONAL PREFERENCE. And in the rear comes the caboose— that which follows along but is not really necessary. The caboose today is FAITH. Upside down!

Just a few examples, which will be treated in completeness in the full chapter on this abomination, are things such as self being elevated to the highest importance. Or, the blurry lines that now exist between Creator and creature, human and animal, male and female. Or, the wicked being justified and the righteous being condemned. And, it's not just in the humanist culture. The church has done its share of turning things upside down also. Seeker-sensitive churches or today's given title, the "attractional church paradigm," has turned "go and tell" into "come and see." Paul's prediction of a depraved mind in Romans 1 is upon us.

An Unwillingness to Embrace Suffering

C.S. Lewis has said: "Pain insists upon being attended to. God whispers to us in our pleasures, speaks in our conscience, but shouts in our pains. It is His megaphone to rouse a deaf world."[17]

Pain is disagreeable to most people, but it is often one of God's best sanctifying tools. Generally, what suffering infringes upon is our comfort and convenience. I would say categorically that those two things are the biggest idols of the day. And, they need to be smashed. When adverse times are upon people, what I hear most is complaining and whining, but often the best lessons of all are learned during times of loss, bereavement, physical challenge, financial downfall, relational rifts and everyday disappointments.

Probably one of my pet peeves is when I hear a follower of Jesus say something like the following. "Yes, I am trying my best to keep my head above water with these present difficulties, but, you know, it beats the alternative." REALLY! It beats death which ushers the Christian into the arms of God? What? You cannot possibly mean that.

Once again, it is James who instructs us. And, his is a hard word. In James 1:2 NKJV he states: *"My brethren, count it all joy when you fall into various trials."* And, Solomon, the wisest of all, states in Proverbs 17:22 *"A merry heart does good, like medicine."*

How will the watching world ever know that all of what God allows is from a good and faithful and loving heart, if His own people complain when things are adverse? God's remnant needs to be intentional about avoiding complaint in the midst of trial. And, if complaining is to take place, it must be TO the living God, not ABOUT the living God.

Little Regard for the Sanctity of Life
Albert Einstein once said "The world will not be destroyed by those who do evil, but by those who watch them—without doing anything."[18] Abortion is one of those evils. Since Roe v. Wade in 1973 we have increasingly become a land of bloodshed. It is happening in our schools, workplaces, media outlets, movie theaters, concert venues, military posts, job sites and places of worship.

We have groups devoted to saving eagles' eggs, but those same members think nothing of late-term abortions. If we continue to be a nation that does not protect the lives of its most vulnerable citizens, then we cannot be surprised that life itself will be cheapened and any innocent bystander will be fair game. God's remnant must be intentional about reverencing and protecting all life.

People Not Maintaining God's Unity
God's ways are ones of reconciliation and restoration. His intentional remnant needs to be working toward unity; learning to disagree agreeably. Paul David Tripp affirms that "The only thing that

divides human beings is what or whom they worship."[19] If self is at the center of the universe, self is what will be worshiped and anyone disagreeing with self will be seen as an enemy.

God has called His own people a "priesthood." (See 1 Peter 2:9.) The root word for priest in Latin is "pontus." It means "bridge." God's remnant is to be intentionally working at building bridges; not burning them. That's not easy in the culture in which we live. Republicans cannot work with Democrats. Democrats call Republicans "deplorable." And, people in the church divide over doctrine, worship styles, the pastor's haircut, the paint selection for fellowship hall, sprinkling or emersion in baptism, and gluten-free or regular bread for communion. Fundamentalists disdain Pentecostals. Calvinists can't abide Arminian thinking.

A.W. Tozer has said: "One hundred pianos all tuned to the same fork are automatically tuned to each other. To be in harmony with other believers, we must be in tune with Christ."[20]

And, being in tune with Christ will help with our patience with disagreeable unbelievers as well.

God's Own People Not Living in His Power

Our current culture is full of wimps and whiners. Victimhood has been elevated to an all-time high position. There are those who even feign being a victim just to receive attention. God's remnant needs to be intentional about not being a victim. Victimhood was never God's plan. We can be people who live out of His enabling power. Then any situation, any circumstance becomes HIMpossible!

"His divine power has given us everything we need for life and godliness." (2 Peter 1:3)

Conclusion

With all of these abominations staring us down, how should the intentional remnant of God proceed? God's direction is clear in

65

Psalm 37:3. *"Trust in the Lord, and do good. Dwell in the land, and feed on His faithfulness."*

The whole of Psalm 37, penned by David, is a roadmap for dwelling in a land where wickedness abounds. In this one verse, four directives are found. 1. Trust in the Lord. 2. Do Good. 3. Dwell in the land. And, 4. Feed on His faithfulness. Though verse three provides the dots on the roadmap, the whole of the psalm gives the specifics of the journey.

<u>Trust in the Lord.</u>
Fretting and trusting are contrary bed-fellows. Fretting, as verse one in the psalm suggests, is when you keep your focus on the problem instead of the solution. When you and I trust in the Lord, we look to Him. We can, as verse four suggests, *"delight in the Lord."* And though evil is all around, God *"will give us the desires of our hearts."* I don't think that means that we get everything we want out of this life, but that God will direct our hearts into the desires He wants us to have. When we *"commit our way to the Lord"* (Psalm 37:5) the results are inevitably *"righteousness"* and *"justice."* (Psalm 37:6) Committing ourselves to Him is another way of saying trust Him. Verse seven tells us to *"rest in the Lord"* and verse 34 echoes the need to *"wait on the Lord."* Verse 40 confirms that *"because they trust in Him, He shall deliver them from the wicked and save them."* Trust in God is imperative.

<u>Do Good.</u>
The following are several verses from this psalm that give a detailed picture of what doing good looks like.

Verse 8 says *"Cease from anger. Forsake wrath."*
Verse 19 instructs: *"Do not be ashamed in the evil time."*
Verse 23 reminds: *"The steps of a good man are ordered by the Lord."*
Verse 27 commands: *"Depart from evil and do good."*

And, Verse 37 says: *"Mark the blameless man, and observe the upright for the future of that man is peace."*

Dwell in the Land.

The psalmist in this case propels his readers into the New Testament with reference to Jesus' teaching on the Mount in Matthew 5:5. In Psalm 37:11 we are told *"the meek shall inherit the earth and delight themselves in the abundance of peace."* Compare that word with Jesus' words in the same verse in The Message. *"You're blessed when you're content with just who you are—no more, no less. That's the moment you find yourselves proud owners of everything that can't be bought."* That's some way to dwell in the land and grace makes it possible.

Psalm 37:39-40 tell us how it is possible for us to dwell in a wicked land that is not thrilled with our biblical worldview. *"He is their strength in the time of trouble."* And, *"The Lord shall help them and deliver them from the wicked and save them."*

Feed on His Faithfulness.

The secret to feeding on God's faithfulness is by living according to His Word. Psalm 37:31 states: *"The law of his God is in his heart; none of his steps shall slide."* What follows in the remainder of the psalm is one piece of evidence after another about how God will deal with the wicked and how He helps the righteous in the land. Consider the following.

The Faithfulness of God Regarding the Wicked

- They will be cut down and wither – verse 2
- They will be cut off – verses 9, 22, 28, 34, 38
- He laughs at them – verse 13
- Their sword shall enter their own hearts – Verse 15
- Their bows will be broken – Verse 15
- Their arms will be broken – Verse 17

- They will vanish like smoke – Verse 20
- They will be no more – Verse 36

The Faithfulness of God Regarding the Righteous

- He will bring forth their righteousness as a light – Verse 6
- There will be justice – Verse 6
- They will inherit the earth – Verses 9, 22, 34
  (Proud owners of everything that can't be bought.)
- They will be upheld – Verse 17
- They will have an eternal inheritance – Verse 18
- They will have no shame – Verse 19
- They will be satisfied in famine – Verse 19
- Though they fall they will not be utterly cast down – Verse 24
- They will be upheld – Verse 24
- They will not beg for bread – Verse 25
- They will not be forsaken – Verse 28
- The Lord will not leave them in the land of the wicked – Verse 33
- There will be a future of peace – Verse 37
- God will be their strength in trouble – Verse 39
- God will deliver them – Verse 40

Though the current abominations are big and looming, our God is bigger than all the adversity we see around us. And, He remains with us. He will not forsake us. We need to trust Him, do good, dwell in the land and feed on His faithfulness. *"Listen, listen to Me, and eat what is good, and you will delight in the richest of fare."* (Isaiah 55:2 NIV)

Follow along in the following chapters as each abomination is explored in depth. In each instance we will explore examples of cultural and church abuse, God's admonitions to us, some Biblical examples and how God's remnant can intentionally live His way in this fallen world.

Prayer Points To Consider

1. Of the contrasting list on page 55 of things esteemed by men and by God, ask God where you personally fit most often. If a course correction is necessary, ask for the Father's help.

2. Pray through the list of current "abominations" in places where you see them operating. (Perhaps even in your own life.) Again, ask God for His help. *"Let us therefore come boldly to the throne of grace, that we may obtain mercy and find grace to help in time of need."* (Hebrews 4:16 NKJV)

   - Not many of God's own people are passionate to spend time with Him in prayer.
   - No Fear of God.
   - Little Gratefulness.
   - Little attention to absolute Truth.
   - Little regard for God's Word.
   - A lack of responsible shepherds.
   - Upside-down thinking.
   - An unwillingness to embrace suffering.
   - Little to no purity.
   - Little regard for the sanctity of life.
   - People not maintaining God's unity.
   - God's own people not living in His power.

3. Pray for God's wisdom in following His directions to

   - Trust Him.
   - Do Good.
   - Dwell in the Land.
   - Feed on His Faithfulness.

4. As the Holy Spirit leads.

CHAPTER FIVE –
ONE THING MATTERS

God's Remnant Spends Extravagant
Time with Jesus In Prayer

> **"To get nations back on their feet, we must first get down
> on our knees."**
> **—Billy Graham—**

Corrie ten Boom is credited with asking a heart-stirring question. *"Is prayer your steering wheel or your spare tire?"[21]* I think she meant, "Do you only pray when you have trouble or is it the breath that leads to the next breath of your everyday existence? Someone once said: "He who does not pray when the sun shines will not know how to pray when the clouds roll in." To answer Corrie ten Boom's query, one must honestly examine how much time is spent with the One who answers prayers. I am learning that the one thing that matters is extravagant time in God's presence. In his exuberant declaration of faith in Psalm 27:4 NKJV, David agrees with me. *"One thing I have desired of the Lord, that will I seek: that I may dwell in the house of the Lord all the days of my life, to behold the beauty of the Lord, and to inquire in His temple."*

It is not only David who concurs. Paul, in his letter to the Philippian church, confessed this truth. *"...one thing I do: Forgetting what is behind and straining toward what is ahead, I press on toward the goal to win the prize for which God has called me heavenward in Christ Jesus."* (Philippians 3:13-14 NIV) He had just explained that above all else he wanted to know Jesus and that everything else was considered rubbish to him except that one thing. The prize was his God.

Jesus also agrees. In speaking to Martha in her complaint of her sister who was not helping with the chores of hospitality, Jesus said the following words in Luke 10:41-42 NKJV. *"Martha, Martha, you are worried and troubled about many things, but one thing is needed, and Mary has chosen that good part, which will not be taken away from her."* What was the one thing Mary had chosen? Mary was sitting at Jesus' feet, taking in every word. In Luke 10:40 the report was that *"Martha was distracted with much serving."*

I get that, because I, too, am easily distracted with "much serving." It seems easier, somehow, than sitting still, looking at Jesus eye to eye, and dealing with the stuff of life. He made me aware of this in a strange fashion when I had known Him about twenty-five years. I was sitting at the piano singing and playing my favorite Broadway musical, "Fiddler on the Roof." My favorite song in the musical is "Do You Love Me?" It is a wonderful interchange between the principle characters of the story; a husband, named Tevye, and his wife, Golde. Tevye is a Russian Jew, experiencing persecution. He has an astounding relationship with his God, speaking to Him personally many times every day. He knows what it means to spend extravagant time with his God. This couple has five daughters, all of whom are getting married, and, they are marrying men whom they love and who love them. This is a foreign concept because Tevye and Golde had an arranged marriage. Tevye begins to muse. "I wonder if my wife loves me." So he asks her. Persistently. "Do you love me?

Golde responds. "Do I what?"

Tevye: "Do you love me?"

Golde: "Do I love you? With our daughters getting married and this trouble in the town, you're upset. You want out. Go inside. Go lie down. Maybe it's indigestion."

Tevye won't leave it alone. He asks yet again. "Do you love me?"

Golde: "For twenty-five years, I've washed your clothes, cooked your meals, cleaned your house, given you children, milked the cow. After twenty-five years, why talk about love right now?"

Tevye asks yet again.

Golde responds. "For twenty-five years, I've lived with him, fought with him, starved with him. For twenty-five years, my bed is his. If that's not love, what is?"[22]

Tevye makes a positive assumption. "Then you love me?"

Golde: "I suppose I do."

The song ends as the two of them go off singing together. "It doesn't change a thing, but even so, after twenty-five years, it's nice to know."

I finished the playing and singing with a flourish and then felt a nudge in my heart. There was no audible voice, but a strong inquiry, nonetheless. "Marilyn, do you love Me?"

My audible response startled me. "Well, for twenty-five years I've taught Your Bible studies, cleaned the church bathroom, helped in the nursery, and sung in the choir." Oh my! I had been doing a lot of odd-jobs for Jesus, being distracted with much serving, but my God wanted to know, "Do you love Me?"

How do you spell LOVE? I believe the answer is: T-I-M-E! We tell Him we love Him when we spend time with Him and then learn to obey Him. Extravagant time with Jesus in prayer is the one thing that matters. I am beginning to understand that unless I spend extravagant time with Him, I have very little to offer anyone else.

Making Him the Number One Priority of our lives even comes with a promise. Matthew 6:33 is clear. *"But seek FIRST the kingdom of God and His righteousness, and all these things shall be added to you."* God notices when we turn aside from all else and give Him the attention He deserves.

One of the best examples I know of this is Moses at the burning bush. In Exodus 3:2-5 NASB the account is clear. *"The angel of the Lord appeared to him in a blazing fire from the midst of a bush; and he looked, and behold, the bush was burning with fire, yet the bush was not consumed. So Moses said, 'I must turn aside now and see this marvelous sight, why the bush is not burned up.' When the Lord saw that he turned aside to look, God called to him from the midst of the bush and said, 'Moses, Moses!' And he said, 'Here I am.' Then He said, 'Do not come near here; remove your sandals from your feet, for the place on which you are standing is holy ground.'"*

Elizabeth Barrett Browning wrote an epic poem titled "Aurora Leigh" in 1857. One stanza of this poem is pertinent to Moses' story. In it she says the following.

"Earth's crammed with heaven,
And every common bush afire with God;
But only he who sees, takes off his shoes,
The rest sit round it and pluck blackberries."[23]

The blackberries represent all the distracting chores we DO, rather than simply BE in the presence of the Holy One. It has taken me a long time—years—to understand that the one thing that matters is seeing the Holy in the common and taking off my sandals. That one response to His presence informs all else. In a sense, I am writing this chapter for you with my shoes off.

Personal Blackberries

I once went blackberry picking with our grandchildren. The fruit we gathered was sweet to the taste, beautiful to the eye, readily available and self-satisfying in the effort expended, not to mention a whole lot of fun. The berries were so large that they made a BIG noise as they went into the bucket. They stained our fingers and the evidence of forbidden tastes was all over our mouths.

I cannot say what your spiritual blackberries look like. They are different for all of us. But, I am beginning to understand what mine look like. They are sweet and big, readily available and so appealing to my fleshly side. They make a big prideful noise in the gathering and they are often lots of fun to handle. The evidence of them is on my stained hands and mouth. And, they are deadly, because they keep me from seeing the fire in the bush and responding to the holiness by taking off my shoes.

Spiritual blackberries are things like being concerned with reputation over repentance. Dignity and honor over deliverance. Human programs over God's presence. Doing instead of being. They are formulas over fresh revelation. Information over transformation. Answers and activity instead of adoration. They are inhibition instead of being inhabited by the Holy Spirit. Spiritual bulliness instead of brokenness. Intellect without intimacy. They are "God all figured out" instead of a heart bowing to the mystery. Endless committee meetings instead of watching after peoples' souls. They are homiletics instead of humility. And, they are "spin" instead of surrender.

There's nothing wrong with a concern for reputation, dignity, information, intellect, programs and homiletics. Nothing, unless those things keep us from the longings of God's heart. And He longs for time with us. Think of it! The Creator of all things wants to spend time with us in close proximity. I'm wondering what you have decided may be your spiritual blackberries; the things that keep *you* from the one thing that matters—precious time with Him. We must all learn to trade what seems good for the best.

A Declaration of Truth

Jonathan Falwell has said: "The greatest possibility we have of turning our culture back to God is not found in words of attack and condemnation but rather in cries from our heart to a holy God in desperate times of prayer. It is high time we take prayer seriously and cry out to God for revival."[24] A.W. Tozer agrees. He states: "To desire revival … and at the same time to neglect prayer and devotion is to wish one way and walk another."[25]

The following are several verses that highlight the importance of prayer, and the woeful lack of it, through the ages. This is not an exhaustive list, but a sobering chronicle, nonetheless.

1 Samuel 12:23 NIV – *"As for me, far be it from me that I should sin against the Lord by failing to pray for you. And I will teach you the way that is good and right."*
2 Chronicles 7:14 NIV – *"If my people, who are called by my name, will humble themselves and pray and seek my face and turn from their wicked ways, then I will hear from heaven, and I will forgive their sin and will heal their land."* A valuable exercise to do with this verse is to circle all the things that are our responsibility and underline the things that God promises He will do in response. Our responsibility is to 1. Humble ourselves, 2. Pray, 3. Seek His face and 4. Turn from wicked ways. What will He do? 1. Hear, 2. Forgive, and 3. Heal our land.
Job 21:15 NIV – *"Who is the Almighty, that we should serve him? What would we gain by praying to him?"*
Romans 3:11 NIV – *"There is no one who understands; there is no one who seeks God."*
Isaiah 43:22 NIV – *"But you have not called upon Me, O Jacob; and you have been weary of Me, O Israel."*
Ezekiel 22:20 NIV – *"So I sought for a man among them who would make a wall, and stand in the gap before Me on behalf of the land, that I should not destroy it; but I found no one."*
Psalm 14:2-3 The Message – *"God sticks His head out of heaven. He looks around. He's looking for someone not stupid—one man, even, God-expectant, just one God-ready woman. He comes up empty. A string of zeroes. Useless, unshepherded sheep, taking turns pretending to be Shepherd. The ninety and nine follow their fellow."*

Examples of Cultural Abuse

Paul David Tripp exclaims: "Prayer is abandoning my addiction to other glories and delighting in the one glory that is truly glorious——the glory of God."[26] Our culture has forgotten that. So, we find prayer out of the public schools and armed police inside them. We hear phrases like the following. "We need more than prayer to protect our children in schools." Really? Perhaps in this lawless culture we do need visible deterrents to violence, but prayer remains a formidable line of defense.

Recently I heard an ad for an online agency that finds recruits for your business in a super-fast fashion. The tag line for the ad was "Goodbye Post and Pray. Hello ZipRecruiter." In other words, prayer is old-fashioned. Out of date. Get with it, buddy. We have something much better for you and your needs.

After the heinous New Zealand attack on people as they worshiped, killing many, a United States legislative representative was reported as saying the following. "What good are your thoughts and prayers when they don't even keep the pews safe?" She went on to assert that "thoughts and prayers" are nothing more than an NRA phrase used to deflect conversation away from policy change. If prayer is only about the results achieved as we desire them, those statements may have some credence. But, prayer is more about the relationship with the One to whom you are praying; a statement of humility that we are all, indeed, dependent on this grace-rescuing Sovereign for our very lives.

Unfortunately, prayer has been turned into other things for many people, including those who would call themselves as Christians. There is something wrong when prayer is just a quick minute before eating or merely the oil that we use to ease daily tensions . We give prayer fancy names like "invocation" and "benediction", but don't really give it much attention.

Once again, it is David Paul Tripp who summarizes the problem. "Prayer often amounts to shopping at the Trinitarian Department Store for things you have told yourself you need with the hope that they will be free."[27] Heaven help us!

God's Reminders To Us

It's no secret. Prayer makes a difference. God underscores its value in many of the Bible verses we are familiar with. The following are just a few.

1 Thessalonians 5:17 NASB – *"Pray without ceasing."*

Romans 12:10-12 NKJV – *"Be kindly affectionate to one another with brotherly love, in honor giving preference to one another; not lagging in diligence, fervent in spirit, serving the Lord; rejoicing in hope, patient in tribulation, continuing steadfastly in prayer."*

Philippians 4:6-7 NIV – *"Do not be anxious about anything, but in every situation, by prayer and petition, with thanksgiving, present your requests to God. And the peace of God, which transcends all understanding, will guard your hearts and your minds in Christ Jesus."*

1 John 5:14-15 NKJV – *"Now this is the confidence that we have in Him, that if we ask anything according to His will, He hears us. And if we know that He hears us, whatever we ask, we know that we have the petitions that we have asked of Him."*

John 17:15 NIV – *"My prayer is not that you take them out of the world but that you protect them from the evil one."* This is a crucial truth. God does not want us OUT of the world. He wants us to penetrate the darkness, all the while praying for protection from the evil one who wants to steal, kill and destroy us. (See John 10:10.)

James 4:1-3 NIV – *"What causes fights and quarrels among you? Don't they come from your desires that battle within you? You desire but do not have, so you kill. You covet but you cannot get what you want, so you quarrel and fight. You do not have because you do not ask God. When you ask, you do not receive, because you ask with wrong motives, that you may spend what you get on your pleasures."* We commit presumptuous sin when we do not pray. Prayer means we have admitted need. We have understood that we are not sufficient for life's struggles in our own strength. The problem is, we will do just about anything BUT pray. We give in to our desires. We covet. We strive. We kill. We scheme. But, we do not pray.

God reminds us over and over that He welcomes our requests and that our prayers do make a difference. Consider the following chart to see the difference that prayer makes.

The Difference Prayer Makes

THE DIFFERENCE	PERSON	SCRIPTURE
Trusting instead of Trembling	The Israelites	Exodus 14:1-31
A Gift instead of Grief	Hannah	1 Samuel 1
Forgiveness instead of Failure	David	2 Sam. 11-12; Ps. 51
Foresight instead of Fear	Elisha's Servant	2 Kings 6:8-20
Healing instead of Hurting	Hezekiah	2 Kings 20:1-11
Rebuilding instead of Rebukes	Nehemiah	Nehemiah 4:1-15
Praising instead of Perishing	Esther/Mordecai	Esther 4
Prosperity instead of Poverty	Job	Job 42
Hope instead of Hostility	David	Psalm 69
Understanding instead of Uselessness	Asaph	Psalm 73
Revelations instead of Revilings	Daniel	Daniel 1-2
Protection instead of Persecution	Daniel	Daniel 6
Deliverance instead of Distress	Jonah	Jonah 2:1-10
Worship instead of Worry	Habakkuk	Habakkuk
Strengthening instead of Sifting	Simon Peter	Luke 22:31-34
Liberation instead of Legalism	Paul	Acts 9:1-22
Cheers instead of Chains	Peter	Acts 12:3-17
Assurance instead of Anguish	David or Epaphras	Psalm 55 or Colossians 4:12-13

It makes no mind if you are at the altar, the battle front, the palace, home at the window, in a lion's den or a whale, in jail, or wherever and whatever you may be encountering. God prays for us (See Hebrews 7:25 and Romans 8:26-27.) And, we must not stop coming to Him in prayer.

A Biblical Example – Nehemiah

The Bible verses are too numerous to count. In a time of rebuilding while the opposition was thriving, Nehemiah led the people. Nehemiah knew that his God was the Restorer of what is broken down. He needed God's strength to approach the King and to rebuild the walls of Jerusalem. He needed a plan. The best of his leadership came in his unrelenting practice of going to his God in prayer. Throughout his ordeal Nehemiah spent extravagant time in the Lord's presence. You can examine the evidence yourself. Following are just a few of the references that find Nehemiah on his knees. Nehemiah 1:4, 11; 2:4; 4:4, 9; 5:19; 6:9, 14; 9:2-3, 5-38; 13:14, 22, 31. What did he ask for?

The list is endless. He asked for mercy, direction, prosperity, favor, for the opposition, for strength, and for God to touch his fear. He asked God to remember him and to spare him. *"Remember me, O God."* Nehemiah listened and followed God's lead.

Can we do any less? Our opposition is fierce in this culture today too. God will remember us as well. You can count on it.

How We Can Intentionally Give Attention To Prayer

The following are several suggestions to motivate a hearty prayer life. They are life-born gleanings from time in the presence of God.

1. LISTEN!

Isaiah 55: 2-3 NIV gives apt direction. *"Why spend money on what is not bread, and your labor on what does not satisfy? Listen, listen to me, eat what is good, and you will delight in the richest of fare. Give ear and come to me; listen, that you may live."* Some time ago the Lord showed me something in His Word that has forever changed me. I will pass it on to you.

In the eighteenth chapter of Genesis we find Abraham bargaining with God over the demise of Sodom and Gomorrah. As was shared in an earlier chapter, in Genesis 18:24 NKJV Abraham dared to say this to God. *"Suppose there were fifty righteous within the city; would You also destroy the place and not spare it for the fifty righteous that were in it?"* Abraham gets more and more bold. What about forty-five? Forty? Thirty? Twenty? Ten? It's the last verse of that chapter, after this interchange between Abraham and his God, that caught my attention. Genesis 18:33 NKJV says: *"So the Lord went His way as soon as He had finished speaking with Abraham; and Abraham returned to his place."*

Did you catch that? Abraham left <u>after God</u> was finished speaking. I wondered how many times I had left conversations with Him when <u>I</u> was finished speaking my list. This taught me the value of listening and not rushing off to my own agenda. Now I am much more likely to linger in His presence to be sure that He has finished saying what is on His heart to me.

That truth from the Word was coupled with an event that reinforced the message. My husband and I were asked to participate in a prayer vigil; twenty-four hours of praying over specific issues at the church. Everyone willing was assigned a forty-five minute time slot and furnished with a list of requests and quiet at the church altar. We arrived for our committed time and started in earnest on the list provided. When the forty-five minutes were up, and I had finished praying the list, I was antsy to leave. After all, other people would soon be showing up for their committed time and I did not want to infringe on their time at the altar. But, my husband continued praying.

"What IS his problem?" I wondered. "Doesn't he know it's time to leave?" I went out to the narthex and paced and cleared my throat—loudly—so he would surely hear. I tapped my foot and I paced some more. After some time had passed, he finally emerged from the sanctuary with a smile on his face. My first words were anything but cordial. "What WERE you doing?" I thrust. His gentle, but firm, answer still resounds in my ears. "I was listening, Marilyn." I sheepishly left, realizing I had a lot to learn.

God gave us two ears and only one mouth. I think it's so that we could actually understand His direction through James 1:19 NKJV. *"So then, my beloved brethren, let every man be swift to hear and slow to speak."*

2. ASK GOD HOW HE IS ALREADY PRAYING AND JOIN HIM!

It has not taken long to realize that my prayers are sometimes insufficient. One day I decided that it would be prudent to ask God how He was praying about something concerning me and then log in to His request on the matter. It made sense. He is a God who prays. We are told in multiple places in the scriptures that our God intercedes for us. In Hebrews 7:25 NIV we are told that *"He (Jesus) always lives to intercede"* for us. In Romans 8:26-27 NIV the record states the following. *"In the same way, the Spirit helps us in our weakness. We do not know what we ought to pray for, but the Spirit himself intercedes for us through wordless groans. And he who searches our hearts knows the mind of the Spirit, because the Spirit intercedes for God's people in accordance with the will of God."*

Allow me to share an anecdote to illustrate. A few years ago I was experiencing difficulty with my lungs. I had gotten pneumonia while traveling to lead a women's retreat in Georgia, and it was causing some lasting problems. The pulmonologist ordered several tests to determine treatment. All of them seemed extraordinarily dreadful and I worked myself up to a level of anxiety not previously experienced. Several weeks before this fateful time, I had remembered the wonderful truth that Jesus and the Spirit pray for me. So, I began asking God, *"Show me how You are already praying."* In recalling that marvelous dialogue with God, I now wondered how He might be praying about this lung situation.

The answer was clear. *"I am praying that you will make this problem situation about Me and My interests, and not focus totally on yourself."* Now, that's a novel thought. I knew it would NOT be how I would proceed. I asked further. *"How would I do that?"* The answer was quick to come. *"You will be going into a hospital waiting room full of people more afraid than you of the tests they are to encounter. I care about them. Pray for them. And, when you are called back into your private room, there just may be a nurse in there who needs encouragement. You could do that! And, at the hardest part of the test, would you be willing to offer Me praise?"* I was astounded with that answer but followed through with the directions given. The fateful testing day came and it was not a burden. It turned into an adventure with peace in my heart and glory going to God.

3. BE PREPARED TO GO TO WAR!

Again, it is Jonathan Falwell who informs us. He has said: "Prayer is battle. It is where our victories are won, our enemies are defeated and our hope is refreshed."[28] Ephesians 6:10-18 NKJV maps out the battle plan and even tells us what we should wear in the skirmishes we face. *"Finally, my brethren, be strong in the Lord, and in the power of His might. Put on the whole armor of God, that you may be able to stand against the wiles of the devil. For we do not wrestle against flesh and blood, but against principalities, against powers, against the rulers of darkness of this age, against spiritual hosts of wickedness in the heavenly places. Therefore take up the whole armor of God, that you may be able to withstand in the evil day, and hav-*

ing done all, to stand. Stand therefore, having girded your waist with truth, having put on the breastplate of righteousness, and having shod your feet with the preparation of the gospel of peace; above all, taking the shield of faith with which you will be able to quench all the fiery darts of the wicked one. And take the helmet of salvation, and the sword of the Spirit, which is the word of God; praying always with all prayer and supplication in the Spirit, being watchful to this end with all perseverance and supplication for all the saints."

I am sure you have noticed that we all have many pieces of armor that God has supplied for our use. Hopefully you have also noticed that none of them is fitted for our backs. That is because we have been told to RESIST the enemy. We are not to run, but to hold our ground. So, we gather, on separate hangers, each piece of armor: truth, righteousness, the gospel, faith, salvation and the sword of the Spirit, and, we cover them all with the garment bag, which is PRAYER! Then we put them on. That is what makes us ready for the battle being waged in the heavenlies over our culture today.

4. TRUST!

Proverbs 3:5-6 NIV wins the day yet again. *"Trust in the Lord with all your heart and lean not on your own understanding; in all your ways submit to him, and he will make your paths straight."* My eyes are drawn to the times in those two verses where a little word with a big impact is used. The word is "ALL." God wants ALL of our heart engaged in this, and ALL of our own ways surrendered to Him.

Only God is Sovereign. Princes and rulers of this world are in His hands. (See Isaiah 40:23-24.) *"All nations before Him are as nothing."* (Isaiah 40:17 NKJV) We can trust our land and our culture into His hands. We can learn to make our ways His ways by spending extravagant time with Him and surrendering to His will. We can disdain the world's way of being big and puffed up by choosing to be small before our big God, but lifted up.

We trust Him when our eyes are on Him. We don't look to ourselves as sufficient to handle the problems of the day. That only creates anguish. And, we should not stare at the problems and challenges. That generally serves to make us angry. We need to opt for looking to our God; to fix our eyes on Jesus. We agree with David's affirmation in Psalm 55:23 NKJV. *"Bloodthirsty and deceitful men shall not live out half their days; but I will trust in You."*

5. JUST DO IT!

God's Word tell us that we may enter the Holy Place with confidence. How is that possible? *"By the blood of Jesus."* (See Hebrews 10:19.) Ephesians 3:12 NIV says: *"In Him and through faith in Him we may approach God with freedom and confidence."* This means that nothing on the outside can rob us of our freedom to spend extravagant time with Him and nothing on the inside can steal our confidence in coming to Him. How can this be? Ephesians 2:13 NIV makes it clear. *"But now in Christ Jesus you who once were far away have been brought near by the blood of Christ."*

Another verse that tells us we may approach God for help is found in Hebrews 4:16 NIV. *"Let us then approach God's throne of grace with confidence, so that we may receive mercy and find grace to help us in our time of need."* Once again. How can we be this confident? The verses preceding verse sixteen give the answer. *"Therefore, since we have a great high priest who has ascended into heaven, Jesus the Son of God, let us hold firmly to the faith we profess. For we do not have a high priest who is unable to empathize with our weaknesses, but we have one who has been tempted in every way, just as we are—yet he did not sin."* (Hebrews 4:14-15 NIV)

We have no excuse. The way is clear. Nothing can hinder us …… but us. I believe God's favorite word is "COME". He says it with a smile on His face and with arms open wide. For you. Just do it!

Conclusion

There is one thing that matters! Nothing compares with extravagant time in the presence of the Lord. In Psalm 84 the sons of Korah penned this confession. *"How lovely is your dwelling place, Lord Almighty! My soul yearns, even faints, for the courts of the Lord; my heart and my flesh cry out for the living God. Even the sparrow has found a home, and the swallow a nest for herself, where she may have her young—a place near your altar, Lord Almighty, my King and my God. Blessed are those who dwell in your house; they are ever praising you."* (Psalm 84:1-4 NIV)

As the psalm continues, the writers add emphasis. *"Better is one day in your courts than a thousand elsewhere; I would rather be a doorkeeper in the house of my God than dwell in the tents of the wicked."* (Psalm 84:10 NIV)

I have been discovering some things that are noticeable if, indeed, we do spend extravagant time with God in prayer. The first is that those who are inclined to follow Jesus will notice our time with God and want to imitate what we do. A prime example of that is in Exodus 33:7-11. Moses set up a tent calling it *"the tent of meeting."* A tent becomes The Tent when the presence of God moves into its dwelling. Moses goes there to inquire of the Lord, much like David writes about in Psalm 27:4 mentioned at the outset of this chapter. But, Moses does not go alone. He takes Joshua with him and, there, the two of them meet in lavish time spent with the Most Holy God. Exodus 33:11 expresses what happens to Joshua as he joins Moses in The Tent. *"The Lord would speak to Moses face to face, as one speaks to a friend. Then Moses would return to the camp, but his young aide Joshua son of Nun did not leave the tent."* (Exodus 33:11 NIV) Joshua was inclined to follow God. He saw Moses spending extravagant time in God's presence and he wanted it for himself too. Nowadays, when I say yes to mentoring anyone, God needs to affirm in my heart that they are people who do not want to leave The Tent; people who have a passion for His presence.

The second thing I have noticed is that folks who are not inclined to follow Jesus can also notice that you have spent extravagant time in His presence and, if they do and it is disagreeable to them, they will attempt to persecute you. In the book of Acts there is an account of some religious folks from the Sanhedrin—the full assembly of the elders of Israel—who noticed that Peter and John had been with Jesus. *"Now when they saw the boldness of Peter and John, and perceived that they were uneducated and untrained men, they marveled. And they realized that they had been with Jesus."* (Acts 4:13 NKJV) What did these religious people do? They called a meeting to figure out a way to shut Peter and John up. They commanded them not to speak in the name of Jesus and they threatened them. It is also worth noting that they had to let them go because they could not find a way to punish them further. Why? *"Because of the people, since they all glorified God for what had been done."* (The healing of a lame man. Acts 4:21 NKJV)

The third thing I have noticed is that spending extravagant time with God in prayer may not change your circumstances, but it will change you! In Psalm 73 Asaph writes of his personal dilemma with wicked, rich people who seem to have no troubles. He confesses in Psalm 73:2 NIV: *"But as for me, my feet had almost slipped."* At the end of his psalm, he offered the following testimony. *"Those who are far from you will perish; you destroy all who are unfaithful to you. But as for me, it is good to be near God."* (Psalm 73:27-28 NIV)

Nothing had changed. The wicked were still wicked. They were free of burdens. They were arrogant and full of malice. So, what changed? Asaph changed. How did it happen? He spent extravagant time with God. Psalm 73:16-17 records his turning point. *"When I tried to understand all this, it troubled me deeply till I entered the sanctuary of God; then I understood their final destiny."* (NIV)

When I speak of extravagant time with Jesus, I am not asking you to become a monk and chant all day. However, I am challenging you to access more of Him. If you sit still with Jesus fifteen minutes a day now, how hard would it be to double the time? If you have mastered memorizing the phrase, *"Jesus wept,"* perhaps you could now do one whole verse, or one chapter and allow His words to *"remain in you."* (See John 15:7.) If you have fasted and prayed for one hour, maybe twenty-four hours or three days would not be too great a stretch to seek His face. Would you be willing to say "yes" to be overcome by His presence? Would you be willing to host God's presence everywhere you go at all times?

You and I have to make a choice. Will it be blackberry picking or bare feet? Will we continue to skirt the real issues by staying busy, OR will we become still; still enough in His presence so we can know this God? (See Psalm 46:10) God's hands are open. I invite you to give Him whatever represents your "blackberries." Do you dare to put them in His hands?

Moses' encounter at the burning bush informs our hearts. We must watch for the divine initiative. We must not discount common things. Everything is spiritual. God is everywhere; in everything. We must take steps toward God no matter where we are at present. Why? Because He notices. We must ask God to open our eyes to see the fire. We must beg Him to open our ears so we can hear Him call our names. We must be ready for whatever marching orders He has in mind to fulfill His purpose for us in our own generation. We must respond immediately. And, we must be assured that in His presence we are standing on holy ground. So, dear reader, take off your shoes and forget the blackberries.

Ravi Zacharias says: "In the end, life is like a balance sheet of gains and losses. The real battle lies in knowing what we can afford to lose and what we must uncompromisingly hold onto."[29] I can lose my blackberries but I must hold uncompromisingly to the holy in the common; the times when it is mandatory to kick off my shoes. And, I must beg God for the understanding to know the difference. I would challenge you to the same. As I see it, there are only two choices: blackberries or bare feet. By His grace, like Moses, we can choose bare feet as our priority; extravagant time in His presence.

Prayer Points To Consider

1. Ask God to help you make prayer your "steering wheel" and not your "spare tire."

2. Read 2 Chronicles 7:14. Ask God to help you with your responsibilities of humility, praying, seeking His face and turning from any evil way. Then, ask God to hear, forgive and heal our land.

3. Ask God to raise up unified prayer warriors that will cross denominations to seek His face for the church universal and for the United States of America.

4. As the Holy Spirit leads.

CHAPTER SIX –
ONLY ONE FEAR

God's Remnant Maintains Awe and Respect for the Living God in the Big and Small Things of Life

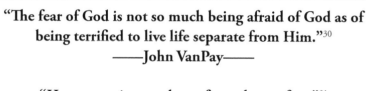

"The fear of God is not so much being afraid of God as of being terrified to live life separate from Him."[30]
——John VanPay——

"Have room in your heart for only one fear."[31]
——Dick Brogden——

Solomon—declared as the wisest man of all—made this statement in Ecclesiastes 12:13 NKJV. *"Let us hear the conclusion of the whole matter: Fear God and keep His commandments for this is man's all."* The only problem is, he did not live by his own advice. Foreign women led him astray and he became a half-hearted king. I suppose this is in the scriptures to remind us that to live in the fear of God we all need God's grace and it must be our intention to surrender to it. It's easy to have fear of other things: people, situations, the future, of being found out, hopelessness and helplessness, just to name a few. Brogden's advice is note-worthy. "Have room in your heart for only one fear."

There are many examples in the Bible, in global history and in our current culture of those who have feared God more than man or circumstance. Consider just a few of them. There was Abraham who left his land and traveled at the bidding of his God. It was said of Noah that *"he moved with godly fear."* (Genesis 6:8) He was followed by Moses who took the first step into the Red Sea. The prophet Ezekiel spoke God's message whether people listened or failed to listen. Daniel continued to pray to his God, as was his daily practice, <u>in front of his window</u> when he was told that dire consequences would follow if he bowed to any other than Nebuchadnezzar. Shadrach, Meshach and Abednego declared on the steps of the fiery furnace that their God was able to save them, *"but even if not, let it be known that we do not serve your gods nor will we worship the gold image which you have set up."* (Daniel 3:18 NKJV) Stephen put the Sanhedrin on notice as being "stiff-necked Holy Spirit resisters." It cost him his life. (See Acts 7 and 8.)

In the annals of history William Wilberforce stood against the slave trade in his native England. Eric Liddell was an Olympic runner who refused to compete on the Sabbath at great personal loss. Jackie Robinson broke racial barriers in major league baseball in the United States, standing firm in his faith.

On the scene in recent times there are stellar examples of those with only one fear in their hearts. Jack Phillips, a Colorado baker, has stood firm in choosing not to bake cakes for LGBTQ and Transgender people even with court actions against him. Bremerton, Washington football coach, Joe Kennedy, lost his job after inviting—NOT coercing—his high school players to pray at the fifty-yard line following every game. Kevin Cochran, Fire Chief in Atlanta, Georgia, lost his job because of a self-published book he wrote on his own time for a Bible study at his church on human sexuality. In it he confirmed his belief of same-sex marriage before God. And, we, along with thousands of others, watched on TV as Andrew Brunson, a missionary to Turkey, released from prison on trumped-up charges, was in the Oval Office on his knees praying for the leader of the free world.

The flourishing of the church depends on their attention to the fear of God. In Acts 9:31 NKJV we are told: *"Then the churches throughout all Judea, Galilee and Samaria had peace and were edi-fied. And walking in the fear of the Lord and in the comfort of the Holy Spirit, they were multiplied."* Other versions translate it as being strengthened and increasing in numbers. The Message reports the same verse this way. *"All over the country—Judea, Samaria, Gali-lee—the church grew. They were permeated with a deep sense of rever-ence for God. The Holy Spirit was with them strengthening them. They prospered wonderfully."* The results of fearing God were 1. Peace, 2. Edification or Strengthening and 3. Growth. The growth was most certainly in numbers, but the encouragement of the Holy Spirit went much deeper than just numbers. These new believers needed depth because they were now thrown into a hostile environment where Christians were not received well; much like today. The fear of God—this *"deep sense of reverence for God"*—made all the differ-ence.

A Declaration of Truth

There are many places in the scriptures that draw attention to the fact that the people in question had no fear of God. One such place is in Romans 3:18 NKJV. Paul declared *"There is no fear of God before their eyes."* The apostle had just spent time showing the church in Rome that they were not glorifying God, nor being thankful to Him. Their hearts were darkened and they *"exchanged the truth of God for a lie."* (See Romans 1:21-25.) He continues in Romans 2 to tell the people that they were either *"accusing"* or *"excusing"* and *"defending"* unseemly behavior. (See Romans 2:15.) And in chapter three of Romans he came to the conclusion, as the psalmist of old had done, that *"there is none righteous, no, not one; there is none who understands; there is none who seeks after God."* (See Romans 3:10-11.)

In the Old Testament, the psalmist wrote a scathing review in Psalm 36:1-4 NIV. *"I have a message from God in my heart con-cerning the wickedness of the sinful. There Is no fear of God before their eyes. In their own eyes they flatter themselves too much to detect or hate their sin. The words of their mouths are wicked and deceitful; they fail to act wisely or do good. Even on their beds they plot evil; they commit themselves to a sinful course and do not reject what is wrong."* In that song the psalmist made it clear. When there is no fear of God in a person's heart, it affects many things, including their spiritual blindness or awareness, their words, their actions, their plans, their choices and their destinies. Fear of God—or the lack of it—is indeed an important thing. It is crucial because fear of God is what leads us into a "trust and obey" lifestyle.

Cultural Abuse

Our pastor is often quoted, saying "Everything is spiritual." Everything we do, say or think is important. It all matters. Sometimes you can see the lack of fear of God in the smallest of things. But, then, if we cannot obey in small matters, we will be tempted to disobey in big things. Consider the following true story to see what I mean.

I drove into a fast food line for a Diet Coke at the local Burger King. The perky clerk at the window said this to me. "Oh, you don't have to pay because you had to wait so long." I thought how nice a policy that was and I was grateful that the infringement of my time was rewarded with a freebie. However, the next time I went to the same place the same girl was at the window. I did not wait at all, yet she again said with a wink, "You don't need to pay. Let this be my little treat." Now, her age would tell me that she did not own that franchise and it was not within her authority to give anything away, even a diet coke. I told her I could not accept her "gift" and was sure that the owners would want to be recompensed for the dispensing of soda from their machines. She sheepishly took my money. My intention was not to make her feel uncomfortable, but my God knows when I cheat anyone out of anything—big or small. Everything is spiritual, indeed.

In the chapter introducing all of today's abominations, it was mentioned that online research on "the fear of God" yielded only one entry about the true fear of God. All the rest concerned a clothing design line called "Fear of God". When the designer, Jerry Lorenzo, was asked why he chose that name, he said that as a child he grew up with devotions every day. His favorite was from Oswald Chambers, "My Utmost for His Highest." He said "I decided you had to stand for something."

In Luke 18:1-8 there is an account concerning a persistent widow who felt the need to approach a judge regarding justice from an adversary. By his own admission the judge said he *did not fear God nor regard man."* (Verse 4) He was labeled an "unjust judge." Today there are many who feign great compassion on homeless people and illegal immigrants but because their lives do not exhibit fear of God, I contend that they don't really care for man either. They're in it for their own benefit somewhere along the line. Their feigning to care for others is exposed as a lie because they do not fear God. This lack of fear of God is pervasive in our culture and harmful in many ways. And, in the church, I see many who have *"pointing fingers and malicious talk"* (See Isaiah 58:9.) and that behavior is Exhibit A of no fear of God. One who truly fears God is more concerned about his or her own sin than the sin of another.

God's Reminders

The following listing of scripture is not an exhaustive study on this matter but a smattering of evidence to show the Father's heart on this matter. Consider the following.

Psalm 112:1-2 – *"Blessed is the man who fears the Lord, who delights greatly in His commandments. His descendants will be mighty on earth; the generation of the upright will be blessed."*
Proverbs 31:30 – *"Charm is deceitful and beauty is passing, but a woman who fears the Lord shall be praised."*

1 Peter 5:5 – *"Be clothed with humility. God opposes the proud but gives grace to the humble."*
Luke 12:5 – *"Fear Him who after He has killed, has power to cast into hell; yes, I say to you, Fear Him!"*
Psalm 25:14 NIV – *"The Lord confides in those who fear Him; He makes His covenant known to them."*

Would you like to be counted among those who are confidantes of God? Then ….

Fear Him!

Biblical Examples

Both the Old and New Testaments carry examples of those who operated without a fear of God in their hearts. Both stories end in death—physically and spiritually—but the Old Testament account records a change of behavior. Follow along for both of these scenarios to play out.

In 2 Samuel 6 the record shows the account of David bringing the Ark of God back to Jerusalem. The Ark was the symbolic presence of the Most High God, containing only three things: Moses' tablets, Aaron's rod that budded, and manna. These three things represented the on-going personal presence of God; His commandments, His protection and His provision. It was only about four feet long and two feet wide and deep; made of wood and overlaid with gold. It had loops on the ends meant for carrying.

The Ark had been captured and held by the Philistines for thirty years and David wanted it back. He was now king and he wanted Jerusalem to be the center of His rule and the worship of his God. The Ark was in the little village of Kiriath-Jearim. The priest Abinadab resided there with his two sons, Ahio and Uzzah. You could see Jerusalem from that vantage point. It was the last leg of any pilgrimage before that holy resting site. All was in place, but it is here that the story takes a dramatic turn.

2 Samuel 6 records two attempts at moving the ark; the sec-

ond just three months after the first try. Both endeavors were accompanied with pomp, excitement, and worship, but only the latter attempt to move it was also accompanied with the fear of God. The attempts to move the ark were met with vastly differing results as well. In the first endeavor, death was the result. In the second attempt, dancing was the result. Consider Eugene Peterson's thoughts in his celebrated classic, "Leap Over A Wall."

"Sometimes I think that all religious sites should be posted with signs reading, 'Beware the God.' The places and occasions that people gather to attend to God are dangerous. They're glorious places and occasions, true, but they're also dangerous. Danger signs should be conspicuously placed, as they are at nuclear power stations. Religion is the death of some people. The story of Uzzah and David posts the warning and tells the glory. Uzzah and David share the story. Uzzah died; David danced. The Ark of the Covenant was the occasion for the death and the dance. Uzzah's death and David's dance."[32]

What were the difficulties that brought on Uzzah's death? The problems are multiple. God had given specific instructions for the manner in which the Ark should be carried from place to place. (See Numbers 4:5-15.) Poles were to be inserted into the gold rings on the box and the Ark was to be carried with the poles on the shoulders of only the Levitical priests. The first transport system devised in this case from Kiriath-Jearim to Jerusalem was on a new cart. That was how the culture did things; not how God did things. One of the priest's sons, Ahio, went in front of the ark. God is the first cause of all things. Nothing or no one should go before Him. And when the ox stumbled in a rut and the Ark was about to be bounced off of the cart, Uzzah reached out a hand to help. But, we are not to help God out. He is the One who helps us.

As I see it, there were at least four things that were glaring pieces of evidence that this move of the Ark was not accompanied by the fear of God. The four are: 1. Disobedience. 2. Presumptuous

Sin. 3. Irreverence and 4. Making God Impersonal. Consider one more word from the heart of Eugene Peterson on the matter.

"Uzzah is the patron saint of those who uncritically embrace technology without regard to the nature of the Holy. Uzzah was in charge (he thought) of God, and meant to stay in charge. Uzzah had God where he wanted him and intended to keep him there. The eventual consequence of this kind of life is death, for God will not be managed. God will not be put and kept in a box, whether the box is constructed of crafted wood or hewn stone or brilliant ideas or fine feelings. We don't take care of God; God takes care of us."[33]

The scriptures tell us that *"David became angry because of the Lord's outbreak against Uzzah"* and *"David was afraid of the Lord that day."* (2 Samuel 6:8-9 NKJV) In a pout, he stopped the procession and left the Ark at the home of Obed-Edom while he returned to Jerusalem.

But, God had placed a fire in David's heart that the Ark should find its rest in Jerusalem. Scholars believe that the psalm that chronicles this event is Psalm 132. Listen to David's heart in verses 3-9. *"Surely I will not go into the chamber of my house, or go up to the comfort of my bed; I will not give sleep to my eyes or slumber to my eyelids, until I find a place for the Lord, a dwelling place for the Mighty One of Jacob. Behold, we heard of it in Ephrathah; we found it in the fields of the woods. Let us go into His tabernacle, let us worship at His footstool. Arise, O Lord, to Your resting place, You and the Ark of Your strength. Let Your priests be clothed with righteousness, and let Your saints shout for joy."* While in the household of Obed-Edom for three full months, it was noted that blessings abounded. So, David returned. And, this time the Ark was brought to the City of Gladness with obedience, no presumptuous sin, no impersonal relationship and no irreverence. The lesson had been learned. The priests picked up the poles inserted in the loops and as 2 Samuel 6:13 reports: *"And so it was, when those bearing the Ark of the Lord had gone six paces, that he sacrificed oxen and fatted sheep."* I don't know how far Obed-Edom's home was from Jerusalem, but despite the exact distance, it would have taken careful handling to walk six steps, stop and sacrifice; walk six steps, stop and sacrifice; walk six steps, stop and sacrifice; walk six steps, stop and sacrifice. You get my point.

And, David danced. Oh, how he danced. The scriptures define it as *"undignified"* (2 Samuel 6:22) dance. He danced like the placards of today suggest: "DANCE LIKE NO ONE IS WATCHING!" David said *"I will be humble in my own sight."* (Vs. 22) He could say that, because this movement of the Ark was not about him. It was not about how things appeared. It was not about the pomp and circumstance. It was not about any religious trappings. It was about the mysterious, intimate, personal, non-presumptuous, reverent fear of a Mighty, Good and Faithful God.

This kind of fear of God will always bring loathing from those who do not understand the importance of what is at hand. Michal, the daughter of Saul, was disgusted at David's dancing. The record states: *"Therefore Michal the daughter of Saul had no children to the day of her death."* The inevitable result of this lack of fear of God is barrenness. It can happen to any of us. Alexander Whyte comments on Michal with the following words. "Those who are deaf always despise those who dance."[34] Let it be a word to the wise.

The New Testament example occurs in the beginning of the early church after the resurrection of Jesus. Acts 4:32-34 tells us some facts about these early believers. They *"were of one heart and one soul."* *"Great grace was upon them all."* *"Nor was there anyone among them who lacked."* They all opened their hearts and pockets and shared with those in need.

Everyone, that is, except Ananias and Sapphira. Ananias, with full knowledge of his wife, Sapphira, sold some possessions to be part of the giving group. However, with no fear of God in his heart, Acts 5:2 reports that *"he kept back part of the proceeds."* Peter took no time in exposing this deed and calling it what it was. Peter said in Acts 5:3-4 *"Ananias, why has Satan filled your heart to lie to the*

*Holy Spirit and keep back part of the price of the land for yourself? …
"You have not lied to men but to God."* Ananias died on the spot. The
result was predictable. *"Great fear came upon all those who heard
these things."* (Acts 5:5)

Three hours later Sapphira appears on the scene, not knowing
what had just occurred. Peter gives her a chance, asking about the
amount they had received from the land sale. She answered as her
husband had and Peter's response was equally as swift and pointing. *"How is it that you have agreed together to test the Spirit of the
Lord? Look, the feet of those who have buried your husband are at the
door, and they will carry you out."* (ACTS 5:9) Sapphira dies also
and *"great fear came upon all the church and upon all who heard these
things."* (Acts 5:11)

God will not be mocked. We can fool human beings, but we
cannot fool Him. When we lie, we display a heart that has no fear
of Him and we test His Spirit. Death is the result. Ananias and
Sapphira may have thought that their actions and testimony were
just "a little white lie." How could that hurt? But, God is concerned
with the heart, and a heart that tries to manipulate and hide truth
is not pleasing to Him. Even in seemingly small things.

How We Can Intentionally Live in the Fear of God

With the biblical examples in my rearview mirror, I am more than
ever motivated to live wisely as I move forward—in the fear of
God. The scriptures speak clearly of several things God's remnant
can do to intentionally live His way and show a watching world
a better way. Following are ten action points for the Intentional
Remnant.

1. **Trust in God and Do Not Lean On Your Own Understanding.** – Proverbs 3:5-6 NIV

"Trust in the Lord with all your heart and lean not on your own understanding; in all your ways submit to Him, and He will make your paths straight." God's intentional remnant must be all in; all their heart and mind engaged in what would please God. If you don't know what that is in any circumstance, ask Him.

2. **Humble Yourself.** 1 Peter 5:5-6 NIV – *"All of you, clothe yourselves with humility toward one another, because, 'God opposes the proud but shows favor to the humble.' Humble yourselves, therefore, under God's mighty hand, that He may lift you up in due time."* Humility is not thinking less of yourself. It is thinking of yourself less. And, if you and I think of ourselves less, we have opportunity to think of God and His desires more. Humility is a necessary path to the fear of God. There is only One God, and we are not Him. When we give Him His rightful place in our hearts, fear of God is working well.

3. **Let Your Words Be Few.** Ecclesiastes 5:7 NIV – *"Much dreaming and many words are meaningless. Therefore fear God."* Today's culture puts much stock in words. The more the better. But, a glib mouth does not display fear of God.

4. **Rely on God.** Isaiah 50:10 NIV – *"Who among you fears the Lord and obeys the word of His servant? Let the one who walks in the dark, who has no light, trust in the name of the Lord and rely on their God."* The operative question at this point is what is the difference between trusting God and relying on God? Trust, I believe, is having confidence in the character, the ability, the desire and the power of God. It is a focus issue. Will I trust in God or will I trust in myself or others? Relying on God, on the other hand, is actually putting action alongside the confidence. To illustrate this contrast, I offer an illustration of years ago. A man was asked if he believed that the man before him could push a wheelbarrow

over a tight-rope across Niagara Falls. His reply was a hearty affirmative. The same man was asked if he would then get in the wheelbarrow. Believing the man could do the stunt was having trust in his character, his ability, his desire and his power to get the job done. Getting in the wheelbarrow is when the man actually relied on the stuntman.

5. **Hold Nothing Back From God.** – Genesis 22:12 NIV – *"'Do not lay a hand on the boy,' he said. 'Do not do anything to him. Now I know that you fear God, because you have not withheld from me your son, your only son."* I am sure you have heard it often. The old saying goes: "If you're not ALL IN, then you're not in at all." God gave His all for us, and He expects the same in return. If there is an area of disobedience in your life, and you are aware of it, it needs to be surrendered. This scripture is in the middle of the account of Abraham's sacrifice of his promised son, Isaac. When asked, Abraham obeyed immediately, and God noticed. He notices when you and I hold back or surrender all also.

6. **LISTEN!** – Psalm 34:11 NIV – *"Come my children, listen to me; I will teach you the fear of the Lord."* If the fear of the Lord is a learned thing, then it is not natural to our natures. We are much more prone to fearing ourselves, or other people, or situations that appear to be in control. A good biblical example of one who understood this was, again, Abraham. In Genesis 18 we read of the famous dialogue he had with God over the fate of Sodom and Gomorrah. "Will you save the land for fifty righteous?" "40?" "30?" "20?" "10?" Abraham was engaging in a tough bargaining point with his God, but the last verse of chapter 18 says much about his fear of God. *"As soon as He (God) had finished speaking to Abraham the Lord departed, and Abraham returned to his place."* (Genesis 18:33 NASB) Did you catch that? Abraham left after GOD was finished speaking. It makes me wonder how many times

I have abandoned the fear of God and left when I, MYSELF, was finished speaking.

7. **Gather Together To Learn To Hear and Fear.** Deuteronomy 31:12-13 NIV - *"Assemble the people—men, women and children, and the foreigners residing in your towns—so they can listen and learn to fear the Lord your God and follow carefully all the words of this law. Their children, who do not know this law, must hear it and learn to the fear the Lord your God as long as you live in the land you are crossing the Jordan to possess."* One of the reasons corporate worship is so important to our growth in godliness is because it is there that we are reminded to listen and learn the fear of God. Hear and fear. I love seeing the sign that is posted to the entry of our church sanctuary. It reads: "NO FOOD OR DRINK PAST THIS POINT." It reminds me every Sabbath that I am entering a holy place; this place of assembly is for God; not my comfort and convenience.

8. **Be Willing To Change Your Ways.** – Psalm 55:19, 1984 NIV – *"God who is enthroned forever will hear them and afflict them—men who never change their ways and have no fear of God."* A sure piece of evidence that a heart is not in fear and awe of God is that the person is sure of his own ways, and WILL NOT change for anyone; not even God.

9. **Submit To One Another.** – Ephesians 5:21 – *"Submit to one another out of reverence to Christ."* In Peter's first letter to the scattered church he speaks boldly of submission; citizens to governing officials, wives to husbands, husbands to wives, children to parents, workers to bosses. In other words, all people to all people. It is a mark of humility to allow another authority over us, and when we act in such a manner, we are in the proper posture to fear our God who has authority over us all.

10. **Shun evil.** Job 1:1 – *"In the land of Uz there lived a man whose name was Job. This man was blameless and upright; he feared God and shunned evil."* What a statement! Don't you long for someone to say that about you? Shunning evil means what Paul said in his letter to the Romans that we would *"hate was is evil and cling to what is good."* (Romans 12:9 NKJV) That means in big and small things; maybe especially small things. When you are given more change at the store than you should receive, giving back the amount that is not yours is fearing God. People may not notice, but God does.

Conclusion

One of the most awe-inspiring chapters of scripture is Exodus 19. The fear of God is all over the account of the Israelites camped in front of the mountain of God. It is the hinge chapter of the whole book. All the chapters and verses that go before are about Moses taking the Israelites out of Egypt. All the chapters and verses that follow concern God taking Egypt out of the Israelites. In this one place is the account of God meeting with His people at the mountain. The trumpet has sounded. The "third day" is upon them. Mystery envelops the entire encounter. The people are warned to be prepared, to cleanse themselves, to not touch the mountain for danger of death. This is serious business. The time is dripping with awe, reverence and, yes, the fear of God.

In the chapter God makes some things crystal clear. He wants His people set apart; ready for His personal use. He calls for consecration of living. He invites a careful approach. He longs to be near us, but on His terms. He is a God who washes and sanctifies; a God who sets boundaries. And, in one verse, He expresses His heart longing of nearness to us. In Exodus 19:20 it is said: *"The Lord descended to the top of Mount Sinai and called Moses to the top of the mountain. So Moses went up.*" For a long time God kept drawing my attention to this one verse and for a long time I didn't get why it was special. Then the insight came. No one descends to the top of anything; no one, unless you are God. God descends to the highest we can know and calls us up to be with Him. That one verse alone informs us of the need of the fear of God—the Most High God who is above all things—and His longing for connection with the likes of us. It also tells us that this true God will not be tamed. All things will be done in His way in His timing.

C.S. Lewis wrote of this paradox—the need to both fear and be in awe of God and the desire to draw near—in his Narnia tales of the great Christ figure, the lion, Aslan. It was the first time the Penvensie children had ever heard of Aslan. Susan and Lucy engage in dialogue with Mrs. Beaver. Consider the following dialogue to see what I mean.

"Ooh!" said Susan. "I'd thought he was a man. Is he—quite safe? I shall feel rather nervous about meeting a lion."

"That you will, dearie, and no mistake," said Mrs. Beaver. "If there's anyone who can appear before Aslan without their knees knocking, they're either braver than most or else just silly."

"Then he isn't safe?" said Lucy.

"Safe?" said Mr. Beaver. "Don't you hear what Mrs. Beaver tells you? Who said anything about safe? 'Course he isn't safe. But he's good. He's the King, I tell you."[35]

Prayer Points to Consider

1. Ask the Lord to show you how to take Him seriously.

2. Ask Him to examine your heart. Allow Him to show the ways you have not honored and reverenced Him. Confess and repent. (Give God time to speak. Listen carefully. Act appropriately.)

3. Ask God to show you how to live intentionally in a healthy fear of Him.

   a. Trusting You
   b. Humbling myself
   c. Letting my words be few
   d. Relying on You
   e. Holding nothing back from You
   f. Listening well
   g. Gathering with those who love You to learn fear of You
   h. Willing to change my ways as You dictate
   i. Submitting to others who know and live Your way
   j. Shunning evil

4. Ask for His help to submit/surrender ALL to Him.

5. As the Holy Spirit leads.

CHAPTER SEVEN –
"WHERE ARE THE NINE?"

God's Intentional Remnant Shows the Watching World How to Be Grateful to a Good God for All His Benefits

> "Everything we do should be gratitude for what God has done for us."
> ——Anonymous——
>
> "I would maintain that thanks are the highest form of thought, and that gratitude is happiness doubled by wonder."[36]
> ——G. K. Chesterton——

Gratefulness brings with it reward and, conversely, the lack of a thankful heart yields results as well. The truth of this is born out of years of struggle in the Caribbean island of St. Croix. The island is tiny and at the mercy of the weather. Hurricanes blow through on occasion and bring devastating results. The faithful on the island decided that they would have concerted prayer efforts to their God, thanking Him for His protection from the wind and waves and petitioning for safety in the seasons known to stir up trouble. For decades Christians gathered in houses of worship to thank God and to plead for the Lord's protective hand on them. For many years God spared the little island. But, time past and the threat did not seem as dire. So, first the congregants coming for prayer were whittled to a meager number, and then the church leaders decided it was no longer necessary. You guessed it. When they stopped thanking God and asking for help, the winds became boisterous and destructive. Now, it is true. Our hearts are not to be grateful just to stay adversity, but the facts speak for themselves.

Gratefulness is learned. I grew up in a home with much complaining. Nothing was ever enough. And, though I was taught to say "please" and "thank you" at an early age, the model I observed was anything but grateful. Then, I married a man who is grateful for every little thing. When he prays, he always begins by thanking God for His many undeserved blessings. In Old Testament times the priests would remind the people to be grateful. Psalm 136:1-4 NKJV proclaims the following. *"Oh, give thanks to the Lord, for He is good! For His mercy endures forever. Oh, give thanks to the God of gods! For His mercy endures forever. Oh, give thanks to the Lord of lords, for His mercy endures forever. To Him who alone does great wonders, for His mercy endures forever."* These very words were read antiphonally; first, the priest and then the people. In essence, the priest was asking "Is there a reason to give thanks to God?" The people would respond with the words of Psalm 136, The Great Hallel.

This event was highlighted in the scriptures at least twice. In 2 Chronicles 5 when the Temple was completed and the Levites brought the Ark inside, God's glory filled the place. The priests asked: "Is there a reason to give thanks to God?" The Great Hallel was proclaimed. Again, in 2 Chronicles 20 when Jehoshaphat was coming against a mighty army, the singers and musicians were placed on the front line. The question was raised. "Is there a reason to give thanks to God?" They worshiped God with all their might. Their praise was a weapon and the opposing army was routed.

Psalm 100:4 NKJV urges us. *"Enter into His gates with thanksgiving, and into His courts with praise. Be thankful to Him, and bless His name."* We have the habit of entering His gates and courts with complaints, sighs, selfish requests, demands and instructions on how God ought to be running things. But, the Word of God says to approach Him with thanksgiving and praise.

Contemporary Cultural Ungratefulness

God's Word is clear that times will come when men and women will be ungrateful. I believe that such a time is now. Romans 1:21 NKJV says: *"...although they knew God, they did not glorify Him as God, nor were thankful, but became futile in their thoughts, and their foolish hearts were darkened."* Paul goes on in 2 Timothy 3:1-5 NKJV to list the character qualities of those who live in the perilous *"last days."* *"But know this, that in the last days perilous times will come: For men will be lovers of themselves, lovers of money, boasters, proud, blasphemers, disobedient to parents, unthankful, unholy, unloving, unforgiving, slanderers, without self-control, brutal, despisers of good, traitors, headstrong, haughty, lovers of pleasure rather than lovers of God, having a form of godliness but denying its power."* (Underlining mine.) What was his advice with such people? *"And from such people turn away!"*

We live in a culture that is entitled. The dictionary defines the adjective "entitled" as "believing oneself to be inherently deserving of privileges or special treatment." That has at its core a self-focus. The world revolves around ME! One does not have to go far to see this attitude fostered, especially in the midst of youth sports. Current protocol has it that everyone is a winner. So, a student athlete, no matter his skill or commitment to the team, is given a "participation trophy." Gone are the days in preparatory gymnastics when gold, silver and bronze medals are given to those children who have worked hard and earned the honor. Now the honors go down even as far as thirteenth place. No one understands the reward that hard work deserving of such an honor affords. You just need to show up. At high school graduations, valedictorians are being replaced by recognition for many students attaining a high GPA. We wouldn't want to hurt anyone's feelings. And, as a result, youngsters today have a hard time congratulating those who have truly earned recognition, and they think they are deserving of privilege and special treatment just because they exist.

In doing research for this book, I read many studies—Christian and secular alike—of the value of gratefulness in a person's life. I was astounded by what I read. All the studies agree. Having a thankful heart is key to good mental, emotional, relational and even physical health. The astounding part came when those writing the studies confessed that though they knew gratefulness was important, they did not know who to be grateful to. Make no mistake. There is One to whom we can declare our gratefulness. He is the Lord God, Maker of heaven and earth; the author of all blessing!

God's Admonitions To Be Grateful

Many places in the scriptures remind us to be grateful. Here are just a few.

1. **Psalm 107:8, 15, 21, 31** – These verses all say the same thing. *"Oh, that men would give thanks to the Lord for His goodness."* The psalm is an exposition of four different kinds of people in differing circumstances. The first are those who wander in the wilderness. They are hungry and thirsty. The psalmist says God fills the hungry. Then the reminder is given. *"Oh, that men would give thanks to the Lord for His goodness."* The second group are those who have rebelled, who sit in darkness and in the shadow of death. The psalmist states that God has brought them out of those dark places. The third group represents sinning fools who are full of iniquities. But God sent His Word and healed them. And, the fourth group are those who have business on the waters and are experiencing storms and strong winds. But God quieted their storms and guided them into safe havens. In each case

the reminder is lodged. *"Oh, that men would give thanks to the Lord for His goodness."*

2. **Philippians 4:6-7** – In this verse we are given the "formula" for the *"peace which surpasses all understanding."* When we are anxious we can bring everything to God *"in prayer and supplication".* The key is to add *"thanksgiving"* in our requests. ALL SURPASSING PEACE = Prayer + Thanksgiving. J. B. Phillips paraphrases it this way. *"Don't worry over anything whatever; tell God every detail of your needs in earnest and thankful prayer, and the peace of God which transcends human understanding, will keep constant guard over your hearts and minds as they rest in Christ Jesus."*

3. **Ephesians 5:18-21 NKJV** – *"And do not be drunk with wine, in which is dissipation, but be filled with the Spirit, speaking to one another in psalms and hymns and spiritual songs, singing and making melody in your heart to the Lord, giving thanks always for all things to God the Father in the name of our Lord Jesus Christ, submitting to one another in the fear of God."*

4. **1 Chronicles 16:8 NKJV** – *"Oh, give thanks to the Lord! Call upon His name; make known His deeds among the peoples."*

5. **Psalm 30:4** – *"Sing praise to the Lord, you saints of His, and give thanks at the remembrance of His holy name."*

6. **1 Corinthians 15:57 NKJV** – *"But thanks be to God, who gives us the victory through our Lord Jesus Christ."*

7. **1 Thessalonians 5:18 NKJV** – *"…in everything give thanks, for this is the will of God in Christ Jesus for you."*

8. **Hebrews 13:15 NKJV** – *"Therefore by Him let us continually offer the sacrifice of praise to God, that is, the fruit of our lips, giving thanks to His name."* Did you catch that? The fruit of

our lips can be the giving of thanks to the only One who is worthy.

A Biblical Example

In Luke 17:17 Jesus asked a piercing question: *"Where are the nine?"* The account is about Jesus on His way to Jerusalem. He passes through Samaria and Galilee and there finds ten lepers who *"stood afar off."* (Verse 12) All ten of them asked for mercy from Jesus, whom they recognized as Master. Jesus told them to go to the priests for cleansing. They obeyed and they were all healed. But, only one of them returned *"and with a loud voice glorified God. He fell down on his face at His feet, giving Him thanks. And he was a Samaritan."* (Verses 15-16) Jesus asked the logical question. *"Were there not ten cleansed? But where are the nine? Were there not any found who returned to give glory to God except this foreigner?"* (Verses 17-18) Jesus' final words to the one thankful man were *"Arise, go your way. Your faith has made you well."* (Verse 19)

It sounds like things have not changed much in the human heart from New Testament times until now. There are many who have a hard time remembering to give thanks for blessings given.

Why Gratitude Is Important

In a Psychology Today article dating back to 2015 Amy Morin writes of "Seven Scientifically Proven Benefits of Gratitude."[37] They are as follows.

1. **Gratitude opens the door to more relationships**. The sobering truth is that sour people don't have as many friends.

2. **Gratitude improves physical health**. Gratitude is known to lower stress, which reduces inflammation in the body, which,

in turn, makes people less susceptible to disease. Dr. Mark Liponis, the Medical Director at Canyon Ranch Health Resort asserts that grateful people take better care of themselves and have fewer aches and pains.

3. **Gratitude improves psychological health**. A leading gratitude researcher, Robert Emmons, has found that gratitude increases happiness, reduces depression, envy, resentment, frustration and regret.

4. **Gratitude enhances empathy and reduces aggression**. In a 2012 study at the University of Kentucky it was discovered that grateful people are less likely to retaliate or seek revenge.

5. **Grateful people sleep better.**

6. **Gratitude improves self-esteem**. In a 2014 study in the Journal of Applied Sport Psychology, it was found that having a thankful heart reduced social comparisons and offered the ability to appreciate the accomplishments of others.

7. **Gratitude increases mental strength**. A 2006 study of Vietnam vets yielded results that said those with more gratitude experienced lower rates of PTSD. Stress levels were reduced and the service people were helped to overcome trauma and increase their resilience.

Winston Churchill once said that "Attitude is a little thing that makes a BIG difference."[38]

The truth is that life is much less about circumstance and much more about our attitude about the circumstance. A short anecdote will explain what I mean. A few months ago I went to my doctor's office for a well check-up. Unfortunately, the elevator in that building is the slowest anywhere. So, lots of people gather waiting for the doors to open and rise to the destination needed. I like bounding up the stairs but the number of floors that need conquering is just too daunting in that building. So, waiting is the name of the game. As I anticipated the arrival of the elevator there was a gentleman about my age impatiently tapping his foot. I smiled at him and said "How are you today, sir?", to which he replied—with a scowl on his face—"I'm old and I feel old!" I wasn't quite sure what to do with his answer, so I kept quiet. Before long he queried, "Well, what about you?" It was my opportunity. I smiled and with a twinkle I said, "Oh, I have been young for a very long time and I'm grateful for every year." His reply startled me. He said enthusiastically: "I LIKE THAT!" Turns out he was going to the same office I was headed for, and I noticed he smiled the rest of the time. A grateful attitude is a little thing that makes a big difference.

Ten Biblical Reasons Why Gratitude Is Important

1. **Thanksgiving is an open door to God's Presence.** Psalm 95:2 - *"Let us come before His Presence with thanksgiving."* Ps. 100:4 – *"Enter into His gates with thanksgiving, and into His courts with praise. Be thankful to Him and bless His name."*

2. **Thanksgiving highlights the character of God. –** Ps. 100:4-5 – *"Enter into His gates with thanksgiving and into His courts with praise. Be thankful to Him and bless His name. For the Lord is good; His mercy is everlasting and His truth endures to all generations."* Our God is good and merciful and full of Truth.

3. **The end result of thanksgiving is God's glory. –** 2 Cor. 4:15 – *"For all things are for your sakes, that grace, having spread through the many, may cause thanksgiving to abound to the glory of God."*

4. **Giving thanks is God's will. –** 1 Thess. 5:18 – *"In everything give thanks; for this is the will of God in Christ Jesus for you."*

5. **Having an attitude of gratitude enhances wisdom and light.** – Consider the opposite of Romans 1:21 – *"…although they knew God, they did not glorify Him as God, nor were they thankful, but became futile in their thoughts, and their foolish hearts were darkened."*

6. **Thankfulness will be missing in the last days.** – 2 Tim. 3:1-5 – *"But know this, that in the last days perilous times will come: For men will be lovers of themselves, lovers of money, boasters, proud, blasphemers, disobedient to parents, unthankful, unholy, unloving, unforgiving, slanderers, without self-control, brutal, despisers of good, traitors, headstrong, haughty, lovers of pleasure rather than lovers of God, having a form of godliness but denying its power. And from such people turn away."*

7. **Thankfulness is the pathway to peace.** – Phil. 4:6-7 – *"Be anxious for nothing, but in everything by prayer and supplication, with thanksgiving, let your requests be made known to God; and the peace of God, which surpasses understanding, will guard your hearts and minds through Christ Jesus."*

8. **Thanksgiving is part of the process of "loosing/unbinding"; coming out of a place of death into life.** – In John 11 the account of the raising of Lazarus is reported. Jesus employed six things to see this work of deliverance into completion. In verses 34 through 38 we see the compassion of Jesus for His friend, Lazarus. He groaned. He was *"troubled in His spirit."* He wept. He groaned yet again. He showed great compassion. I have a wise friend who always says "Love releases God's power." Jesus lived that truth is this account. In verse 39 Jesus made a command. *"Take away the stone."* He asked someone else to move the obstacle that would be in the way of Lazarus' return to life. In prayer, we can do the same thing for someone needing deliverance. We can ask God to send someone who will remove the barrier.

What past event or mindset occurred to block abundant life? Jesus then employed gratefulness. In verse 41 He said: *"Father, I thank You that You have heard Me."* Unbinding happens in the midst of a thankful heart. Verse 42 states: *I know that You always hear Me, but because of the people who are standing by, I said this, that they may believe that You sent Me."* Jesus called on Belief. In verse 43 He forcefully said *"Lazarus, come forth!"* He did not just say "Come forth." He attached a name to it. It was a personal word for a specific situation. Often when deliverance is needed in someone's life, I pray for God to speak a personal word to that person and that they would hear it. In verse 44 Jesus said to those standing by, *"Loose him, and let him go."* He was asking for people to be part of the process of healing and freedom. The six components Jesus utilized for deliverance were: 1. Compassion, 2. The Stone Removed, 3. Gratefulness, 4. Belief, 5. A Personal Word and 6. Loosing/Unbinding.

9. **Being Thankful is part of the Character of the New Man and Woman.** – Col. 3:12-17 –Being thankful is mentioned twice, along with holiness, kindness, humility, meekness, longsuffering, bearing with one another, forgiving, love, letting the Word dwell in you richly, teaching and singing.

10. **Being thankful is evidence of one filled with the Holy Spirit.** – Eph. 5:18-21 – "Do not be drunk with wine, but be filled with the Spirit….giving thanks always for all things to God."

What We Have To Be Grateful About

Ephesians 1:3 speaks with clarity. *"Blessed be the God and Father of our Lord Jesus Christ, who has blessed us with every spiritual blessing in the heavenly places in Christ."*

The following is an A to Z listing of our promises in Christ. It has been compiled by Pastor Charity Rose and is used by permission.

OUR PROMISES "IN CHRIST"

A to Z	Jesus Is Our ...	Scripture
A	Advocate	1 John 2:1
B	Bondage-Breaker	Galatians 5:1
C	Courage	Romans 8:15
D	Discipline	Hebrews 12:10
E	Enough	Ephesians 3:19-21
F	Friend	John 15:14
G	Griever's Companion	John 11:33-35
H	Health	2 Corinthians 4:16-18
I	Immutable	Psalm 102:25-27
J	Joy	1 Peter 1:8-9
K	Keeper	1 Corinthians 1:7-9
L	Light	Isaiah 9:2
M	Majesty	2 Peter 1:16
N	Near (Brought Us Near)	Ephesians 2:12-13
O	Orchestrator	Ephesians 1:11
P	Peace	Philippians 4:6-7
Q	(Doesn't) Quit	Philippians 1:4-6
R	Refiner	1 Peter 1:6
S	Shame-Destroyer	Romans 8:1-2
T	Truth	John 8:31-32
U	Understanding	1 John 5:20
V	Victory	1 John 5:3-5
W	Wisdom	1 Corinthians 1:30
X	eXtravagant	Ephesians 2:4-7
Y	Yes! To All His Promises	2 Corinthians 1:20
Z	craZy About Us	Romans 8:38-39

Surely there is something in that list that makes your heart soar and pound with gratitude. If it's not enough, consider the next chart of exchanges made for us in Christ.

Exchanges Made on the Cross For Us

JESUS...	So That We Might...	Scripture
Died	Live	John 10:10
Suffered	Be Comforted	2 Cor. 1:3-7
Was Rejected	Be Accepted	Ephesians 1:6
Was Separated from the Father	Be Brought Near	Eph. 2:13; John 3:16; Psalm 23:6
Bore a Shameful Death	Know No Shame	Psalm 25:3; 34:5
Was Crucified Naked	Be Clothed in Righteousness	Isaiah 61:10; Ephesians 6:14
Thirsted	Drink Living Water	John 4:13-14; John 7:37-38
Bones Out of Joint	Be Unified	John 17:22-23; Ephesians 4:3
Tongue Stuck To His Jaw	Sing A New Song of Praise to our God	Psalm 107:1-2; 34:1-3; 40:3
Hands and Feet Were Pierced	Draw Near and Be the Feet who bring Good News	James 4:8; Isaiah 52:7; Ephesians 6:15
Answered Nothing Back to His Accusers	Have an Advocate and An Intercessor	1 John 2:1; Hebrews 7:25
Carried the Heavy Cross	Have a Light and Easy Yoke	Matthew 11:28-30; 1 Pet. 5:7; Ps. 68:19
Was Crucified Between Two Thieves	Minister to the "Least of These"	Matthew 25:40; 1 John 3:16
Was Buried in a Borrowed Grave	Live in Eternal Mansions Prepared for Us	John 14:2-4
Rose from The Dead	Know Living Hope And Victory	1 Peter 1:3; 1 Cor. 15:42-44, 50-58

Suggestions for Intentional "ThanksLIVING"

The following are eight ideas to help each of us cultivate a more grateful attitude.

1. **Keep a Gratitude Journal.** I discovered the immeasurable value of this during a time of surgery for one of our adult sons. It had been a particularly difficult week with trips back to the hospital to treat complications. Frustrations were building and tempers flared at awkward moments. I began writing. "Thank you for excellent medical care." Thank you for a church family that cares and provides family food." I am grateful, Lord, for Your faithfulness at crucial moments." On and on the list went. And, by the time I finished dumping my grateful heart onto paper, I felt better, the atmosphere had cleared and progress began.

2. **Be a Gracious Receiver.** When you give to another, you are in charge. When you receive, it requires humility. I discovered this during a recent illness. I learned that I love taking care of others, but I do not like others taking care of me. That's a pride issue and it has to go! When you receive well it motivates gratefulness. Everything becomes a blessing, no matter how small.

3. **Share With Others.** Our home church leadership is masterful at sharing with others who have needs. Every year on the first Saturday in December we host "A Touch of Christmas." It is advertised for months. Folks line up in the middle of the night for the doors to open at ten a.m. Once inside families with need are greeted with love and new winter coats and Christmas gifts for every child under eighteen. Medical screening is offered through a local hospital. Family photos are taken. Lunch is served. And, groceries—one bag for every family member—are given. All with a sweet spirit. All with

Marilyn Anderes

no strings attached. And, to top it off, a Christmas musical production is shared with a gospel presentation at the end. Most years, hundreds of people come to know Jesus. And, gratefulness abounds; not only from thankful recipients, but in the hearts of those with the privilege of putting those things into the hands of people who need them.

4. **Be Exposed To Real Need.** Two summers ago, our youngest son, a pastor, took his whole family on a missions trip to Peru. They cleaned, they painted, they built new facilities, they shared the gospel, and they exposed their children to the obvious needs of others. Upon their return, all three of our grandchildren independently told us of the time they visited a village. The youngest of them said these words. "Did you know, Meemaw, that some people live in houses with dirt floors? I have a carpet in my bedroom at home, but they walked, and sometimes slept, on dirt." It made a huge impact. And, it made them grateful for what they had; not as apt to complain about what they did not have.

5. **Do Not Allow Complaining in Yourself or Anyone Else.** The truth is: what you say affects how you feel. Philippians 2:14-16 NIV says: *"Do everything without grumbling or arguing, so that you may become blameless and pure, children of God, without fault in a warped and crooked generation, so that you will shine like stars in the universe as you hold out the word of life."* The mouth will speak what is in the heart, so if you complain, it merely reveals an unthankful heart.

6. **Do Not Allow Entitlement in Yourself or Anyone Else.** Statements of pride sound like the following. "I deserve better!" Or, "I deserve more!" Both of those phrases have a me-center. The truth is that neither you nor I nor anyone else deserves anything; no special treatment. Yet the God of all grace showers us with blessings.

120

7. **Know That Everything is From God.** Our God is a good God. 1 Chronicles 29:14 NKJV says: *"...all things come from You, and of Your own we have given You."* 1 Timothy 6:6 NKJV asserts: *"Godliness with contentment is great gain."*

8. **Focus on the Good and Ample in Every Situation.** You have a choice on which perspective to agree with. You can either think "I have too much laundry to do" or you can think "I am thankful for the many clothes that God has provided." It is reported of the great violinist, Itzhak Perlman, that he once played a concerto with a renowned orchestra under adverse conditions. As the movement began, one of the strings on his violin broke. He had a choice. He could complain in disgust, go to the wings and get a new string, or he could do what he did. He chose to play the entire concerto with only three strings. If you know anything about Mr. Perlman's life, you understand that due to polio as a child, he has a difficult time walking. He makes his way with steel structures clamped to his arms. The concert ended with shouts of bravo. It was magnificent; even with only three strings. The violinist went to the nearest microphone and expressed these words to the listening audience: "Sometimes it is the artist's task to find out how much music you can still make with what you have left."[39] That's gratitude.

Conclusion

Being grateful is vastly important. And, it is valuable for those who are part of God's intentional remnant to show the watching world, which is usually not very thankful, that there is a better way to live.

To illustrate the importance of gratefulness and the motivator that it can be in the lives of others, I submit to you this true account of Doug Conant, a past CEO of the Campbell Soup Company. It seems that the corporation had been floundering in the months prior to Mr. Conant's appointment to leadership. He quickly realized that production was not up to par and the morale of company workers was low. He wisely called a meeting of all the heads of divisions around the world and made a simple request. He asked for them to supply names and addresses of those within the company—high executives down to fork-lift operators—who had done exemplary work. This CEO wrote ten to twenty thank you notes six days a week to deserving employees. He did it for ten years. The result? The bottom line improved and the morale was off the charts.

Mr. Conant had a bad car accident some years into his tenure of company leadership. Many notes arrived at his home from around the world from people thankful for his grateful notice earlier of their contributions to the corporate success. One man, low on the totem pole, is reported to have claimed that he kept the CEO's original note to him on his refrigerator for years. He was a grateful man.[40]

Prayer Points To Consider

1. Begin by thanking God for His goodness to you personally.

2. Ask God to help you be a person intentionally engaged in "THANKSLIVING".

3. Ask God to touch any "Entitlement Mentality" in you and in the culture around you.

4. Write a psalm/prayer of thanksgiving to God.

5. As the Holy Spirit leads.

CHAPTER EIGHT –
TRUTH OR CONSEQUENCES

God's Intentional Remnant Is Able To Stand For True Truth in A Culture That Will Fall For Anything

> "There is no neutral ground in the universe.
> Every square inch, every split-second, is
> claimed by God and counter-claimed by Satan."[41]
> ——C. S. Lewis——

The first game show ever introduced to the American public started in 1940 on NBC Radio. It was first hosted by Ralph Edwards and later by Bob Barker. It had an illustrious run of forty-eight years, ending in 1988. The show was called Truth or Consequences. The premise of the show was to offer a contestant two seconds to answer a zany, off-the-wall question that no one was likely to get. The answer needed to come before Beulah the Buzzer sounded her alarm. If, by some strange coincidence, the contestant actually got the answer correct, a second and third part was added. The point was to make the contestant pay the consequence for not answering the question with a truthful answer. The consequences were always embarrassing stunts arranged to make the person playing the game look silly. Everyone had a good laugh; even the contestants.

In this world there are consequences for not living by the truth as well. God asked a piercing question of the church at Galatia through the apostle Paul. *"O foolish Galatians! Who has bewitched you that you should not obey the truth?"* (Galatians 3:1 NKJV) Bewitched indeed! Because the Bible, the very Word of God, is not honored by our culture today, we have become a nation of fools. John 17:17 declares that we are sanctified by the truth. *"Your word is truth."* Immediately following Paul's daunting list of bad character qualities of men and women that we should stay away from in the perilous last days in 2 Timothy 3:1-5, he writes these words. *"For of this sort are those who creep into households and make captives of gullible women loaded down with sins, led away by various lusts, always learning and never able to come to the knowledge of the truth. Now as Jannes and Jambres resisted Moses, so do these also resist the truth: men of corrupt minds, disapproved concerning the faith; but they will progress no further, for their folly will be manifest to all, as theirs also was."* (2 Timothy 3:6-9 NKJV)

There are several facts evident of those in these "perilous last times." 1. People are always learning, but never able to come to the knowledge of the truth. 2. They are resisters of truth. 3. They have corrupt minds. And, 4. They make no forward progress. We are living in those "perilous last times." But there is hope because Truth is a Person, His name is Jesus and He reaches to touch our lives——to testify to the Truth. He is a stumbling block to some but The Way, The Truth, and The Life to many others. It is the mission of the Intentional Remnant to prepare the way for Jesus to have encounters with the Father's Love, Truth and Power. That will mean a heart change for many. There are only eighteen inches between the head and heart, but sometimes the journey is long and arduous. In this age of information and readily accessible knowledge, there are many who are *"always learning"* BUT *"never able to come to the knowledge of the truth."*

Declarations of Truth

God's Word is clear about the deadly condition of man's heart. Human beings actually think they know better than God and only God's grace can rescue them from themselves and their faulty thinking. Consider the following scriptures to see God's assessment.

Hosea 4:1 NKJV – *"There is no truth or mercy or knowledge of God in the land."*

John 3:19-21 The Message – *"The one who comes from above is above all; the one who is from the earth belongs to the earth, and speaks as one from the earth. The one who comes from heaven is above all. He testifies to what he has seen and heard, but no one accepts his testimony. The man who has accepted it has certified that God is truthful. For the one whom God has sent speaks the words of God, for God gives the Spirit without limit. The Father loves the Son and has placed everything in His hands. Whoever believes in the Son has eternal life, but whoever rejects the Son will not see life, for God's wrath remains on him."*

Romans 1:18, 25 NKJV – *18. "For the wrath of God is revealed from heaven against all ungodliness and unrighteousness of men, who suppress the truth in unrighteousness."*
25. "(they) exchanged the truth of God for the lie, and worshiped and served the creature rather than the Creator, who is blessed forever."

Isaiah 59:4 NKJV – *"No one calls for justice, nor does any plead for truth. They trust in empty words and speak lies; they conceive evil and bring forth iniquity."*

Jeremiah 5:1 NKJV – *"Run to and fro through the streets of Jerusalem; see now and know; and seek in her open places if you can find a man, if there is anyone who executes judgment, who seeks the truth. And I will pardon her."*

1 John 1:8 NKJV – *"If we say that we have no sin, we deceive ourselves, and the truth is not in us."*

Jeremiah 9:3 NKJV – *"And like their bow they have bent their* *tongues for lies. They are not valiant for the truth on the earth. For they proceed from evil to evil, and they do not know Me, says the Lord."* **Psalm 145:18 NIV** *– 'The Lord is near to all who call upon him, to all who call upon him in truth."*

Examples of Cultural Abuse

A recent cartoon illustrates the difficulty we face in our culture today. It pictures a movie theater with two feature films. One movie is titled "A Reassuring Lie". The line to view this picture winds around the block. The other movie showing is one called "An Inconvenient Truth." No one is standing in that line to buy tickets.

In a culture of situational ethics and "feel good" scenarios, reassuring lies are easy to fall for. Our culture—and some in the church today—have trouble distinguishing between what feels good and what is good, between what seems kind and what is healthy and leads to life. No one wants to be seen as a "bad person"; one who would not love on another. However, we can love people according to the world's definition or we can love them well, according to God's definition. God will always opt for truth with grace.

We get mixed up with people-centered faith as opposed to a Person-centered faith; between viewing life from humanity up instead of from the Kingdom down. It's no secret that the mainline United Methodist Church is near a split. The argument is over sexual ethics. There are some within the denomination willing to throw off the truth of God's Words for a more progressive leaning view of sexuality and marriage. The Rev. Carolyn Moore writes the following in Good News magazine.

"Let's talk Christologically. Does the conversation about the future of the United Methodist Church begin with Jesus? In my experience, the Lordship of Jesus is where we part ways long before we ever get to the topic of sexual ethics. For those of us who embrace an orthodox understanding of faith and truth, Jesus is the most true being. Those of us who are committed to absolute truth also believe deep in our spirits that the people we like and the people we have feelings for and the people for which we have great compassion and the people we want to see living holy lives and the people we want to see in Heaven are not the authors of our faith. The author of our faith is Jesus Christ. We have a Person-centered faith, not a people-centered faith. Our conversations must reflect this 'Kingdom-down' perspective while resisting the urge of a 'humanity-up' perspective. If we start with Jesus Christ, I suspect we will find plenty to discuss and (grievously) much on which we fundamentally disagree."[42]

What We Can Do With the Truth

The scriptures are clear to reveal to us that we all can have a negative response to the truth or a positive response to the truth. Dr. Henry Cloud has said the following. "When Truth presents itself, the wise person sees the light, takes it in, and makes adjustment. The fool tries to adjust the Truth so he does not have to adjust to it."[43] Let's look first at the negative responses possible and the scriptures that tell us these truths.

<u>Negative Responses to the Truth:</u>

- **We Can Suppress the Truth – Romans 1:18 NKJV –** *"For the wrath of God is revealed from heaven against all ungodliness and unrighteousness of men, <u>who suppress the truth in unrighteousness.</u>'*

- **We Can Distort the Truth – Acts 20:28-31 NIV –** *"Keep watch over yourselves and all the flock of which the Holy Spirit has made you overseers. Be shepherds of the church of God, which He bought with His own blood. I know that after I leave, savage wolves will come in among you and will not spare the flock. Even*

129

from your own number men will arise and <u>distort the truth</u> in order to draw away disciples after them. So be on your guard! Remember that for three years I never stopped warning each of you night and day with tears."

- **We Can Exchange the Truth for a Lie – Romans 1:25 NKJV** – *"…(they) <u>exchanged the truth of God for the lie</u> and worshiped and served the creature rather than the Creator, who is blesses forever."*

- **We Can Bring the Truth Into Disrepute – 2 Peter 2:2 NIV** – *"Many will follow their depraved conduct and will <u>bring the way of truth into disrepute</u>."*

- **We Can Refuse to Love and Live the Truth – 2 Thessalonians 2:9-10 NIV** – *"The coming of the lawless one will be in accordance with how Satan works. He will use all sorts of displays of power through signs and wonders that serve the lie, and all the ways that wickedness deceives those who are perishing. They perish because <u>they refused to love the truth and so be saved</u>."* **2 Timothy 3:7 NIV** – *"…always learning but never able to come to a knowledge of the truth."* **1 John 1:6 NIV** – *"If we claim to have fellowship with him and yet walk in the darkness, we lie and <u>do not live out the truth</u>."* **Hebrews 10:26-27 NIV** – *"<u>If we deliberately keep on sinning after we have received the knowledge of the truth, no sacrifice for sins is left,</u> but only a fearful expectation of judgment and of raging fire that will consume the enemies of God."*

- **We Can Reject the Truth – Romans 2:8 NIV** – *"But for those who are self-seeking and who <u>reject the truth and follow evil</u>, there will be wrath and anger."*

- **We Can Oppose the Truth – 2 Timothy 3:8 NIV** – *"Just as Jannes and Jambres opposed Moses, so also these teachers <u>oppose the</u>*

truth. They are men of depraved minds, who, as far as the faith is concerned, are rejected." These two men of old mentioned in Exodus 7:10-12 are the magicians sent by Pharaoh to duplicate Moses' throwing down of his staff that turned into a snake. But, God had the last word. Aaron's staff swallowed up their staffs. God's True Truth will always stand firm.

Positive Responses to the Truth:

- **We Can Acknowledge and Accept the Truth – 1 Timothy 2:3-4 NKJV –** *"For this is good and acceptable in the sight of God our Savior, who desires all men to be saved and <u>to come to the knowledge of the truth</u>."*

- **We Can Build on the Truth – 1 Corinthians 3:10-15 NIV** – (Remember: Truth is a Person. His name is Jesus.) *"By the grace God has given me, <u>I laid a foundation as a wise builder, and someone else is building on it.</u> But each one should build with care. For no one can lay any foundation other than the one already laid, which is Jesus Christ. If anyone builds on this foundation using gold, silver, costly stones, wood, hay or straw, their work will be shown for what it is, because the Day will bring it to light. It will be revealed with fire, and the fire will test the quality of each person's work. If what has been built survives, the builder will receive a reward. If it is burned up, the builder will suffer loss but yet will be saved—even though only as one escaping through the flames."*

- **We Can Correctly Handle the Truth – 2 Timothy 2:15 NIV –** *"Do your best to present yourself to God as one approved, a worker who does not need to be ashamed and <u>who correctly handles the word of truth</u>."*

- **We Can Obey the Truth – 1 Peter 1:22 NIV –** *"Now that <u>you</u>*

have purified yourself by obeying the truth so that you have sincere love for each other, love one another deeply, from the heart."

What the Truth Offers Us

Once again it is the scriptures that inform us of what exactly living by God's absolute truth offers us. The following is the short list.

- **The Truth Offers Us FREEDOM – John 8:32 NKJV –** *"You shall know the truth, and the truth shall make you free."*

- **The Truth Offers Us STABILITY – Ephesians 6:13-14 NKJV –** *"Therefore take up the whole armor of God, that you may be able to withstand in the evil day, and having done all, to stand. Stand therefore, having girded your waist with truth...."*

- **The Truth Offers Us JOY – 1 Corinthians 13:6 NKJV –** *"(Love) does not rejoice in iniquity, but rejoices in the truth."*

- **The Truth Offers Us SANCTIFICATION – John 17:17 NKJV –** *"Sanctify them by Your truth. Your word is truth."*

- **The Truth Offers Us INTIMACY WITH GOD – Psalm 145:18 NKJV –** *"The Lord is near to all who call upon Him, to all who call upon Him in truth."*

- **The Truth Offers PERSECUTION –** Yes! The truth offers us many good things, but you need a heads up. It also brings persecution. **John 8:37 NKJV –** *"I know that you are Abraham's descendants, but you seek to kill Me, because My word has no place in you."* **John 15:18-21 NKJV –** *"If the world hates you, you know that it hated Me before it hated you. If you were of the world, the world would love its own. Yet because you are not of the world, but I chose you out of the world, therefore the world hates you. Remember the word that I said to you, 'A* *servant is not greater than his master.' If they persecuted Me, they will also persecute you. If they kept My word, they will keep yours also. But all these things they will do to you for My name's sake, because they do not know Him who sent Me.'"* That is true truth. But, be of good cheer! In the next breath Jesus declared: *"In the world you will have trouble. But take heart! I have overcome the world."* (John 16:33 NIV)

God's Admonitions To Us

Through Solomon God reminds us of His stellar counsel of truth to us. *"Have I not written to you excellent things of counsels and knowledge, that I may make you know the certainty of the words of truth, that you may answer words of truth to those who send to you?"* (Proverbs 22:20-21 NKJV) This question seems similar to me to the question God asked through the prophet Isaiah when He had declared that He had done everything He could do to make them fruitful. He had dug up the ground, cleared it of stones, planted it with choice vines, built a watchtower to protect it and had an expectation of fruitfulness. But He only saw bad fruit. He said: *"What more could have been done for My vineyard than I have done for it?"* (Isaiah 5:4 NIV) God is looking for a remnant that will take advantage of the tools He has offered to ingest truth, to rely on it, to obey it and to offer it to others.

You may ask, "What are those tools?" Good question! I believe God has given us His "Dynamic Duo"——the Word of God and the Spirit of God——to aid in our certainty of knowing His truth and passing it on. John 17:17 NIV says *"Sanctify them by the truth; Your word is Truth."* The rest of scripture tells us this is so. 2 Timothy 3:16-17 tells us the Word is able to teach us, to rebuke us, to correct us and to train us. Psalm 19:7-11 testifies that this Word of Truth revives us, makes us wise, gives us joy and offers us light. All of Psalm 119 speaks of the benefits of the Word of God. In verses 169-176 we are told that it touches our minds, our mouths, our wills, our emotions and our consciences. A good exercise to do for a quiet time is to read all of Psalm 119 and make two lists: "What the Word Can Do For Me" and "What I Can Do With the Word."

John 16:13 NIV declares: *"But when He, the Spirit of truth comes, He will guide you into all truth."* The following is a list of the many things the Spirit accomplishes in our lives along with the Bible references that say it is so. It should be an encouragement to you.

The Holy Spirit …

- Convicts - John 16:8-11
- Helps me Remember – John 14:26
- Counsels – John 14:26
- Seals – 2 Corinthians 1:21-22
- Reveals – Ephesians 1:17
- Intercedes – Romans 8:26; Ephesians 6:18
- Teaches – John 16:12-15; John 14:26
- Regenerates – Titus 3:5
- Comforts – John 14:1, 27
- Comes Alongside – John 14:18
- Gifts – 1 Corinthians 12:1-11; Romans 12:6-8
- Equips – Hebrews 2:4; Ephesians 4:11-13
- Assures – Romans 8:16
- Guides – Romans 8:14

My friend, Tikki Grace Jefferson, now with Jesus, always said the following: "If you have the Word without the Spirit, you dry up. If you have the Spirit without the Word, you blow up. But, if you have the Word AND the Spirit, you grow up." Dr. Luke must have understood this when he wrote the gospel of Luke. In the very beginning of his book, he wrote the following words. *"Since I myself have carefully investigated everything from the beginning, I too decided to write an orderly account for you, most excellent Theophilus, so that you may know the certainty of the things you have been taught."* (Luke 1:3-4 NIV) Luke was conscientious with the truth. He investigated it carefully. He made an orderly presentation of it to someone else. And the hoped-for result was that that person would be certain of the same truth. The True Truth.

A Biblical Example

In John 18:28-38 NIV the account is recorded of Pilate's questioning of Jesus in His last week. His queries were many. *"Are you king of the Jews?" "What is it you have done?"* Jesus patiently answered. *"My kingdom is not of this world." "You are right in saying I am a king. In fact, for this reason I was born, and for this I came into the world, to testify to the truth. Everyone on the side of truth listens to Me."*

The same is true today. If you and I align with Jesus and His Word and Spirit, we are automatically on the side of truth. The problem is that people now and then try to wiggle away from that uncomfortable Truth. So they ask what Pilate asked. *"WHAT IS TRUTH?"* Folks are always hoping that some other politically correct, "progressive", Woke reasoning will replace what is uncomfortable and inconvenient. Not much has changed in the centuries.

Once again, the Word of God makes things quite clear. In Jesus' explanation to Nicodemus in John 3:19-21 NKJV He said: *"And this is the condemnation, that the light has come into the world, and men loved darkness rather than light, because their deeds were evil. For everyone practicing evil hates the light and does not come to the light, lest his deeds should be exposed. But he who does the truth comes to the light, that his deeds may be clearly seen, that they have been done in God."* God in His grace sent His light so that we might see the error of our ways. That's important because if we do not see that how we live is in error, we cannot ache over it; how it affects us or God's heart. And that's vital because if we do not ache over it, we cannot agree with God and confess it. Confession is invaluable because without it we cannot repent and turn from bad ways.

Paul David Tripp says it this way. "Sin turns all of us into citizens of the night. Sin causes all of us to be committed to low-light living. We hide, we deny, we cover, we lie, we excuse, we shift the blame, we rationalize, we defend, and we explain away. These are all acts of darkness by people who fear exposure. Grace shatters our darkness. (God) dispels our self-inflicted darkness because he knows that we cannot grieve what we do not see, we cannot confess what we have not grieved, and we cannot turn from what we haven't confessed."[44]

We must not play games with the truth. We must allow God's light to makes us AWARE of how we live or do not live aright in the light of God's truth. We must ACHE over any departure from it. We must AGREE with God and confess our shortcomings to Him. And, we must APOLOGIZE with correct behavior; a turning. Repentance.

How We Can Intentionally Live in Absolute Truth

In Revelation 14:1-5 NKJV a picture is painted of a final remnant of God living in the midst of the bowls of judgment. The account is about the famed 144,000. *"Then I looked, and behold, a Lamb standing on Mount Zion, and with Him one hundred and forty-four thousand, having His Father's name written on their foreheads. And I heard a voice from heaven, like the voice of many waters, and like the voice of loud thunder. And I heard the sound of harpists playing their harps. They sang as it were a new song before the throne, before the four living creatures, and the elders, and no one could learn that song except the hundred and forty-four thousand who were redeemed from the earth. These are the ones who were not defiled with women, for they are virgins. These are the ones who follow the Lamb wherever He goes. These were redeemed from among men, being firstfruits to God and to the Lamb. And in their mouth was found no deceit, for they are without fault before the throne of God."*

These are ones who are "all in." Every part of their lives is controlled by the truth of the living God. Their minds are affected for the word tells us *"their Father's name is on their foreheads."* Their feet are touched by this truth because *"they follow the Lamb wherever He goes."* Their tongue is involved because the report is that *"in their mouth was found no deceit."* Their hearts are touched. They are seen as undefiled ones who *"are without fault before the throne of God."* And their ears are affected because we are told they *"heard a voice from heaven."* This is a great motivator for us to be "all in" as well.

As was discussed earlier, we will become people of the Truth to the degree that the Word and the Spirit——God's Dynamic Duo——have sway over our hearts and minds.

Also, our prayers can keep us pursuing truth and passing it on to others. Take to heart the passionate prayer of the psalmist in Psalm 43:1-2a, 3 NKJV. *"Vindicate me, O God, and plead my cause against an ungodly nation. Oh, deliver me from the deceitful and unjust man! For You are the God of my strength. Oh, send out Your light and Your truth! Let them lead me; let them bring me to Your holy hill and to Your tabernacle."*

Another way to live God's Truth is to continue to speak God's truth. Again, it is the psalmist——David——who proclaims God's ways and His Truth. *"I have not hidden Your righteousness within my heart; I have declared Your faithfulness and Your salvation. I have not concealed Your lovingkindness and Your truth from the great assembly."* This harkens back to Ezekiel telling us we must "sigh and cry".

And, finally, love wins the day. Paul exhorts the church at Ephesus in Ephesians 4:15 NKJV. *"Speak the truth in love. Grow up in all things into Him."* We are told of Jesus that He was *"full of grace and truth."* (John 1:14 NKJV) We must never bludgeon people with truth and leave them untouched by God's grace. And, we must not lavish grace and turn a blind eye to truth. Dick Brogden, missionary in the Middle East, has said: "Just as truth without mercy kills, mercy without truth corrupts."[45] We need both.

Conclusion

Sometimes it is in difficult times that we learn truth best; those times that stir up tears and cause angst in our hearts. It is in those moments that lies are exposed. Things like God needs my help. Or, I cannot possibly let go of my problems. Or, God is just not present when darkness and emptiness loom in my life. Or, I will have to work hard to keep any of my longings alive. Or, I am what I have done in the past. Or, when things are really hard, God must be punishing me for some awful sin I am not aware of. But, the truth is God wants us to put ourselves in His hands, not try to help Him out. And, I actually make forward progress by holding an open hand to God, not clutching my life with a white-knuckle grip. And, when things are really dark and empty, God's light shines best and fills the empty spaces. And, rest comes from being in God's everlasting arms. I do not have to strive. I can live His longings. And, God has promised me a future and a hope. The past is not a problem for Him. And, there may be disciplining going on in my life but it is only ever from the hand of a loving Father who wants what is best for me.

Yes! Things that bring us to tears are ready tutors for Truth lessons.

"Then Jesus said to those Jews who believed Him, 'If you abide in My word, you are My disciples indeed, and you shall know the truth, and the truth shall make you free." (John 8:31-32 NKJV)

On close observation it seems that the consummate Alpha Male—the apostle Paul—paid attention to tears. Tears are tiny; made up largely of water and lipids and sodium and potassium and glucose. They protect our eyes and warn of us of irritants, like smoke and onions, and they are wardens of emotion. They appear when we are happy and when we are sad; like others have said, safety valves on a heart with too much pressure on it. And, the scriptures tell us that Paul noticed them. He was aware of the tears of Timothy. (See 2 Timothy 1:4.) And, he noticed the tears of those who pleaded with him not to go to Jerusalem. (See Acts 21:13.) He himself cried in love for the Corinthian church that he needed to rebuke over unforgiveness for a brother. (See 2 Corinthians 2:3-11.) He cried warning the Philippians about *"enemies of the cross."* (See Philippians 3:18-19.) And, he wept over the distortion of Truth in Acts 20:29-31 NIV. *"I know that after I leave, savage wolves will come in among you and will not spare the flock. Even from your own number men will arise and distort the truth in order to draw away disciples after them. So be on your guard! Remember that for three years I never stopped warning each of you night and day with tears."*

It seems that God notices tears also. In Psalm 56:8 NASB the prayer of the psalmist indicates that God finds them so valuable that He collects them in a bottle. *"You have taken account of my wanderings; put my tears in Your bottle. Are they not in Your book?"* William Shakespeare is credited with saying that "tears water our growth." So, my question is: Do YOU cry over the distortion of True Truth in our culture today?

Prayer Points To Consider

1. Ask God for His Truth to set you free in whatever areas He deems appropriate. Listen for His responses.

2. Ask God to help you be a person who obeys His Absolute Truth.

3. Ask God to utilize the "Dynamic Duo"——the Word of God and the Holy Spirit——in your life to live in Truth.

4. However the Spirit leads.

CHAPTER NINE –
DECORATION OR LIFE?

God's Intentional Remnant Devours God's Word and Finds Sustenance 365 Days A Year from This Daily Bread.

> "We must allow the Word of God to confront us, to disturb our security, to undermine our complacency and to overthrow our patterns of thought and behavior."[46]
> ——John R. W. Stott——

My husband and I have now been married nearly fifty-five years. I know, we're old. In our early years as newly married folks in the 1960's, it was still acceptable to honor the Bible. When I set about decorating our first apartment I thought it might be nice to have the family Bible on the coffee table. It looked so ...... you know, impressive. The only problem was we never opened it. We were church-goers, so we heard the Word, but we did not read it for ourselves. Studying it was out of the question. We had so many more important things to do and a whole life ahead of us to pursue. In essence, the Bible was a decoration in our home. It wasn't until after I came to know Jesus as my Lord and Savior in 1972 that His Word held any real significance for me. In Deuteronomy 32:46-47 NIV Moses declared: *Take to heart all the words I have solemnly declared to you this day, so that you may command your children to obey carefully all the words of this law. They are not just idle words for you—they are your life.* (Underlining mine.) *By them you will live long in the land you are crossing the Jordan to possess."*

Today folks would not say they disdain the scriptures, but neither are they respected as more than nice children's stories by most of our culture. Even in the church, the interest in Bible study has waned. Memorizing the Bible is close to being a lost art. And, many inside the church check off a "Quiet Time" on their "To-Do" list, but never actually meet the God of the Word when they sit with their Bibles in their laps. Usually they are not still long enough to know God's presence or to hear His voice. Centuries ago Martin Luther said the following. "The Bible is the cradle that holds the Christ; without Him it is nothing more than wood and straw."[47]

A true story is told of a godly woman, an elderly saint, who all her life had held the Bible in high esteem. She knew that if she wanted a grasp on the scriptures, she would need to invest time hearing it, reading it and studying it. And, if she desired the Word to get a grasp on her, she would need to memorize and meditate on it, as Joshua declared in Joshua 1:8. So, her habit was to memorize. She did it with zeal and encouraged anyone willing to follow her example. Her favorite verse was 2 Timothy 2:12. *"I am not ashamed for I know whom I have believed and am persuaded that He is able to keep what I have committed to Him until that Day."* As the years wore on, her mind started playing tricks. The once favorite verse became more and more difficult to remember. Phrases would come out of her mouth, but not the whole verse. *"I am not ashamed."* And then, *"I am persuaded".* Finally, *"He is able."* Soon even the phrases became an impossibility and the word she was left with was …… *"HIM."*

At this point, I want to give a plug for scripture memory. In 1984, over thirty-six years ago, God impressed on me the need to get the Bible in my heart, not just before my eyes. A verse from the prophet Amos riveted my soul. In Amos 8:11-12 NIV he said: *"'The days are coming,' declares the Sovereign Lord, 'when I will send a famine through the land—not a famine of food or a thirst for water, but a famine of hearing the words of the Lord. They shall wander from sea to sea, and from north to east; they shall run to and fro, seeking the word of the Lord, but shall not find it.""* At the time, I thought, "That will never happen." But, today, I am not so sure that such a time is not just around the corner. Therefore, God's own people need to be prepared. Perhaps there will be a day when people will not know us by our given names, but by the portion of the Bible inside our heart ready to be shared with others hungry to know it. You may be known as the book of 1 Peter or as Psalm 84. Surely you will be known for more than: *"Jesus wept."* The Word is eternal, (See 1 Peter 1:23) so God will not allow it to disappear. But, His remnant is going to need to be intentional about keeping it in their hearts for their good, the growth of others and the glory of God.

The truth is the Bible was never meant to be a mere decoration. It was meant to be life, to give life, to sustain life and to transform life. Hebrews 4:12 NIV reminds us of God's assessment of His own Word. *"For the word of God is alive and active. Sharper than any double-edged sword, it penetrates even to dividing soul and spirit, joints and marrow; it judges the thoughts and attitudes of the heart."* It is alive, not dead. It is active, not passive. It is sharp, not dull. It penetrates, never bull-dozes. It judges. It is not a benign word. It is life because it reveals God and His character and ways. It also gives life as it reveals our need for a Rescuer, a Savior, and then meets our need with Jesus. *"For God so loved the world that He gave His only begotten Son, that whoever believes in Him should not perish but have everlasting life."* (John 3:16 NKJV)

Not only IS the Word life. Not only does the Bible GIVE life. It also SUSTAINS life. It provides food, encouragement and pro-tection for the journey. Job said: *"I have treasured the words of His mouth more than my necessary food."* (Job 23:12 NKJV) Jesus said: *"It is written, man shall not live by bread alone, but by every word that proceeds from the mouth of God."* (Matthew 4:4 NKJV) Not only is the Bible life. Not only does it give life. Not only does it sustain life. It TRANSFORMS life by the renewing of our minds. *"Do not be conformed to this world, but be transformed by the renewing of your mind, so that you may prove what the will of God is, that which is good and acceptable and perfect."* (Romans 12:2 NASB) Paul exhorted the Colossian church with these words. *"Let the word of Christ dwell in you richly in all wisdom...."* (Colossians 3:16 NKJV)

A Declaration of Truth

Many of the prophets, major and minor, shouted a heads up to us long ago about the disinterest that would develop for God's own word by His own people. Just a few of those verses are listed below.

Jeremiah 6:10, 19b NKJV – *"To whom shall I speak and give warning that they may hear? Indeed, their ear is uncircumcised and they cannot give heed. Behold, the word of the Lord is a reproach to them; they have no delight in it."* 19. *"I will certainly bring calamity on this people——the fruit of their thoughts, because they have not heeded My words nor My law, but rejected it."*

Hosea 5:11 NKJV – *"Ephraim is oppressed and broken in judgment because he willingly walked by human precept."* That statement hits home in today's culture.

Jeremiah 8:9 NKJV – *"The wise men are ashamed. They are dismayed and taken. Behold, they have rejected the word of the Lord; so what wisdom do they have?"* Indeed!

Hosea 8:12 NKJV – *"I have written for him the great things of My law, but they were considered a strange thing."*

Amos 2:4-5 NKJV – *"Thus says the Lord: 'For three transgressions of Judah, and for four, I will not turn away its punishment, because they have despised the law of the Lord, and have not kept His commandments. Their lies lead them astray, lies which their fathers followed. But I will send a fire upon Judah, and it shall devour the palaces of Jerusalem."*

Isaiah 30:9-12 NKJV – *"This is a rebellious people. Lying children, children who will not hear the word of the Lord; who say to the seers,*

'Do not see.' And to the prophets, 'Do not prophesy to us right things; speak to us smooth things, prophesy deceits. Get out of the way, turn aside from the path, cause the Holy One of Israel to cease from before us.' Therefore thus says the Holy One of Israel: 'Because you despise this word, and trust in oppression and perversity, and rely on them, therefore this iniquity shall be to you like a breach ready to fall, a bulge in a high wall, whose breaking comes suddenly, in an instant."

The Intentional Remnant is aware that the bulge is growing like an aneurism ready to burst. It will be sudden. In an instant.

Examples of Cultural and Church Abuse

As mentioned in chapter four, in an April, 2018 issue of GQ Magazine, the following article, titled "21 Books You Don't Have To Read", was touted as great journalism. Of the books mentioned many were classics; volumes you and I were obligated to read by teachers of yore. The overall statement that commenced the explanation for the piece were these words. "Some (of these books) are racist and some are sexist, but most are just really, really boring. So we—a group of unboring writers—give you permission to strike these books from the canon." You guessed it. The Bible was among those listed.

One of the editors, Jesse Ball, continues in his explanation of why the Bible was stricken. "The Holy Bible is rated very highly by all the people who supposedly live by it but who in actuality have not read it. Those who *have* read it know there are some good parts, but overall it's certainly not the finest thing that man has ever produced." (I will stop here to point out the ignorance of these "unboring" editors. The Bible is <u>God</u>-breathed; not written by men. 2 Peter 1:20-21 NKJV is clear. *"No prophecy of Scripture is of any private interpretation, for prophecy never came by the will of man, but holy men of God spoke as they were moved by the Holy Spirit."*)

The editor continues. "It (the Bible) is repetitive, self-contradictory, sententious, foolish, and even at times ill-intentioned. If the thing you heard was good about the Bible was the nasty bits, then I propose Agota Kristof's "The Notebook", a marvelous tale of two brothers who have to get along when things get rough."[48] An ill-gotten opinion at best.

In January and February of 2017, Barna Research did a study on the State of the Bible. They came up with five different "Bible Engagement Definitions." They are as follows.

1. **Bible Engaged**. These are people who "view the Bible as a) the actual or b) the inspired word of God with no errors or as c) the inspired word of God with some errors." The folks in this category said they "read, used or listened to the Bible four times a week or more." Twenty per cent of those polled fell in this category.

2. **Bible Friendly.** These are men and women who "view the Bible as a) the actual or b) the inspired word of God with no errors. They read, used or listened to the Bible fewer than four times per week." The largest percentage of those polled were in this category logging in at 38%.

3. **Bible Neutral.** This category accounted for 23% of those polled. They "view the Bible as the inspired word of God with some factual or historical errors OR it is not inspired but tells how the writers understood the ways and principles of God. They read, used or listened to the Bible one time a month or less."

4. **Bible Skeptic.** These people "viewed the Bible as 'just another book of teachings written by men.'" 19% of those polled fell in this slot.

5. **Bible Hostile.** This group was defined as "a subset of the Bible Skeptic group. They viewed the Bible as a book written by men and intended to manipulate and control

others." 13% were found in this category. This study also revealed that most Skeptics were Hostiles.

Further, it was shown that in 2011 25% of the American public polled NEVER read, listened to or prayed with the Bible. In 2017 that number had grown to 32% (That's almost one-third of people.) And, not surprisingly, it was also revealed that as age increased, so did Bible Engagement. 24% of millennials were Bible Skeptics while only 12% of elders fell in that category.[49]

Lest you think this is only a cultural problem and that the church is somehow immune, I draw your attention to another study conducted by Barna in 2018. The following question was asked of Churchgoers. "Have you heard of the Great Commission?" 6% reported: "I'm not sure." 25% said: "Yes, but I can't recall the exact meaning." 17% confidently stated: "Yes, and it means …." And 51% said: "No." Churchgoers! 51% saying "NO!" Appalling.

God's Reminders To Us

God speaks to us in His Word and reminds us of the value of respecting His words and living them out. The following are just a few places in the Bible that tell us of its priceless worth.

Psalm 12:6 NKJV – *"The words of the Lord are pure words, like silver tried in a furnace of earth, purified seven times."*
Hebrews 4:12 NIV – *"For the word of God is alive and active. Sharper than any double-edged sword, it penetrates even to dividing soul and spirit, joints and marrow; it judges the thoughts and attitudes of the heart."*
Psalm 19:7-11 NKJV – *"The law of the Lord is perfect, converting the soul; the testimony of the Lord is sure, making wise the simple; the statutes of the Lord are right, rejoicing the heart; the commandment of the Lord is pure, enlightening the eyes; the fear of the Lord is clean, enduring forever; the judgments of the Lord are true and righteous*

altogether. More to be desired are they than gold, yea, than much fine gold; sweeter also than honey and the honeycomb. Moreover by them Your servant is warned, and in keeping them there is great reward."

Deuteronomy 8:3b NKJV – *"Man shall not live by bread alone; but man lives by every word that proceeds from the mouth of the Lord."*

Proverbs 13:13 NKJV – *"He who despises the word will be destroyed, but he who fears the commandment will be rewarded."*

1 Peter 1:23-25 NIV – *"For you have been born again, not of perishable seed, but of imperishable, through the living and enduring word of God. For, 'All people are like grass, and all their glory is like the flowers of the field; the grass withers and the flowers fall, but the word of the Lord endures forever.' And this is the word that was preached to you."*

A Biblical Example

"Good Kings Come in Small Packages." That was the title of a children's musical of the 1980's. It was the story of Josiah who became king at the ripe old age of eight. At age twenty-six, when he had now sat on the throne for eighteen years, he gave the command to repair and clean up the Temple. As his command was being carried out, the Book of the Law was found and brought to the young King Josiah. He read it. He wept. He tore his robes. He knew that he and his people had grieved the heart of the Lord by not keeping this law. His heart was tender toward the Book and all it contained. He humbled himself in the reading and, as a result, God gave peace to the land during his reign.

Josiah not only had his heart touched by the Word of God; his outward actions reflected the transformation God had commenced on the inside. Josiah called all the people together and he read it before them. Can you imagine what it might be like if the leader of our land were to call the people together to read the Bible before them? That is power! 2 Chronicles 34:32 NKJV says: *"And he* (Josiah) *made all who were present in Jerusalem and Benjamin take a stand. So the inhabitants of Jerusalem did according to the cove-*

nant of God, the God of their fathers." Verse 33 goes on to say *"Thus Josiah removed all the abominations from all the country that belonged to the children of Israel, and made all who were present in Israel diligently serve the Lord their God. All his days they did not depart from following the Lord God of their fathers."*

Why the Word is so Important

The following is a chart that explains Psalm 19:7-11.

What It's Called	A Descriptor	The Result
The Law Of the Lord	It is PERFECT	It Converts The Soul
The Testimony Of the Lord	It is SURE	It Makes Wise The Simple
The Statutes Of the Lord	They are RIGHT	They Rejoice The Heart
The Commandment Of the Lord	It is PURE	It Enlightens The Eyes
The Judgements Of the Lord	They are TRUE And RIGHTEOUS	It is Desirable And Sweet

THE WORD WARNS AND GIVES GREAT REWARD

The rewards that the Word of God gives us are immeasurable. In the column on "Results" in the preceding chart, I will share a few personal illustrations.

- **It Converts the Soul** – In my life one of the Bible verses that most clearly helped in the conversion of my soul in 1972 was Jeremiah 31:3-4. As an adult coming out of a dysfunctional childhood, not assured of the love that I hoped for but did not experience consistently, that verse drew me into the arms of Jesus. *"The Lord has appeared of old to me, saying: "Yes, I have loved you with an everlasting love; therefore with lovingkindness I have drawn you. Again I will build you, and you shall be rebuilt, O virgin of Israel!"*

- **It Makes Wise the Simple** – Hebrews 10:19-25 NIV made me wise by showing me simple, authentic discipleship. Three commands are given in these verses. They all encompass the three big things of our journeys with God: Faith, Hope and Love. We are told to 1. <u>Draw Near</u> with full assurance of faith, 2. <u>Hold Unswervingly</u> to the hope we profess, and 3. <u>Spur one another</u> on toward love. Sometimes the most profound things are the simplest. Because Jesus made the way, I can draw near to the Father. Then I am to hold on tight with His perseverance. And, I can help someone else do the same thing. *"We love, because He first loved us."* (1 John 4:19 NASB) That's being a disciple.

- **It Rejoices the Heart** –As a child I did everything I knew to do to find acceptance; to be brought near. Often my attempts were rebuffed. One day I found a verse in the Bible that gave me great joy. Ephesians 2:13 NIV says: *"But now in Christ Jesus you who once were far away have been brought near by the blood of Christ."* Drawn in. Held. Accepted. Loved. Oh, what joy!

- **It Enlightens the Eyes** – Isaiah 26:8-9a NIV turned the light on for me to show me what it looks like if someone was a "Yes, Lord" person. *"Yes, Lord, walking in the way of your laws, we wait for you; your name and renown are the desire of our hearts. My soul yearns for you in the night; in the morning my spirit longs for you."* I began to see that if I wanted to be someone God could count on to say a wholehearted "Yes" to

Him, no matter what the cost, there would be four things I would need do. l. I need to be obedient; not just to talk about walking His way, but actually walk in God's ways. 2. I would need to wait for Him; not run ahead, not lag behind. I would need to be aware of His timing and His agenda. 3. I would need to be humble; making all of life about Him——His name and His renown. And, 4. I need to be passionate about pursuing God; yearning and longing for Him 24/7.

- **It is Desirable and Sweet** – Psalm 119:103 NIV says *"How sweet are your words to my taste, sweeter than honey to my mouth."* We have three children and two of them have been insulin-dependent diabetics since they were very young. One was diagnosed at age eleven and the other at age six. It always bothered me that they could not have candy. Upon reading this verse in Psalm 119 I decided to start praying that when they craved sugar, they would go to the Word of God, which is the sweetest thing they could ingest. Today, one of them is a Christian Counselor, helping many through trauma with the Word of God. The other is a pastor who loves to preach when he gets the chance and is most discerning with the Word. The Bible is definitely sweeter than honey, and I have been told that honey is the sweetest natural thing we can know.

The Bible gives great reward. Revelation 1:3 affirms this truth. "Blessed is the one who reads aloud the words of this prophecy, and blessed are those who hear it and take to heart what is written in it, because the time is near."

How We Can Intentionally Regard the Word

The third chapter of Paul's second letter to Timothy (2 Timothy 3) starts with a list of the many things that will describe the character of men and women in the last days. The list is daunting and real. We see it every day. It's enough to make you throw up your hands, surrender to the downward spiral and put a blanket over your head. But, take heart. The end of the same chapter, 2 Timothy 3:16-17, tells us we are equipped to handle any of the garbage that the culture dishes out. That verse in the NIV says: *"All Scripture is God-breathed and is useful for teaching, rebuking, correcting and training in righteousness, 17 so that the servant of God may be thoroughly equipped for every good work."* Did you get that? We are "thoroughly equipped." That means entirely ready. Meticulously prepared. Scrupulously armed. Comprehensively outfitted. Fully capable. The Word will teach us how to live, rebuke us when we depart from God's way, correct us by exposing wayward paths and convincing us that God's way is best, and by training us with discipline to get it right.

When Paul wrote the Philippian church in Philippians 2:15-16 he was writing to folks who lived in a generation much like ours today. It was crooked and depraved. But, once again, the Word becomes the tool to overcome. The NIV verse exhorts us. *"Do everything without grumbling or arguing, 15 so that you may become blameless and pure, "children of God without fault in a warped and crooked generation." Then you will shine among them like stars in the sky 16 as you hold firmly to the word of life."*

In the Old Testament the prophet Isaiah told us a startling truth. Isaiah 66:2b NIV reports: *"These are the ones I look on with favor: those who are humble and contrite in spirit, and who tremble at my word."* When I first read that verse and took it to heart, I had to ask myself: "Do I *tremble* at God's Word?" The Lord reminded me of a time not long ago when I was attempting to memorize Acts 17:16-34 (Paul's amazing apologetic at Mars Hill in Athens) that I did indeed tremble in the face of what I was seeing before my eyes. In that passage there are three things that Paul noticed about the culture around him. You read about them in chapter three. 1. They were full of idols. 2. They gave themselves only to thinking and talking about the latest ideas. And, 3. They were very religious; always resisting the Holy Spirit. It didn't take long to realize that describes our culture today. I trembled. And I asked God what to do. This look at the Intentional Remnant is part of His answer. The logical question at this point is: "Do YOU tremble at God's Word?"

I have mentioned Psalm 119 often in this chapter. At the very end of this longest of the psalms, we are told that the Word of God touches everything in our lives. Psalm 119:169-176 NIV says: *"May my cry come before you, Lord; give me understanding according to your word. May my supplication come before you; deliver me according to your promise. May my lips overflow with praise, for you teach me your decrees. May my tongue sing of your word, for all your commands are righteous. May your hand be ready to help me, for I have chosen your precepts. I long for your salvation, Lord, and your law gives me delight. Let me live that I may praise you, and may your laws sustain me. I have strayed like a lost sheep. Seek your servant, for I have not forgotten your commands."*

It touches our minds because it says *"give me understanding."* Our mouths are affected for it declares *"my lips overflow with praise"* and *"my tongue will sing of Your word."* Our wills are touched because it reports *"I have chosen your precepts."* Our emotions are tapped for it says *"I long for your salvation"* and *"your law gives me delight."* And our feet are touched for the confession is *"I have strayed like a lost sheep."* The Word of God is important in that it touches all of our being.

God paints wonderful pictures in His Word. He even places strokes on canvas for how His Word looks. I call this "Pictures At An Exhibition." God says His Word is "like" many things. The things are commonplace. We understand them. Things like honey and lamps. And when we consider that His Word is "like" those things, we have more understanding as to exactly what this amazing Word has to offer. Honey is sweet. The Word is sweet. Lamps light up dark places. So does the Word of God. Following is a list of these pictures from the brush of the Almighty. The references are next to them so you can check it out for yourself. Consider walking through the gallery with me, enjoying each masterpiece.

- A Well-Driven Nail – Ecclesiastes 12:11
- A Treasure – Psalm 19:10-11; 119:72
- A Lamp – Psalm 119:105
- A Mirror – James 1:22-25
- Food – Job 23:12; Jeremiah 15:16
- Life – Deuteronomy 32:46-47
- An Equipper – 2 Timothy 3:16-17
- A Hammer and A Fire – Jeremiah 23:19
- A Scalpel – Hebrews 4:12
- A Sword – Ephesians 6:17
- Honey – Psalm 119:103
- A Wise Investment (A present expenditure for a future dividend) – Isaiah 55:11
- A Teacher – Psalm 119:99; Proverbs 7:2
- Rain Water – Deuteronomy 32:1-3
- An Ice Breaker – Psalm 147:18

If you look carefully at all of these pictures you begin to realize that the Word hits the nail on the head. It gives exactly what is needed at exactly the right moment. It is treasure to be mined. It offers light for each step. It helps you see yourself. It feeds and sustains you. It prepares you. It hits you over the head, if you need it. It is a skilled physician's tool; a scalpel that might hurt, but then heal. It fights our enemies. It gives us understanding and wisdom and discernment. It helps us grow. And, it breaks down walls. How could we not be people who want to jump in, sit on the Father's lap daily, and allow Him to underline the parts that are just for us?

Conclusion

A true story is told of a remote jungle tribe reached by missionaries in the early part of the twentieth century. Cannibalism was their regular practice. As missionaries translated God's Word into the tongue of the people there, a change occurred. The Bible came alive to them and transformed the tribe from the inside out, starting with the chief. Some time elapsed after the conversions took place and God caused growth in their hearts. Some gawkers from the United States and the United Kingdom arrived in their midst to see if it was all true. One man, especially skeptical of what was reported about God's touch on this people group, sneered and shouted "I don't believe the words of the Book you say changed you. They are mere fairy tales." The chief replied confidently, "You may not believe in the power of the God-breathed Word to change the lives of men, sir, but it is what is keeping me from eating you!"

Power indeed. God's Intentional Remnant holds His Word in high regard, patterning all of life after its words. It is a beacon to anyone who will notice and change their own ways.

Prayer Points To Consider

1. Confess any lack of interest in or obedience to the Word of God.

2. Ask God to help you make the Word "your life." Ask Him for a plan to implement that.

3. Ask God to touch your mind, your mouth, your will, your emotions and your feet with the truth of His Word. Keep a journal of what He accomplishes.

4. Pray Psalm 19 and/or Psalm 119, making it personal to you.

5. Ask God what He wants you to memorize of His Word and then follow through with obedience.

6. As the Holy Spirit leads.

CHAPTER TEN – SHEPHERDS, NOT SHEEP RUSTLERS

God's Intentional Remnant is Reliable in its Shepherding

> "God has entrusted us with His most precious treasure—people. He asks us to shepherd and mold them into strong disciples with brave faith and good character."[50]
> ——John Ortberg——
>
> "It is the duty of a good shepherd to shear his sheep, not to skin them."[51]
> ——Tiberius——

One of the abominations that I believe grieves the heart of God is the unreliability of shepherds in the modern church. There are those who love to preach, leaders with business acumen, and those with counseling ability, but God is looking for those who will humbly feed and lead at His direction. He wants men and women who will have a heart for those under their care, sacrificing for them as needed. He wants His under-shepherds to be Jesus-centered; under the authority of the Good Shepherd.

"Let me set this before you as plainly as I can. If a person climbs over or through the fence of a sheep pen instead of going through the gate, you know he's up to no good—a sheep rustler! This is the declaration made in The Message by its writer, Eugene Peterson. It is in John 10:1. There are aliases given in this passage as well. The sheep

rustlers are also called thieves, robbers, strangers and hired hands that don't care about the sheep. It isn't long before we are told that Jesus is The Gate. We must come through Him. No other way will do. A.W. Tozer is credited with saying "Without the Holy Spirit you have to get by with business practices, human effort and psychology."[52] Noted global speaker, Duffy Robbins, asserts: "What you draw people with is eventually what you draw them to." In the NIV the same verse says: *"Very truly I tell you Pharisees, anyone who does not enter the sheep pen by the gate, but climbs in by some other way, is a thief and a robber."* "Some other way" could be entertainment, celebrity attention, programs or spin. But God is saying …… Only Jesus.

Sheep rustling is nothing new. BBC News writer, Lauren Potts, reports that "it is one of the oldest felonies on record, but it shows no signs of abating."[53] The practice of sheep rustling is thousands of years old. In medieval times the motive was most often poverty. Today the motive is greed. It has become a target for organized crime and is especially prevalent in countries like the United Kingdom, Northern Ireland, Australia and even the United States. Farmers lose big financially and emotionally. Spiritual sheep rustling is also a matter of greed. Leaders wanting notice and acclaim rise up with competitive notions of being the biggest church in town and the sheep lose emotionally and spiritually.

A Declaration of Truth

God knows about sheep rustlers. Through His prophets He has sent multiple messages to warn people who may be victims of such unreliability and to give woe to perpetrators. The following verses declare what I mean.

Ezekiel 34:1-10 NKJV – *"And the word of the LORD came to me, saying,* [2] *"Son of man, prophesy against the shepherds of Israel, prophesy and say to them, 'Thus says the Lord GOD to the shepherds: "Woe to* *the shepherds of Israel who feed themselves! Should not the shepherds feed the flocks?* [3] *You eat the fat and clothe yourselves with the wool; you slaughter the fatlings, but you do not feed the flock.* [4] *The weak you have not strengthened, nor have you healed those who were sick, nor bound up the broken, nor brought back what was driven away, nor sought what was lost; but with force and cruelty you have ruled them.* [5] *So they were scattered because there was no shepherd; and they became food for all the beasts of the field when they were scattered.* [6] *My sheep wandered through all the mountains, and on every high hill; yes, My flock was scattered over the whole face of the earth, and no one was seeking or searching for them."* [7] *Therefore, you shepherds, hear the word of the LORD:* [8] *"As I live," says the Lord GOD, "surely because My flock became a prey, and My flock became food for every beast of the field, because there was no shepherd, nor did My shepherds search for My flock, but the shepherds fed themselves and did not feed My flock"—* [9] *therefore, O shepherds, hear the word of the LORD!* [10] *Thus says the Lord GOD: "Behold, I am against the shepherds, and I will require My flock at their hand; I will cause them to cease feeding the sheep, and the shepherds shall feed themselves no more; for I will deliver My flock from their mouths, that they may no longer be food for them."*

Jeremiah 10:21 – *"For the shepherds have become dull-hearted, and have not sought the LORD; therefore they shall not prosper, and all their flocks shall be scattered."*

Jeremiah 23:1 – *"Woe to the shepherds who destroy and scatter the sheep of My pasture!" says the LORD"* **Jeremiah 50:6** – *"My people have been lost sheep. their shepherds have led them astray; they have turned them away on the mountains. They have gone from mountain to hill; they have forgotten their resting place".*

Examples of Church Abuse

The abuses in this abomination are church related. The culture doesn't understand the significance of being a shepherd, but neither do many who occupy pulpits across the land. One example of egregious misuse comes through an article posted in a Seattle newspaper a few years ago. An editor was interviewing a PCUSA pastor who was on the brink of retirement. He had served his congregation for decades. The most telling thing was the answer to this simple question. "What is the most significant contribution you have made in your many years as minister?" He replied: "I took a little Bible-believing congregation and turned it into a multi-faith community. The greatest moment in my personal spirituality was the moment I discovered Jesus is not God, not Savior, not even an historical individual; but the concept of love." I need to tell you; I would die for Jesus, but I would not die for "a concept of love." I said this in an earlier chapter and I am not ashamed to repeat it again.

The scary part of all this surfaced when I did a little research on the church he was serving. Their Mission Statement reads as follows. "We are a community of people encouraging each other, seeking to be like Jesus, serving God by loving generously, proclaiming boldly, and giving with grace and humility." Just reading that statement would make any strong believer want to belong to that faith community. But the truth is that insidious lies were lurking. The pastor did not even believe in Jesus, so there is no way he could lead his flock in biblical ways. A little more information on their website raised red flags. There was a FAQ, Frequently Asked Questions, tab with these questions and answers. "How long has the church been in business?" A: 61 years. "How many work there?" A: 10. "What are the annual sales?" A: $460,000. "How big is your facility?" A: 14,242 sq. ft. That makes you know something is amiss. The church is not a business and should not be run as such.

A 2020 Pastoral Care Inc. study indicated some interesting findings. I will share just a few items. 80% of pastors believe the pastoral ministry has negatively affected their families. Many pastor's children do not attend church now because of what the church has done to their parents." "90% of pastors report the ministry was completely different that what they thought it would be like before they entered the ministry." 95% of pastors report <u>not</u> praying daily or regularly with their spouse." "80% of pastors and 84% of their spouses have felt unqualified and discouraged as role of pastors at least one or more times in their ministry." "80% of pastors expect conflict within their church." 70% of pastors report they have a lower self-image now than when they first started." 34% of pastors wrestle with the temptation of pornography or visit pornographic sites." "One out of every ten pastors will actually retire as a pastor." "The profession of 'Pastor' is near the bottom of a survey of the most-respected professions, just above "car salesman."[54]

That is a woeful picture considering God is looking for those full of life who will feed the flock, strengthen the weak, heal the sick, bind up the broken, and bring back the ones who have been driven away. He wants shepherds who will seek the lost and rule with love and humility.

God's Reminders To Us

There is a word from Matthew, the gospel writer, that shows us the depth of Jesus' heart for His people who have no shepherd. Matthew 9:36 NKJV states: *"But when He saw the multitudes, He was moved with compassion for them, because they were weary and scattered, like sheep having no shepherd."*

The best place in the Word to find God's heart on shepherding is the chapter in John where He reveals Jesus as the Good Shepherd. It is a clear I AM statement. Jesus, of course, is our model. John 10:1-16 (The Message) follows. *"Let me set this before you as plainly as I can. If a person climbs over or through the fence of a sheep pen instead of going through the gate, you know he's up to no good——a sheep rustler! The shepherd walks right up to the gate. The gatekeeper opens the gate to him and the sheep recognize his voice. He calls his own sheep by name and leads them out. When he gets them all out, he leads them and they follow because they are familiar with his voice. They won't follow a stranger's voice but will scatter because they aren't used to the sound of it."*

"Jesus told this simple story, but they had no idea what he was talking about. So he tried again. 'I'll be explicit then. I am the Gate for the sheep. All those others are up to no good——sheep stealers, every one of them. But the sheep didn't listen to them. I am the Gate. Anyone who goes through me will be cared for——will freely go in and out, and find pasture. A thief is only there to steal and kill and destroy, I came so they can have real and eternal life, more and better life than they ever dreamed of.'"

"'I am the Good Shepherd. I know my own sheep and my own sheep know me. In the same way, the Father knows me and I know the Father. I put the sheep before myself, sacrificing myself if necessary. You need to know that I have other sheep in addition to those in this pen. I need to gather and bring them, too. They'll also recognize my voice. Then it will be one flock, one Shepherd.'"

Today's pastors/shepherds are dealing with the same things that were mentioned in the seven churches in the book of the Revelation. There are people in each congregation that mirror the attitudes and character of those in Ephesus, Smyrna, Pergamos, Thyatira, Sardis, Philadelphia and Laodicea. The people these shepherds need to help are loveless, some are persecuted, some compromise, some are down-right corrupt, some are dead in their spirits, some are faithful and passionate for Jesus, and some are lukewarm. What are the messages the shepherds need to impart? Missives that echo the guidance given to the seven churches of long ago will do nicely. *"Remember from where you have fallen and repent."* (Revelation 2:5 NKJV) *"Be faithful until death. Do not fear".* (Revelation 2:10 NKJV) *"Hold fast until I come."* (Revelation 2:25 NKJV) *"Repent."* (Revelation 3:3 NKJV) *"Hold fast what you have."* (Revelation 3:11 NKJV) *"Be zealous and repent."* (Revelation 3:19 NKJV) Shepherds need to encourage repentance, faithfulness, perseverance, and wake-up calls.

For the Intentional Remnant to be reliable shepherds they need to cultivate the essence of those who are whole-hearted, who love God with all of their heart and mirror Jesus.

A Biblical Example

Peter is a perfect example of one who "got it." He was brash and impulsive and when the going got rough, he bailed out. He betrayed Jesus, not once, but three times. In John 21:15-17 we have a bird's eye view of what restoration looks like. Jesus asked Peter three times if he loved Him. That used to bother me. I thought "Get off of his case. He told you he loved You more than all else. Why ask him an insulting second time, and then a third?" But then I understood. Jesus' three questions covered the three times Peter had said "I don't know this man." What grace!

The first time Jesus asked Peter: *"Do you love Me more than these?"* Peter replied affirmatively. Jesus' immediately gave him a mission. He said *"Feed My lambs."* The second time Jesus asked Peter *"Do you love Me?"* Peter answered in the positive. *"You know that I love You."* Again a direction was given. *"Tend My sheep."* The third question echoed the second—*"Do you love Me?"* Peter said *"You know all things. You know I love You."* The third task assigned was *"Feed My sheep."* Apparently, loving Jesus involves feeding and loving His flock.

Peter understood. How we know that he "got it" is what he wrote in his first letter to the scattered church. 1 Peter 5:1-4 NIV says *"To the elders among you, I appeal as a fellow elder, a witness of Christ's sufferings and one who also will share in the glory to be revealed: Be shepherds of God's flock that is under your care, serving as overseers——not because you must, but because you are willing, as God wants you to be; not greedy for money, but eager to serve; not lording it over those entrusted to you, but being examples to the flock. And when the Chief Shepherd appears, you will receive the crown of glory that will never fade away."*

How We Can Intentionally Be
Reliable Shepherds

Wherever <u>you</u> are serving as a shepherd——as a pastor, in small groups at church, with children, caring for elderly parents or neighbors or work associates, or in a classroom—God is asking you to be three things: 1. Willing. 2. Eager to serve. And, 3. A good example. Peter says it is so.

Ezekiel 34:4 is a place we have looked at before in this chapter. He has five dictates for shepherds who intend to do things God's way. They are: 1. Strengthen the weak. 2. Heal the sick. 3. Bind up the injured. 4. Bring back the strays. And, 5. Search for the lost. That sounds simple enough but it will take the power of the Holy Spirit to accomplish.

And, what we read in John 10:1-16 just a bit earlier applies in this section of understanding also. Over the years I have gone to many "Leadership Conferences." I have been puzzled by many of them, concerned at some, and downright against what I was hearing at others. It seemed to me that the main messages were consistently "Be a Pizzazzy Leader." "Learn to be articulate for Jesus." "Manage people to get the work of the church done." Red flags would go off. I wasn't being a rebel, I just could not believe that this was what was being peddled. And, then I realized, that's what sold tickets. How many people would you get lined up for a conference that promised to teach you how to be a good follower, how to listen before you speak, and how to work hard yourself before you ask anyone to do anything?

John 10:1-16 answered my concern. In that passage we are told that Jesus, the Good Shepherd, Leads, Speaks and Serves. We are to Follow, Listen and learn to Serve also. So, the message was threefold: 1. Follow Jesus before attempting to lead anyone. 2. Listen to Jesus before you speak for Him; and, when you do, use His very words, not your own. And, 3. Roll up your sleeves before you ask anyone else to serve. If we truly followed Jesus' example we would know that a bona fide shepherd is personal. They know their sheep and their sheep know them. They take initiative. They go before the sheep. A good shepherd gives the sheep freedom. They come in and go out. A shepherd who cares offers provision and protection. The "pasture" is open to them. Reliable shepherds are sacrificial, laying down their lives for the sheep. They care; it's not just another job. They persevere. They don't run away. And they are unifiers, bring together sheep from other pens. In other words, they choose to be authentic, God-ordained shepherds; not a sheep-rustlers.

Conclusion

In the Preface to this book I shared two photos. One was of a large ten-foot stump. Plain. Stark. Ugly. Dying. The other was a wood carving of Jesus holding His sheep created by a master chainsaw artist. Alive. Meaningful. Heart-stirring. I told you of the transformation. What I didn't share with you was what lays at the feet of Jesus in that prominent spot in the front yard of my friends and why the items laying there are there at all. So, the story continues. It illustrates the heart of a Reliable Shepherd.

My husband and I were down-sizing and moving from our family home into an apartment that our oldest son had built for us in his home. Purging years and years of belongings is a tiresome task, as any who have engaged in it will tell you. One such item that needed a new home was a large box of potato sized stones. I know. You're wondering, what on earth is anyone is doing with such a collection? They were props for altar responses for a talk I had given to retreat groups on leaving their burdens with the Lord. The instruction was to help build a memorial altar to our God with each stone. The stones represented heavy things in our lives that we were still carrying. When once the stone or stones were released from our open hands, we were to pick up a feather, representing Jesus' light and easy yoke.

I did not know what to do with these stones. And, then I

remembered that our friends used stones of like size to line their gardens and help with water run-off. These are the same friends with the Jesus statue in the middle of their front yard. I made a phone call. "Would you like my whole box of stones?" The reply was a resounding "Yes!" So, I made the hour-long trek to get to their home. The man of the house was ready with his wheelbarrow and the car was soon unloaded. He asked me how I had gotten so many of these stones, and I told him the story of the retreat encounters with Jesus at the altar.

He said that all that night he tossed and turned about "the stones." It seemed that water and garden debris run-off made it clear that the stones would be in the wrong place if they were mere liners. He reasoned, "People cried over those stones. Their hearts broke as the remembered the burdens. And, then their hearts leaped at the light and easy replacement Jesus offered them." He asked God what to do with the stones. His shepherd's heart cared about the aches of others, even though they would never know where their stones had been placed. God answered. The stones found a home at the feet of Jesus at the statue in the front yard.

That's a shepherd like Jesus. God's Intentional Remnant needs to imitate the heart of this man who echoes Jesus' work among us. And, lest you think the stones are the only evidence of his shepherd's heart, you might consider the dozens of people he has organized to make beds for children who have no place to lay their heads, and the home he gave to refugees who had no home, the man he picked up on the street who needed a ride to work——a perfect opportunity to share Jesus—and going *toward* ones who need rescue, not being offended by them. A willingness. An eagerness. Being an example to anyone who watches. *"Let your light so shine before men, that they may see your good works and glorify your Father in heaven."* (Matthew 5:16 NKJV)

Prayer Points To Consider

1. Pray for your pastors and ministry leaders.

2. Pray for yourself in whatever spiritual leadership capacity you may have.

3. Ask God to give you the heart of a true shepherd.

4. Ask God to help you identify any ways in which you have been a "sheep-rustler."

5. Ask God to help you be aware of the needs of the following kinds of people, willing to meet their need and share their need with others.

   a. The Weak
   b. The Sick
   c. The Injured
   d. The Straying
   e. The Lost

6. Ask God to help you strengthen, heal, bind up, bring back and search for such ones.

7. As the Holy Spirit leads.

CHAPTER ELEVEN – TOOTHBRUSH THEOLOGY

God's Intentional Remnant Seeks Clean Hands and a Pure Heart

> "We are not the Christ; we are not even mini-Christs. We are not the Word of God. We are the stationary on which He writes, and as such, we need to be clean, pure, holy and true. Nothing must detract from the handwriting of God."[55]
> ——Dick Brogden——

An elderly friend of mine, reaching 104 years of age before he went to glory, reminded me often that living a holy life for God is merely "Toothbrush Theology." He reasoned: You would not want to use anyone else's toothbrush and you would not want anyone else to use yours. That's because your toothbrush is set apart for your personal use. When we speak of sanctification and holiness we are speaking of being set apart for God's personal use. Philip Greenslade is credited with saying: "Holiness implies separateness, being set aside for God's exclusive cause. To be holy is to be as distinctive in our own way as God is in His. It is to dare as God's holy people to be as different as God; to stand out as belonging to Him by our purity and goodness in a sinful society and a corrupt culture."[56]

God's love is for real, but so is His wrath. He is the Just Judge. Hebrews 4:13 NKJV declares: *"And there is no creature hidden from His sight, but all things are naked and open to the eyes of Him to whom we must give account."* Peter echoes that word with his thoughts.

"But they will have to give account to him who is ready to judge the living and the dead." (1 Peter 4:5 NIV) There is an accounting for the people of God first (See 1 Peter 5:17), and then for those who do not bow the knee to Jesus. God is holy and He expects us, who are created in His image, to *"be holy in all you do."* (1 Peter 1:15 NIV) And, for further motivation He adds *"Be holy, because I am holy."* (1 Peter 1:16 NIV) The good news is that it is He who makes us holy. Leviticus 20:8 NIV states: *"Keep my decrees and follow them. I am the Lord, who makes you holy."*

It is Adrian Rogers who makes things a bit more clear. He states: "You were created to know three worlds—the spiritual, psychological, and material worlds. These can be considered the world above us, the world within us, and the world around us. These worlds are related to the three parts of our human nature—spirit, soul, and body. When you are rightly related to the material world with your body, you are healthy. When you are rightly related to the psychological world with your soul, you are happy. And when you are rightly related to the spiritual world in your spirit, you are holy. God's aim is that ultimately you are to experience all three realities: health, happiness and holiness."[57] I would follow his words with a caution. Of faith, hope and love——all of which are important—love is the greatest. (See 1 Corinthians 13:13) In like manner, health, happiness and holiness are all important, but the greatest of these is holiness. God will always work toward our holiness and sometimes uses our measure of health and happiness to reach His goal.

Purity and holiness are struggles of monumental proportions. We cannot do it alone. We need the power of the Holy Spirit to carry us through; one decision at a time. It is an imperative for God's Intentional Remnant. Selwyn Hughes states: "Nothing but an increase of holiness in those who call themselves Christians will make the church a powerful witness in the world."[58] Paul delivers a similar warning in Philippians 2:14-15 NIV. *Do everything without grumbling or arguing, so that you may become blameless and pure,*

'children of God without fault in a warped and crooked generation.'
Then you will shine among them like stars in the sky." I believe one of
the things that God grieves over, that would be labeled an abomination, is the lack of purity and holiness in His own people. The
culture is warped. The culture is crooked. The culture is depraved.
The Intentional Remnant has a burden to show the watching world
a better way; God's way——the way of holiness. Peter declares to
the scattered church that we are *"a chosen people, a royal priesthood, a*
holy nation, a people belonging to God that we may declare the praises
of Him who brought us out of darkness into His marvelous light." (1
Peter 2:9-10 NIV)

A Declaration of Truth

There are many places in the Word of God that make it clear that
purity is a struggle for us. The following verses are only the tip of
the iceberg.

2 Timothy 3:1-2 NIV – Paul informs Timothy, and us, that in the
last days things will be perilous. Here are three descriptors, among
many, of the peril at hand. People will be *"ungrateful, unholy and*
unforgiving."
Ezra 9:11 NKJV – *"The land which you are entering to possess is an*
unclean land, with the uncleanness of the peoples of the lands, with
their abominations which have filled it from one end to another with
their impurity."
Jeremiah 6:15 NKJV – *"'Were they ashamed when they had commit-*
ted abomination? No! They were not at all ashamed, nor did they know
how to blush. Therefore they shall fall among those who fall; at the time
I punish them, they shall be cast down,' says the Lord."
Romans 7:15-24 NIV – *"15 I do not understand what I do. For*
what I want to do I do not do, but what I hate I do. 16 And if I do
what I do not want to do, I agree that the law is good. 17 As it is, it is
no longer I myself who do it, but it is sin living in me. 18 For I know

that good itself does not dwell in me, that is, in my sinful nature. For I have the desire to do what is good, but I cannot carry it out. 19 For I do not do the good I want to do, but the evil I do not want to do—this I keep on doing. 20 Now if I do what I do not want to do, it is no longer I who do it, but it is sin living in me that does it. 21 So I find this law at work: Although I want to do good, evil is right there with me. 22 For in my inner being I delight in God's law; 23 but I see another law at work in me, waging war against the law of my mind and making me a prisoner of the law of sin at work within me. 24 What a wretched man I am! Who will rescue me from this body that is subject to death?" These verses clearly show the struggle that rages in human hearts. The answer to Paul's question in Romans 7:24 comes in Romans 7:25. 25 *"Thanks be to God, who delivers me through Jesus Christ our Lord! So then, I myself in my mind am a slave to God's law, but in my sinful nature a slave to the law of sin."*

In the 1970's I sang in a choir that performed Cam Floria's "The Apostle" about the life of the apostle Paul. He created one song in that musical that depicted these verses in Romans very well. His lyrics went something like this. "That which I would not, that do I do. I wish I wouldn't do it, but I'm already through. The Spirit wars within me and I don't get any rest. I'm doing all these crazy things; my flesh is such a pest. But, I thank God that I am His and He will take me, break me, wash me, save me, heal me, mend me, make me. I am His and He is mine." Indeed!

Examples of Cultural Abuse

Purity and the quest for holiness is under attack in the current culture and the church is not immune. Numbers 32:23 NKJV is startling clear. *"…you have sinned against the Lord; and be sure your sin will find you out."* An echo comes in the New Testament with this word in Luke 12:2 NKJV. *"For there is nothing covered that will not be revealed, nor hidden that will not be known."* Sexual improprieties are being shouted from the housetops in government, the media, academia, the entertainment industry, sports and even in the church. Never before has it been so apparent that there is ecclesiastical pedophilia especially with priests in the Catholic church. The #MeToo movement has made its mark with many women stepping forward to reveal the sexual abuse that has been perpetrated against them for decades.

Pornography is increasing at epidemic proportions. The organization Covenant Eyes cites the following statistics. "90% of teens and 96% of young adults are either encouraging, accepting, or neutral when they talk about porn with their friends." "Just 55% of adults twenty-five and older believe porn is wrong." In the church, "one in five youth pastors and one in seven senior pastors use porn on a regular basis." "64% of Christian men and 15% of Christian women say they watch porn at least once a month." "Only 7% of pastors report their church has a ministry program for those struggling with porn."[59] Pornography is deadly for the stability of the family. Many of those addicted to porn act on it in the form of affairs outside of marriage, which leads to separation and divorce.

Another example of cultural abuse is the alarming rate at which young, unmarried couples are living together before marriage. Most of them claim financial reasons as their primary motivation. In asking a pastor who has served his congregation for many years, the report is that ten years ago only a very few couples were living together and were willing to separate until their wedding day. Today, almost all of the couples coming for mandatory pastoral counseling before marriage are living together and not willing to separate until their wedding day.

Selwyn Hughes is credited with saying: "Holiness is all about taking our place in the world and contributing to it, but being separated for God and living by the laws of His Kingdom."[60] Jesus told us to be sent in but set apart. *My prayer is not that you take them out of the world but that you protect them from the evil one. They are not of the world, even as I am not of it. Sanctify them* (set them apart) *by the truth; your word is truth. As you sent me into the world,*

I have sent them into the world." (John 17:15-18 NIV) As I see it, the answer to Jesus' prayer offers four choices to us. 1. Be partially obedient and be out of the world and not of it. 2. Be half-hearted in obedience and be in the world, but enjoy and take part in its ways. 3. Be totally disobedient and be out of the world but enjoy all its ways. And, 4. Be totally obedient and be in the world but not of it. The following chart will show you what I mean.

John 17:15-18 – Sent In and Set Apart/ In the World but Not Of It

CHOICE	Out of the World/Not Of It	In the World and Of It	Out of the World and Of It	In the World but NOT Of It
FOCUS	Partial Obedience	Partial Obedience	Total Disobedience	Total Obedience
AIM	Safety/ Comfort	Pleasure	Personal Gain	Exalt God
LOVE/ DISDAIN	Disdain World's Ways & People	Love World's People & Ways	Disdain World's People; Love Ways	Disdain World's Ways & Love World's People
SET APART?	Separate From the World	Mingles with the World	Has the World but won't face it	Separate unto God
THE ANSWER	Has it but not sharing it	Too Watered Down for Effect	Getting For Self not God	Has It and Shares It
MIND	So Heavenly Minded No Earthly Good	So Earthly Minded No Heavenly Good	Mind Set on the Flesh	Mind Set on the Spirit
THEME SONG	Sings "Onward Christian Soldiers" on the way to Potluck	Sings "Trust and Obey" at the Pub or in the Lottery Line	Sings "I'd Rather Have Jesus Than Anything" driving a new BMW	Sings all three with meaning
IMPACT	No Impact	No Impact	No Impact	Immeasurable Impact
COMMIT-MENT	50%-ers Lukewarm	50%-ers Lukewarm	0%-ers Cold	100%-ers On Fire for Jesus

God's Admonitions To Us

The following are just a few of the many scriptures that warn us to live in holiness.

- **Philippians 2:14-16a NIV** – *14 Do everything without grumbling or arguing, 15 so that you may become blameless and pure, "children of God without fault in a warped and crooked generation." Then you will shine among them like stars in the sky 16 as you hold firmly to the word of life. And then I will be able to boast on the day of Christ that I did not run or labor in vain."*

- **1 Corinthians 10:13 NKJV** – *13 "No temptation has overtaken you except such as is common to man; but God is faithful, who will not allow you to be tempted beyond what you are able, but with the temptation will also make the way of escape, that you may be able to bear it."*

- **James 1:13-15 NKJV** – *13 "Let no one say when he is tempted, "I am tempted by God"; for God cannot be tempted by evil, nor does He Himself tempt anyone. 14 But each one is tempted when he is drawn away by his own desires and enticed. 15 Then, when desire has conceived, it gives birth to sin; and sin, when it is full-grown, brings forth death."*

- **2 Peter 3:11-12a NIV** – *11 "Since everything will be destroyed in this way, what kind of people ought you to be? You ought to live holy and godly lives 12 as you look forward to the day of God and speed its coming."*

- **Proverbs 22:11 NKJV** – *"He who loves purity of heart and has grace on his lips, the king will be his friend."*

- **James 1:27 NIV** – *"Religion that God our Father accepts as pure and faultless is this: to look after orphans and widows in their distress and to keep oneself from being polluted by the world."*

- **1 Peter 2:11 NIV** – *"Dear friends, I urge you, as foreigners and exiles, to abstain from sinful desires, which wage war against your soul"*

- **1 Peter 1:13-16 NIV** – *"¹³ Therefore, with minds that are alert and fully sober, set your hope on the grace to be brought to you when Jesus Christ is revealed at his coming. ¹⁴ As obedient children, do not conform to the evil desires you had when you lived in ignorance.¹⁵ But just as he who called you is holy, so be holy in all you do; ¹⁶ for it is written: "Be holy, because I am holy."*

- **Romans 13:14 NKJV** – *¹⁴ But put on the Lord Jesus Christ, and make no provision for the flesh, to fulfill its lusts."*

- **1 Thessalonians 4:3-5, 7 NIV** – *³ It is God's will that you should be sanctified: that you should avoid sexual immorality; ⁴ that each of you should learn to control your own body in a way that is holy and honorable, ⁵ not in passionate lust like the pagans, who do not know God"; ⁷ "For God did not call us to be impure, but to live a holy life."*

A Biblical Example: Joseph with Potiphar's Wife

In Genesis chapter 39 the account is given of Joseph in Potiphar's home. Potiphar was an officer under Pharaoh and had bought Joseph from the Ishmaelites who had brought him to Egypt after Joseph's brothers had sold him into slavery. The Word says: *"The Lord was with Joseph, and he was a successful man."* (Genesis 39:2 NKJV) Joseph found favor with Potiphar and was made overseer of the man's house.

The report continues to reveal that *"Joseph was handsome in form and appearance."* (Genesis 39:6 NKJV) Potiphar's wife longed for him and asked Joseph to have sex with her. Joseph's response was first to say that he could not do that to his master who trusted him, but the real motivation came in the following words. *"How then can I do this great wickedness, and sin against God?"* (Genesis 39:9 NKJV) So, time after time Joseph fled from the seduction of Potiphar's wife. He obeyed the command given to all of us in 1 Corinthians 6:18 NASB. *"Flee immorality. Every other sin that a man commits is outside his body, but the immoral man sins against his own body."*

Potiphar's wife continued in lust but Joseph stayed pure. He chose holiness. He did not lose God's favor. He employed self-control and perseverance. He knew his first love was his God. He looked for God's way of escape in the situation. He made moment by moment right decisions and he was aware of the "Esau Syndrome" of *"trading away God's lifelong gift to satisfy a short-term appetite."* (Hebrews 12:14-17 The Message)

Of course, Bible-reading people know the rest of the story. Potiphar's wife continued. One day as he ran from her yet again, she caught his garment and, as a woman scorned, she lied to her husband and accused Joseph of rape. For that, Joseph was unjustly put into prison. What is amazing is that even there, even in prison, the *"Lord was with Joseph and showed him mercy, and He gave him favor in the sight of the keeper of the prison."* (Genesis 39:21 NKJV)

Eventually Joseph enjoyed all the benefits of abstaining from fleshly pursuits. 1 Peter 2:11-17 spells them out. *"[11] Dear friends, I urge you, as foreigners and exiles, to abstain from sinful desires, which wage war against your soul. [12] Live such good lives among the pagans that, though they accuse you of doing wrong, they may see your good deeds and glorify God on the day he visits us. [13] Submit yourselves for the Lord's sake to every human authority: whether to the emperor, as the supreme authority, [14] or to governors, who are sent by him to punish those who do wrong and to commend those who do right. [15] For it is God's will that by doing good you should silence the ignorant talk of foolish people. [16] Live as free people, but do not use your freedom as a cover-up for evil; live as God's slaves. [17] Show proper respect to everyone, love the family of believers, fear God, honor the emperor."* The results of holy living were glory to God, the fear of God, the silencing of the ignorant talk of foolish men and becoming a slave of God.

Issues Involved in Aiming At Purity

Joseph teaches us that there are at least six issues that can impact any one of us in the pursuit of holiness.

1. **Self-Control.** Self-control is a fruit of the Spirit. It is overflow in the life of anyone who chooses to let God call the shots. It is the surrender of personal desires for the desires of God. In Ezekiel 47:3-5 NIV we encounter the river of God. Anyone taking the plunge into the depths of this river finds important truths. One of these truths is that the deeper you go, the less control you have and the more control God has. *"3 As the man went eastward with a measuring line in his hand, he measured off a thousand cubits and then led me through water that was ankle-deep. 4 He measured off another thousand cubits and led me through water that was knee-deep. He measured off another thousand and led me through water that was up to the waist. 5 He measured off another thousand, but now it was a river that I could not cross, because the water had risen and was deep enough to swim in—a river that no one could cross."* First the water is ankle-deep, then knee-deep, then up to the waist, and finally enough to swim in. If you have ever been swimming, you know that if you stand in water ankle-deep, you still have control. At knee-deep level you are a bit less in control. Up to the waist makes you vulnerable to the currents. And, in over your head means that the water has control of you. The same is true with those going to the depths of God. The deeper we go, the less control we have and the more our desires will line up with God's desires.

2. **Perseverance.** 2 Peter 1:4-8 NIV says: *4 "Through these he has given us his very great and precious promises, so that through them you may participate in the divine nature, having escaped the corruption in the world caused by evil desires.5 For this very reason, make every effort to add to your faith goodness; and to goodness, knowledge; 6 and to knowledge, self-control; and to self-control, perseverance; and to perseverance, godliness; 7 and to godliness, mutual affection; and to mutual affection, love. 8 For if you possess these qualities in increasing measure, they will keep you from being ineffective and unproductive in your knowledge of our Lord Jesus Christ."*

   When we add perseverance to self-control we insure a victory. Think about it. If we start a diet but only follow the program for one day, we will probably not lose much weight. But if we persevere, the results will be much more positive. And, if we do not add godliness to the perseverance, it just becomes stubbornness. We need to do it God's way.

3. **First Love.** When Peter was restored after his three betrayals of Jesus, the Lord asked him a pointed question. *"Simon, son of Jonah, do you love Me more than these?"* (John 21:15 NKJV) When we are tempted by anything, we need to ask ourselves which we love more; the things seducing us or our God. It is a first love issue. Jesus spoke hard words to the loveless church in Ephesus in the book of the Revelation. *"I know your works, your labor, your patience, and that you cannot bear those who are evil. And you have tested those who say they are apostles and are not, and have found them liars; and you have persevered and have patience, and have labored for My name's sake and have not become weary. Nevertheless, I have this against you, that you have left your first love."* (Revelation 2:2-4 NKJV) Per-

severance wasn't enough. Working for God didn't cut it. Discernment regarding liars did not make the grade. God wanted to be their first love. And, He wants to be our first love too. The thing that tempts you and me cannot have first place.

4. **The Way of Escape.** God knew that we would be tempted to live less than holy lives, so with each temptation, He provided a way out. Remember the Sunday School song for toddlers mentioned in an earlier chapter? "Be careful little eyes what you see; be careful little eyes what you see. For the Father up above is looking down in love, so be careful little eyes what you see." The song goes on to little ears and what they hear, little mouths and what they taste, little hands and what they touch and little feet and where they go. Our senses are gifts from God but also ripe for the enemy to pervert. 1 Corinthians 10:13 NKJV says: *"No temptation has overtaken you except such as is common to man; but God is faithful, who will not allow you to be tempted beyond what you are able, but with the temptation will also make the way of escape, that you may be able to bear it."*

5. **Holiness Thinking.** 1 Peter 1:15-16 NIV states: *"But just as he who called you is holy, so be holy in all you do; for it is written: "Be holy, because I am holy."* The word "BE" is a powerful word. It is present tense. It is a momentary decision. I used to think that if I was on a diet and I messed up, then it was okay to eat six cookies and resume the work the next day. I reasoned, "I already blew it, so enjoy the sugar." Then I realized that holiness is a present moment decision. Just because I failed an hour ago doesn't mean I need to cave in at this moment. I need to "be holy" because my God "IS holy".

6. **Awareness of the "Esau Syndrome."** Hebrews 12:14-17 in The Message makes things quite clear. *"Work at getting along with each other and with God. Otherwise you'll never get so much as a glimpse of God. Make sure no one gets left out of God's generosity. Keep a sharp eye out for weeds of bitter discontent. A thistle or two gone to seed can ruin a whole garden in no time. Watch out for the Esau syndrome: trading away God's lifelong gift in order to satisfy a short-term appetite. You well know how Esau later regretted that impulsive act and wanted God's blessing—but by then it was too late, tears or no tears."* Not much more needs to be said. God has offered us eternal treasures. Short-term appetites get in the way of His magnificent gifts.

The One Who Helps Us

Malachi 3:1-3 NKJV proclaims truth. *"Behold, I send My messenger, and he will prepare the way before Me. And the Lord, whom you seek, will suddenly come to His temple, even the Messenger of the covenant, in whom you delight. Behold, He is coming," says the LORD of hosts.* [2] *"But who can endure the day of His coming? And who can stand when He appears? For He is like a refiner's fire and like launderers' soap.* [3] *He will sit as a refiner and a purifier of silver; He will purify the sons of Levi, and purge them as gold and silver, that they may offer to the LORD an offering in righteousness".* Our God is a refiner's fire; a launderer's soap. Fire is sometimes understandably fearful for it can be destructive, but in this context it is an agent of purification. The Holy Spirit is known as fire and it is His power that strengthens us in our inner beings so that Christ may dwell in our hearts. (See Ephesians 3:16-17.) When Christ takes up residence in our hearts it is He who is in control and our lives will be bent toward purity. Leviticus 20:8 NIV reassures us. *"I am the Lord who makes you holy."*

Several verses of scripture encourage us with the truth that we are not alone in any quest for holiness. Consider each of the following and let not your hearts be troubled. Belief and trust in Jesus and His power in our lives makes all the difference.

- **Hebrews 4:15 NKJV** – "*For we do not have a High Priest who cannot sympathize with our weaknesses, but was in all points tempted as we are, yet without sin.*"

- **1 Peter 1:18-19 NIV** – *¹⁸" For you know that it was not with perishable things such as silver or gold that you were redeemed from the empty way of life handed down to you from your ancestors, ¹⁹ but with the precious blood of Christ, a lamb without blemish or defect.*"

- **Hebrews 9:14 NKJV** – "*How much more shall the blood of Christ, who through the eternal Spirit offered Himself without spot to God, cleanse your conscience from dead works to serve the living God?*"

- **Romans 8:1-2 NKJV** – "*There is therefore now no condemnation to those who are in Christ Jesus, who do not walk according to the flesh, but according to the Spirit. ² For the law of the Spirit of life in Christ Jesus has made me free from the law of sin and death.*"

- **Philippians 2:13 NIV** – *"for it is God who works in you to will and to act in order to fulfill his good purpose.*"

- **Philippians 4:13 NKJV** – *"I can do all things through Christ who strengthens me.*"

My prayer for all who read this is what is contained in Hebrews 13:20-21 NKJV *"Now may the God of peace who brought up our Lord Jesus from the dead, the great Shepherd of the sheep, through the blood of the everlasting covenant, make you complete in every good work to do His will, working in you what is well pleasing in His sight, through Jesus Christ, to whom be glory forever and ever. Amen."* Amen means "so be it." May it be so in your life!

How We Can Intentionally Live in Purity

We have repeatedly referred to 1 Peter 1:13-16 in this chapter which calls all of us who follow Jesus to *"Be holy as He is holy."* Following that challenge are three directives. 1. *"Prepare your minds for action."* 2. *"Be self-controlled."* And 3. *"Set your hope fully on God's grace."* To do that I offer ten suggestions that will help you and me, as God's Remnant, to intentionally live what is well pleasing in His sight.

1. **Be People of God's Word. – Psalm 119:9 NKJV –** *"How can a young man cleanse his way? By taking heed according to Your word."*

2. **Be People of Prayer. – Psalm 51:10 NKJV –** *"Create in me a clean heart, O God, a renew a steadfast spirit within me."*

3. **Rely on God. – 1 Thessalonians 5:23-24 NKJV –** [23] *"Now may the God of peace Himself sanctify you completely; and may your whole spirit, soul, and body be preserved blameless at the coming of our Lord Jesus Christ.* [24] *He who calls you is faithful, who also will do it."*

4. **Surrender Yourself For Cleansing. – 2 Timothy 2:20-21 NKJV –** *"But in a great house there are not only vessels of gold and silver, but also of wood and clay, some for honor and some for dishonor.* [21] *Therefore if anyone cleanses himself from the latter, he will be a vessel for honor, sanctified and useful for the Master, prepared for every good work."*

5. **Live Soberly. – Titus 2:11-12 NKJV –** [11] *For the grace of God that brings salvation has appeared to all men,* [12] *teach-*

ing us that, denying ungodliness and worldly lusts, we should live soberly, righteously, and godly in the present age."

6. **Wives Submit To Your Husbands – Ephesians 5:25-27 NKJV** – *25 Husbands, love your wives, just as Christ also loved the church and gave Himself for her, 26 that He might sanctify and cleanse her with the washing of water by the word, 27 that He might present her to Himself a glorious church, not having spot or wrinkle or any such thing, but that she should be holy and without blemish."* I know. The word "submit" raises the hair on the back of your neck. But, it is truly God's provision for wives. A godly man in her life will be God's tool to sanctify, cleanse and protect. An incident in my life may help. I had a person that I talked with on the telephone regularly. She was consistently negative and the relationship was toxic at best. My husband observed what was happening and said he would like me to consider not talking to her unless he was on the phone with me. When my husband was on the phone, this woman did not share her vitriolic rhetoric. My husband gave me the opportunity to be sanctified—set apart—the conversation was cleansed and I was protected. Submission is something to seriously consider.

7. **Surrender for a Heart Change. – Joel 2:13 NKJV** – *So rend your heart, and not your garments; return to the Lord your God, for He is gracious and merciful, slow to anger, and of great kindness; and He relents from doing harm."* The practice in the Old Testament when you were grieved over anything was to tear your robes. The prophet Joel was telling the people to tear their hearts, not their clothes. Pastor Adrian Rogers has said: "You're never going to purify the water by painting the pump."[61] It has to go deeper than that.

Romans 12:1-2 The Message – "*So here's what I want you to do, God helping you: Take your everyday, ordinary life—your sleeping, eating, going-to-work, and walking-around life—and place it before God as an offering. Embracing what God does for you is the best thing you can do for him. Don't become so well-adjusted to your culture that you fit into it without even thinking. Instead, fix your attention on God. You'll be changed from the inside out. Readily recognize what he wants from you, and quickly respond to it. Unlike the culture around you, always dragging you down to its level of immaturity, God brings the best out of you, develops well-formed maturity in you.*"

8. **Draw Near to God. – James 4:8 NKJV** – "*Draw near to God and He will draw near to you. Cleanse your hands, you sinners; and purify your hearts, you double-minded.*"

9. **Choose the "Highway of Holiness". – Isaiah 35:8-9 NKJV** – "*A highway shall be there, and a road, and it shall be called the Highway of Holiness. The unclean shall not pass over it, but it shall be for others. Whoever walks the road, although a fool, shall not go astray. ⁹ No lion shall be there, nor shall any ravenous beast go up on it; it shall not be found there. but the redeemed shall walk there.*"

10. **Set Your Minds and Hearts On "Things Above." – Colossians 3:1-3 NIV** – "*Since, then, you have been raised with Christ, set your hearts on things above, where Christ is, seated at the right hand of God. ² Set your minds on things above, not on earthly things. ³ For you died, and your life is now hidden with Christ in God.*"

Conclusion

A story is told of a married couple getting ready for work in the morning. The wife was in the kitchen and the husband was getting dressed in their bedroom. He shouted to his wife: "Honey, is this shirt dirty? I don't know if I should wear it or not." His wife answered immediately with firmness. "It's dirty. Don't put it on!" He countered with: "How do you know? You haven't even looked at it." She responded: "If you had to ask, it's dirty."

The same is true for us and the things we question doing or not doing. If we have to ask, don't do it. If a red flag waves, heed the warning. God's Word tells us that *"all things are permissible"* for us BUT *"not all things are beneficial."* (See 1 Corinthians 6:12 and 10:23 NIV.) Allow me to explain this with a driving illustration. You probably have logged years behind the wheel and you know from your road lessons as a teenager that when a broken yellow line is in the middle of the road, it means you have permission to pass any car in front of you. However, if another car is coming in the opposite direction, it would not be beneficial for you to pass the vehicle in front of you. It would result in a crash and perhaps even death. The same is true for the choices we make about the things we are tempted by. You have the right to do most things, but not all of them are constructive for you …… and for God. To intentionally live a life of holiness and purity, we need to be mindful of what is beneficial to us and to our God. When we do, we see Him more and more and that vision turns into ever increased motivation to live a holy life.

In a recent sermon by Randy Hurst, the Advancement Director for Assemblies of God World Missions, he highlighted some of what the Covid-19 pandemic has taught us. Just as we have been encouraged to social distance and wash our hands during coronavirus times, to be the people God makes holy, we should consider "spiritual distancing". *"Abhor what is evil. Cling to what is good."*

(Roman 12:9) And, *"cleanse your hands, you sinners, and purify your hearts, you double-minded."* (James 4:8) Good wisdom.

Prayer Points To Consider

1. Ask God to search your heart and confess any impure ways that are in your personal life.

2. Make confession before the Lord for the impure, unholy practices that are evident in our nation today.

3. Pray over the "Issues Involved in Aiming At Purity"; that you will be self-controlled, persevering, maintain Jesus as your "first love", employ the "way of escape", train your mind for holy thinking, and be aware of the "Esau Syndrome."

4. Pray over the specific ways we can intentionally live in purity. That you will be a person of the Word and prayer, that you will rely on God, surrendering to Him for cleansing; that you will live soberly in submission, surrendered for a heart change; That you will draw near to God and wash your hands and heart; that you will choose the "Highway of Holiness," and set your heart and mind on "the things above."

5. However the Spirit leads.

CHAPTER TWELVE –
HIGHER THOUGHTS

God's Intentional Remnant Seeks
To Think As God Thinks

> **"We are living in a time when people are listening with their eyes and thinking with their feelings."**[62]
> ——**Ravi Zacharias**——

Three times in the beginning of Paul's letter to the Romans he uses the phrase *"God gave them over."* (Romans 1:24, 26, 28 NIV) What were the people given over to? First, they were given over *"to sexual impurity"*. Second, they were given over *"to shameful lusts"*, exchanging natural sexual relations for unnatural ones. Third, they were given over *"to a depraved mind."* Paul goes on to say that the people in the Roman church had *"no understanding."* (Romans 1:30) They did not know how to think any longer.

Paul refers throughout his letters to a *"darkened understanding."* Romans 1:21 states: *"For although they knew God, they neither glorified him as God nor gave thanks to him, but their thinking became futile and their foolish hearts were darkened."* To the church at Ephesus he spelled it out with even more clarity. *"They are darkened in their understanding and separated from the life of God because of the ignorance that is in them due to the hardening of their hearts."* (Ephesians 4:18 NIV)

We have been experiencing this downward spiral of thinking for several decades in America. In the 1960's we experienced the sexual revolution. God had given us over. In the 1990's we saw the homosexual revolution. God had given us over. And, now, God has given us over to a depraved mind with the inability to think. Today, many think with their feelings. There is no standard elevated and trusted to determine which thoughts are worthy and which are not.

In the scriptures there is no such lack of clarity. In Isaiah 55:8-9 God declares the following. *"For My thoughts are not your thoughts, neither are your ways My ways,' declares the Lord. As the heavens are higher than the earth, so are My ways higher than your ways and My thoughts than your thoughts."*

A Declaration of Truth

Isaiah 5:20-21 NIV states: *"Woe to those who call evil good, and good evil; who put darkness for light, and light for darkness; who put bitter for sweet, and sweet for bitter! Woe to those who are wise in their own eyes and clever in their own sight."*

Decades ago I attended a seminar led by a man named Bill Gothard. He used an illustration that I have never forgotten. Three volunteers were chosen, each of whom held signs that showcased the following words in large letters: "GOOD", "MIDDLE OF THE ROAD," and "EVIL." They stood in the front of the assembled group with "Middle of the Road" of course in the center. As the speaker began to talk, the person holding the sign representing "EVIL" consistently moved further away from the other two people. The leader explained. Good is what God says is good. It will never move. It is unchangeable just as is the character of our good God. Evil, however, will consistently choose a darker persona, working always at getting as far away from God as possible. What was incredible is what happened to the gentleman holding the 'MIDDLE OF THE ROAD" sign. He could not stay where he was originally if he wanted to remain in the middle. To be "in the middle", he needed to move further away from "GOOD," so that as the illustration concluded, he was now in the place that "EVIL" had occupied at the very beginning.

Calling evil good or good evil will not work in God's economy. And, being in a middle of the road position will not suffice either. Evil and middle of the roaders will consistently move further away from what is good. We must learn to think as God thinks if we are to maintain His higher thoughts and be blessed in the obedience.

Just a few other verses will suffice.

Isaiah 65:2 – NKJV – *"I have stretched out My hands all day long to a rebellious people, who walk in a way that is not good, according to their own thoughts."*

Jeremiah 6:19 NKJV – *"Hear, O earth! Behold, I will certainly bring calamity on this people—the fruit of their thoughts, because they have not heeded My words nor My law, but rejected it."*

Genesis 6:5 NKJV – *"Then the Lord saw that the wickedness of man was great in the earth, and that every intent of the thoughts of his heart was only evil continually."*

Micah 4:12 NKJV – *"But they do not know the thoughts of the Lord, nor do they understand His counsel; for He will gather them like sheaves to the threshing floor."*

Psalm 94:11 NKJV – *"The Lord knows the thoughts of man, that they are futile."*

It would be prudent for us to look a bit closer at this mention of futile thinking. Ephesians 4:17-19 NIV gives us an apt picture. *"So I tell you this, and insist on it in the Lord, that you must no longer live as the Gentiles do, in the futility of their thinking. They are darkened in their understanding and separated from the life of God because of the ignorance that is in them due to the hardening of their hearts. Having lost all sensitivity, they have given themselves over to sensuality so as to indulge in every kind of impurity, and they are full of greed."* This "hardening" that is spoken of is translated with other words in varying translations of the scriptures. "Blindness" is one such substitution as is "stubbornness."

When Cru was known as Campus Crusade for Christ, they published little booklets called The Transferable Concepts. In one of them a train illustration was used to explain godly thinking. Pictures of a train engine, fuel car and caboose were employed. The engine—what drives the train—were the Facts. The facts were meant to be God's promises in His Word. The fuel car—what keeps the engine running—was Faith; trust in God and His Word. The caboose—what comes behind it all—is Feelings. Feelings are nice—gifts from God—but they are not what should steer us from point A to point B.

Today the engine is Feelings, the fuel car is Personal Preference and the caboose is Faith———maybe; nice, but not sufficient to run things. The Ravi Zacharias quote at the outset of the chapter states: "We're living in a time when people are listening with their eyes and thinking with their feelings." I believe he means that what people are listening to is informed only by what they see. So, they look to the temporal, the seen; things that can be counted and stacked and quantified. The unseen, eternal elements do not propel people today. And, they think with their feelings. That's why "being safe" and giving attention to what "looks kind and loving" is exalted over true Truth. People have to demand safety with a stomping foot and a raised fist if they do not know *The name of the Lord is a strong tower. The righteous runs into it and is safe."* (Proverbs 18:10 NASB) Folks have to settle for the temporal if they do not understand the truth of the eternal. *"...we look not at the things which are seen, but at the things which are not seen; for the things which are seen are temporal, but the things which are not seen are eternal."* (2 Corinthians 4:18 NASB)

We, as a nation, have difficulty thinking as God thinks because we have become *"dull of hearing"* (Hebrews 5:11 NASB). We do not listen to His counsel. We devise our own wisdom; that which satisfies our longings and caresses our feelings. Other translations render this condition of deafness in the following manner. The New Living Translation says *"You are spiritually dull and don't seem to listen."* The Message says *"You have a bad habit of not listening."* The New International Version says *"you no longer try to under-*

stand." Hebrews 5:12-14 goes on to explain that folks who are dull of hearing revert to needing milk, not solid food, and they lack the discernment of knowing the difference between good and evil.

Commenting on this very truth, missionary Dick Brogden states the following. "Unfortunately, those who walk with Jesus the longest are just as susceptible to become 'dull of hearing' as the unconverted. If we are not careful, the more we know about Jesus, the harder it is for the Spirit to explain things to us. We often regress in intimacy the more we increase in head knowledge, but without intimacy there is no lasting revelation. We tend to regress from 'food to milk.' We lose our spiritual teeth and cannot chew on fresh revelation. We get spiritual dementia and lose the sense of discernment."[63] The truth is that we all have difficulty thinking God's higher thoughts. We need help.

Examples of Cultural and Church Abuse

The prophet Isaiah makes an apt indictment that was true of the people then and it is true of our culture today. *"You turn things upside down, as if the potter were thought to be like the clay! Shall what is formed say to the one who formed it, 'You did not make me'? Can the pot say to the potter, 'You know nothing'"?* (Isaiah 29:16 NIV) We are on dangerous ground indeed when we begin to think we are wiser than God. God's thoughts are "right-side-up thinking" by definition. What He says is right and good stands. His standard is higher than all else. The problem arises when we, like the Israelites of the past, turn things upside-down. When we do that, we prove that our thinking is all the adjectives we have assigned to it in the previous paragraphs: futile, ignorant, alienated, blind, hardened, stubborn.

The following chart will offer a one-glance view of just a few pieces of evidence that we, in the culture *and* in the church, have upside-down-thinking. The scriptures are listed for you to check on it yourself, if you choose.

God's Right-Side-Up Thinking	Scriptures	Cultural Upside-Down Thinking
The government is on God's Shoulders	Isaiah 9:6	God is on the government's Shoulders
Consider Others More Important Than Self	Philippians 2:3-4	Consider Self of Paramount Importance
Treat Others the Way You Want To Be Treated	The Golden Rule Matthew 7:12	Consider ONLY How You Must be Treated
The Precious is Extracted from the Worthless	Jeremiah 15:19 b NASB	The Worthless is Extracted from the Precious
Be Still and Know that I Am God	Psalm 46:10	Do Not Know How To Be Still
Distinctions Made At Creation: Human/Animal Creator/Creature Male/Female	Genesis 1-2	Blurred Lines
Life is Sacred and God-given	John 1:3-4; John 10:10; Deuteronomy 30:19-20	Planned Parenthood calls Abortion "A Sacred Blessing"
The Righteous are Honored; The Wicked "Cut Off"	Proverbs 17:15	The Wicked are Justified; The Righteous Condemned
Real Fellowship (Koininea)= We Need Each Other	Hebrews 3:12-13; 10:24-25; Ephesians 3:18; 1 Cor. 12	Religion = Me + Jesus with No Accountability

Another example of cultural abuse *inside the church* is the thinking that used to carry the label of "Seeker-Sensitive" churches. Today the moniker assigned to that same thinking is "The Attractional Church Paradigm." It makes me wonder if the change in name is motivated by those who need to convince Jesus-followers that this is really okay thinking. This thinking launched several mega-churches and it no doubt has the capacity of growing numbers. But, God wants us to grow deep, not just wide. Making

Christianity more acceptable by ignoring the "messier" parts of theology that are not attractive—like sin—is not how God chooses for His Kingdom to grow. In a chapter from the book "Portraits of A Pastor", Jared C. Wilson writes the following.

"In 1 Corinthians 14 Paul uses the word 'outsider' to describe unbelievers who are present in the worship gathering. He is making the case for our worship services to be intelligible, hospitable, and mindful of the unbelievers present, but his very use of the word 'outsider' tells us that the Lord's Day worship gathering is not meant to be primarily focused on the unbelieving visitor but on the believing saints gathered to exalt their King. In the attractional church paradigm, this biblical understanding of the worship gathering is turned upside down. Consequently, mission and evangelism are actually inverted, because Christ's command to the church to 'Go and Tell' has been replaced by 'Come and See.' Philosophically, many of these churches operate more like parachurches, and the result is that the sheep, the very lambs of God, basically become the outsiders."[64]

Upside-down thinking is not only a problem in the population as a whole. The church has erred as well.

God's Reminders To Us

The following scriptures are God's reminders—heads-up warnings—concerning the importance and value of turning our thoughts in His direction.

Isaiah 55:7-9 NKJV – *"Let the wicked forsake his way, and the unrighteous man his thoughts; let him return to the Lord, and He will have mercy on him; and to our God, for He will abundantly pardon. 'For My thoughts are not your thoughts, nor are your ways My ways,' says the Lord. 'For as the heavens are higher than the earth, so are My ways higher than your ways, and My thoughts than your thoughts.'"*
Proverbs 23:7a NKJV – *"...as he thinks in his heart, so is he."* A per-

son's destiny can be determined by the thoughts he or she allows. Gulp!

<u>Matthew 15:18-20a NKJV</u> – *"But those things which proceed out of the mouth come from the heart, and they defile a man. For out of the heart proceed evil thoughts, murders, adulteries, fornications, thefts, false witness, blasphemies. These are the things which defile a man, ..."*
Evil thoughts are placed on par with the biggies; murders and adulteries. This is a heart issue. Do you have a heart to go after God's higher thoughts or will you reject them for lesser truths?

<u>1 Corinthians 14:20 NKJV</u> – *"Brethren, do not be children in understanding; however, in malice be babes, but in understanding be mature."*

<u>1 Corinthians 2:11-16 NKJV</u> – *"For what man knows the things of a man except the spirit of the man which is in him? Even so no one knows the things of God except the Spirit of God. Now we have received, not the spirit of the world, but the Spirit who is from God, that we might know the things that have been freely given to us by God. These things we also speak, not in words which man's wisdom teaches but which the Holy Spirit teaches, comparing spiritual things with spiritual. But the natural man does not receive the things of the Spirit of God, for they are foolishness to him; nor can he know them, because they are spiritually discerned. But he who is spiritual judges all things, yet he himself is rightly judged by no one. For 'who has known the mind of the Lord that he may instruct Him?' But we have the mind of Christ."*

A Biblical Example

Having the mind of Christ is no small matter. There are those in any culture who will consider the ways of God foolishness and there are those who will embrace God's thoughts as their own. They will not follow man's wisdom but the things that the Holy Spirit teaches. And, when they do, it generally upsets the apple cart for those who refuse to think God's higher thoughts. There is a poignant example in Acts 17 of some who were persuaded of God's truth and some who were not. Those not convinced that God's way was the best way leveled an accusation against those who were Jesus followers. They called them men *"who have turned the world upside down."* (Acts 17:6) In reality, these men were trying to keep the world right-side-up. The full account of these happenings in the city of Thessalonica is as follows.

"But the Jews who were not persuaded, becoming envious, took some of the evil men from the marketplace, and gathering a mob, set all the city in an uproar and attacked the house of Jason, and sought to bring them out to the people. But when they did not find them, they dragged Jason and some of the brethren to the rulers of the city, crying out, 'These who have turned the world upside down have come here too. Jason has harbored them, and these are all acting contrary to the decrees of Caesar, saying there is another king—Jesus.' And they troubled the crowd and the rulers of the city when they heard these things." (Acts 17;5-8 NKJV) Today the church has been turned upside down by the world.

God intends for the church to turn the world upside down; just as in Jason's day.

How We Can Intentionally Think Like God

The following are suggestions of how we can train ourselves to think like God.

1. **Ask God to search you and know your thoughts.** – Psalm 139:23 NKJV – *"Search me, O God, and know my heart; try me, and know my anxieties; and see if there is any wicked way in me, and lead me in the way everlasting."*

2. **Allow God's Word and Spirit to renew your mind.** – Hebrews 4:12 NIV – *"For the word of God is alive and active. Sharper than any double-edged sword, it penetrates even to dividing soul and spirit, joints and marrow; it judges*

the thoughts and attitudes of the heart." And, Romans 12:2 NASB – *"And do not be conformed to this world, but be transformed by the renewing of your mind, so that you may prove what the will of God is, that which is good and acceptable and perfect."* We can know what God's will is by knowing His Word. His Word is alive, not dead. It is active, not passive. It is sharp, not dull. It penetrates; it is not meant to be a bull-dozer. And, it has the power to examine and judge our thoughts and attitudes. Some translations even say, intentions. That's powerful.

The Word and the Spirit are God's "Dynamic Duo." There is power in allowing His Word to change your thinking. And, you and I can echo Paul's prayer in Ephesians 3:16-17 NASB. *"...that He would grant you, according to the riches of His glory, to be strengthened with power through His Spirit in the inner man, so that Christ may dwell in your hearts through faith."* Our inner man and woman is touched by His Spirit and we are strengthened to think His higher thoughts.

3. **Take your thoughts captive to Christ.** – 2 Corinthians 5:10 NIV – *"We demolish arguments and every pretension that sets itself up against the knowledge of God, and we take captive every thought to make it obedient to Christ."* A.W. Tozer has said that "What comes into our minds when we think about God is the most important thing about us."[65] In other translations the words "arguments" and "pretensions" in this verse are traded with other words that reveal that Tozer was right. Other renderings include "speculations", "lofty things," "lofty opinions," proud obstacles," "barriers," and "warped philosophies." Our thoughts must be surrendered to true Truth.

I sometimes employ an unusual tactic just to slow down long enough to allow God to approve or disapprove of a particular thought. I picture myself in a western corral. The wild horse I am trying to tame represents my thought. Jesus sits on the fence of the corral, and, as I attempt to rope in the thought, I look to Him and get either a thumbs-up or a thumbs-down. All the while He has a smile on His face. He is pleased when we take His Word seriously.

4. **Think like Christ.** – Philippians 4:8 NASB – *"Finally, brethren, whatever is true, whatever is honorable, whatever is right, whatever is pure, whatever is lovely, whatever is of good repute, if there is any excellence and if anything worthy of praise, dwell on these things."* Paul wrote that we can have the mind of Christ. If you want to know what the mind of Christ is, the best place to look is this verse. It is what is true and honorable and right and pure and lovely and of good repute, excellent and praiseworthy.

The problem is that we often allow our minds to dwell on just the opposite. The opposite of true is false. "What if thinking" is a good example of this. If you let your mind dwell on the what if's, you are living in falsehood. Those things are not true, at least not now. The opposite of honorable is petty. The opposite of right is wrong. The opposite of pure is stained. The opposite of lovely is ugly. The opposite of good repute—a good report—is a bad report. The opposite of excellence is mediocrity. And, the opposite of praiseworthy is something to complain about.

It was becoming more and more important that I memorize that verse because knew I needed help with my thoughts, but I had a difficult time setting it in my heart. I turned to God for help and He introduced me to a friend of His. His name is F.B. Thrplgrep. That's not a misprint! F.B. stands for *"Finally brethren."* T is for True, H is for Honorable. R is for Right. P is for Pure. L is for Lovely. GR is for Good Repute. E is for Excellence. And, P is for Praiseworthy. When I know I am going off track with my thinking, I partner with F.B. Thrplgrep and, together, we make a right choice.

5. **Set your minds on the things of the Spirit, not the Flesh.** – Romans 8:5 NKJV – *"Those who live according to the flesh, set their minds on the things of the flesh, but those who live according to the Spirit, the things of the Spirit."* And, also, Colossians 3:1-3 NASB – *"Therefore if you have been raised up with Christ, keep seeking the things above, where Christ is, seated at the right hand of God. Set your mind on the things above, not on the things that are on earth. For you have died and your life is hidden with Christ in God."* It's a godly decision of the will.

Conclusion – "Pillow Tag Theology"

In Romans 8:10-14 NASB it is made clear what it is that we have an obligation to obey. *"If Christ is in you, though the body is dead because of sin, yet the spirit is alive because of righteousness. But if the Spirit of Him who raised Jesus from the dead dwells in you, He who raised Christ Jesus from the dead will also give life to your mortal bodies through His Spirit who dwells in you. So then, brethren, we are under obligation, not to the flesh, to live according to the flesh—for if you are living according to the flesh, you must die; but if by the Spirit you are putting to death the deeds of the body, you will live. For all who are being led by the Spirit of God, these are sons of God."*

Allow me to explain it with a mundane illustration. I love to make beds. I know, that's weird! But, I am rarely up for the morning more than fifteen minutes before the bed is made. I like smoothing out the sheets, arranging the pillows and making the bedroom look tidy. The only thing I have learned not to like are the tags that trail off of the pillows. You know. The ones that have the zebra code and offer washing instructions and fiber content. Those tags always seem to hang out unseemly, like they are sticking out their tongues at me. One day I decided to cut all the tags off so I would not have to deal with them anymore. But, as the scissors were ready to make the first snip, I saw the warning: "DO NOT REMOVE UNDER PENALTY OF LAW." I looked around. Perhaps a pillow tag police force would appear out of nowhere, put me in handcuffs and haul me away to the local precinct. Then I realized. Wait a minute! I purchased those pillows; paid a good price for them. They belong to me. I can do whatever I please with them. I found the freedom I needed to cut those offensive pieces of fabric off of every pillow in my possession.

Jesus did that for us. He paid a good price for us. We belong to Him. He has given us freedom from the obligation of living according to the flesh. And, when we live by the Spirit who indwells us, we are given freedom to think the way the Spirit thinks. And, when we do, we please God and find ourselves at peace. *"The steadfast of mind You will keep in perfect peace, because he trusts in You."* (Isaiah 26:3 NASB)

Paul marveled at God's wisdom and declared the following to the Roman church. *"Oh, the depth of the riches both of the wisdom and knowledge of God. How unsearchable are His judgments and unfathomable His ways!"* (Romans 11:33 NASB) Soon after Paul's statement of wonder, he exhorts the church. *"Do not be conformed to this world, but be transformed by the renewing of your mind."* Why does he give the church a heads up about this? Because if their minds are renewed they will then *"prove what the will of God is, that which is good and acceptable and perfect."* (Romans 12:2 NASB)

There are many voices in our culture today who will tempt you to think *their* way. Some of them are louder than others. Some of them carry the current label: "Progressive." But, if their worldview doesn't line up with God's way, they will seduce you away from what God says is *"good, acceptable and perfect."* Our God is everlasting. He is the Alpha and the Omega. That means His thinking was progressive in the past, He is progressive now and He will be progressive in the future.

About the progressive agenda, R. Albert Mohler, Jr., President of The Southern Baptist Theological Seminary, says the following. "Young Christians do not want to appear hateful. They do not want to appear uncool. And by the way, we do not want young Christians to be hateful or unwelcoming. But we can't define those things on the world's terms. There's no middle ground between affirming and denying the bodily resurrection of Christ. There's also no middle ground between defining marriage as the union of a man and a woman and saying it can be something else. So, Christians are going to have to answer with the full measure of conviction, or they're just on a slower track than some others to denying the faith."[66]

"Who is wise? Let them realize these things. Who is discerning? Let them understand. The ways of the Lord are right; the righteous walk in them, but the rebellious stumble in them." (Hosea 14:9 NIV)

Prayer Points To Consider

1. Ask God to show you any ways you have confused good and evil, bitter and sweet, and light and darkness in your thoughts.

2. Ask God to renew your mind through His Word and His Spirit.

3. Ask God to help you take your thoughts captive to Christ.

4. Ask God to help you partner with F.B. Thrplgrep in thinking as He thinks. Be honest. Which most reflects your thinking?

   Truth? _____ Or Falsehood? _____
   What is Honorable? _____ Or What is Petty? _____
   What is Right? _____ Or What is Wrong? _____
   What is Pure? _____ Or What is Stained? _____
   What is Lovely? _____ Or What is Ugly? _____
   A Good Report? _____ Or A Bad Report? _____
   Excellence? _____ Or Mediocrity? _____
   What is Praiseworthy? _____ Or Complaint? _____

   Take your assessment to God in prayer.

5. Ask God to reveal to you the places that you are strong and weak in living Philippians 4:8.

6. As the Holy Spirit leads.

CHAPTER THIRTEEN – SMASHING IDOLS

God's Intentional Remnant Is Willing To Embrace Suffering

> "No words can express how much the world owes to sorrow. Most of the Psalms were born in the wilderness. Most of the Epistles were written in a prison. The greatest thoughts of the greatest thinkers have all passed through fire.
> The greatest poets have learned in suffering what they taught in song.
> In bonds Bunyan lived the allegory that he afterwords wrote and we may thank Bedford Jail for the Pilgrim's Progress.
> Take comfort, afflicted Christian!
> When God is about to make pre-eminent use of a person, He puts them in the fire."[67]
> ——George MacDonald—

Circumstances rarely determine destinies, but responses to situations—especially in adverse times—can steer future hope or despair. Missionary Dick Brogden declares: "Suffering is a gift God gives to His people that they continually refuse to open. Suffering is as much a gift as salvation. Suffering and death are personal gain, for they promote us to the presence of Jesus.[68]

There are at least four things we can do in response to suffering. We can (1) DENY IT. We can pretend it does not exist and, therefore, give it no credence. (2) We can DOUBT GOD in it; questioning His love, faithfulness, goodness and redemptive plan.

(3) We can DESPAIR IN IT. That leads to discontent, ungrateful-ness and complaint which all spiral down to death. Or, (4) we can DRINK THE CUP of suffering knowing with assurance that our Heavenly Father is sovereign and good and crazy in love with us, designing all things for our holiness. We can know that the Son already took not only our sins to the cross but our infirmities and sorrows as well. (See Isaiah 53:4-5.) And, we can be confident that the Holy Spirit has been called alongside as our Comforter.

If you took a tally of any group of fully devoted followers of Christ and asked the following question, you would find unity in a positive response. The question is: "Can you say a solid 'yes' to the fact that sanctification is a good process employed by a good and loving God?" Everyone would wave their hand in affirmation. It follows, then, that if you agree that sanctification is good and that suffering is an apt tool used by our God to accomplish that task, then embracing suffering is actually enlisting it for God's greater glory and our greater good. He is exalted and we begin to look more like Jesus. Unfortunately, often we prefer to take the bat-tleground of suffering and make it into a playground—somehow easier and care free—but God prefers for it to become holy ground.

Once again "Toothbrush Theology" comes into play. If you remember from the chapter on purity, the premise is that you do not want to use anyone else's toothbrush, nor do you want them using yours, because your toothbrush is "set apart for your per-sonal use." Sanctification is the process of being set apart for God's personal use. And, if suffering is one of God's best "setting apart" tools, then we should welcome it as the narrow road designed for us to look like the Son and live God's purpose in our own genera-tion. (See Acts 13:36.)

At this juncture it would be valuable to identify the present areas of suffering in our own lives. They may be spiritual, physical, emotional, relational, financial, or all of the above. These are the things that you think about when you go to sleep at night and the things that are still on your mind when you awake. They are the things that motivate tears and requests for prayer. They are the items that find you crying out to God; lingering for hours at His throne of grace in your time of need.

Have you decided what they are in your personal life right now? In asking you to embrace suffering on the road to holiness, there is no intention of minimizing what you are going through. Rather, this is an invitation for you—and me—to see these things as God's tools of sanctification; setting us apart for His personal use.

Ravi Zacharias writes of our penchant for avoiding suffering in his book "Has Christianity Failed You?" "We resist pain because pain debilitates and forces limitations on us; Jesus, however, willingly followed the path of pain because it would bring us healing and open new horizons for us. We resist pain because we think of the 'now' rather than of life's ultimate purpose; Jesus endured pain in order to restore ultimate purpose to us and to our existence. We resist pain because we are drawn toward that which brings us comfort and a sense of well-being; Jesus experienced pain so that we would find our ultimate comfort and well-being in God and in doing his will."[69]

The willingness to embrace suffering is important for at least four reasons. First of all, as we have just read, embracing suffering makes us more like Jesus. Second, it is, as we have previously ascertained, one of God's best tools for sanctification. Third, if our culture continues its downward plunge into darkness, depravity and lawlessness, persecution of Christians will not be far behind. And, if we refuse to be trained in the everyday sufferings of this world, how will we be ready for future persecution? The prophet Jeremiah says it this way. *"If you have run with the footmen, and they have wearied you, then how can you contend with horses? And if in the land of peace, in which you trusted, they wearied you, then how will you do in the floodplain of the Jordan?"* (Jeremiah 12:5)

The fourth reason embracing suffering is important is because it demolishes the two most prevalent idols of our day: Comfort and Convenience. Let's face it! We don't like to be uncomfortable, and personal inconvenience has pushed the society into two of the greatest social ills of all time—abortion (child sacrifice) and the break-up of the family in divorce. We consume alcohol and use drugs to numb our pain. We engage in endless rounds of meaningless busyness to avoid looking at suffering face to face. We are a people who refuse to be uncomfortable and inconvenienced.

This is nothing new. The Bible is full of accounts when people found themselves in uncomfortable, inconvenient circumstances. Most of their responses were not stellar and certainly not godly. A few were of the godly sort that only grace could accomplish. Consider just a few with me.

Uncomfortable/Inconvenient Bible Circumstances

In Genesis 20:11 we find Abraham fearing for his life in a place where there was *"no fear of God."* His uncomfortable encounter with the pagan King Ahimelech caused Abraham to lie. He passed his beautiful wife, Sarah, off as his sister to save his own neck.

In the fourth chapter of Jonah we see the rebellious, headstrong prophet, who was given a second chance in an uncomfortable, inconvenient situation. God had sent Jonah to the nasty, vicious Ninevites with a divine message of reconciliation and they actually repented. Jonah's response? Anger and a death wish. *"O Lord, please take my life from me, for it is better for me to die than to live?"* (Jonah 4:3)

Peter responded with what I call "Babel Talk" (words to fill space) in his uncomfortable place. He finds himself with another disciple and Jesus on the Mount of Transfiguration. Elijah and Moses appear with the Lord. The record in Mark 9:6 says *"he was greatly afraid"* and *"he did not know what to say."* So, he said something stupid. *"It is good for us to be here and let us make three tabernacles; one for You, one for Moses and one for Elijah."* The narrative goes on to explain that when the disciples opened their eyes, *"only*

Jesus remained. "Jesus fulfilled what the patriarchs and the prophets had come to accomplish. Peter's words just got in the way. What an awkward moment!

Another uncomfortable, inconvenient situation occurred in John 6:1-15 when too many people showed up (5000 men; and that did not even count in the women and children) and there was not enough food to feed them. Three solutions were offered. Phillip advocated striving and earning their way to the answer. Andrew suggested borrowing from the lunch pail of a boy with five loaves and two fishes. They both knew their answers were insufficient. Then Jesus stepped up to the plate and, with a touch, the meager resources were multiplied so that all were fed with leftovers in abundance.

In Acts 9:1-22 a disciple from Damascus named Ananias was called by Jesus to come alongside a man from Tarsus named Saul. This was most uncomfortable because this Saul had been killing and imprisoning followers of Jesus. Ananias registered his complaint to the Lord with these words in Acts 9:13-14 NIV. *"Lord, I have heard many reports about this man and all the harm he has done to your holy people in Jerusalem. And he has come here with authority from the chief priests to arrest all who call on your name."* But, the Lord told him to go because this man, Saul, was his *"chosen instrument to proclaim His name to the Gentiles."* (Acts 9:15) Ananias paid no attention to his personal discomfort. He obeyed the Lord and, oh my, you and I have received riches from his willingness to smash the idol of comfort. Saul, the persecutor of the church, became Paul, the pillar of the church. His letters comprise most of the New Testament and are a watchword for us today.

Probably the Bible character whom we are most like on this issue is Job. He certainly found himself in an uncomfortable spot with all of his losses of life and family and livestock and health. He was known as *"blameless and upright"; "a man who feared God and shunned evil."* (Job 1:1) He started good by embracing the suffering at hand. Job declared: *"The Lord gave and the Lord has taken away;*

blessed be the name of the Lord." (Job 1:21) When his wife said *"Curse God and die!",* his response was: *"Shall we indeed accept good from God, and shall we not accept adversity?"*

But, as Job's sufferings continued, he changed his tune. In Job 7:19-20 he said to the Lord: *"How long? Will You not look away from me and let me alone till I swallow my saliva? What have I done to You, O watcher of men? Why have You set me as Your target, so that I am a burden to myself?"* As time goes on in our difficulties, we start to complain. What I am learning is that if our complaint is to the Lord—as Job's was—it is still a faith action because it is toward the Lord. But, if our complaint is to people about God, then it is sin. And, God is not pleased.

Job's story ends well; as ours can. In Job 42:5 we hear Job's confession. He agrees with God. *"My ears had heard of You; but now my eyes have seen You. Therefore, I despise myself and repent in dust and ashes."* Job may have been upright, a man who feared God, but until he was totally surrendered, God's sanctifying work was not complete. Now the battleground had indeed become holy ground. He lived through the inconvenient, uncomfortable time in his life for God to do a purifying work. Those idols were smashed!

How can you know if you are giving these idols credence in your life? Like the examples above, the evidence is clear. You will know you are bowing to these idols of comfort and convenience by what comes out of your mouth when they are challenged. Are there lies or harsh words or defensive accusations that proceed from your tongue? You can also tell by how your self-image fares when those idols are exposed. Would you rather die than live? Does anger rise up for yourself or your challenger? And, examine your heart. Like Phillip, with the need to feed so many, do you just work harder to appease these controlling idols?

One word of balance. If you are in a comfortable place right now, you need to know that there is nothing wrong with that. Nothing, unless God is allowing something uncomfortable. Then we must follow His lead and surrender to His Spirit for His glory and our greater good.

C.S. Lewis is credited with saying: "Pain insists upon being attended to. God whispers to us in our pleasures, speaks to us in our conscience, but shouts in our pains. It is His megaphone to rouse a deaf world."[70]

A Declaration of Truth

An anonymous writer affirms the truth that "pain is inevitable, but suffering is optional." The following are some truths from God's Word that agree with that anonymous pen.

Job 36:21 NKJV – *"Take heed, do not turn to iniquity, for you have chosen this rather than affliction."* That seems to be a strange trade-off; iniquity instead of affliction. Yet, that is precisely what we do when we refuse to embrace suffering and complain to people about God. And, it is done often——even by Christians. *"I guess God has just forgotten me." "Why pray? God is not listening to me anyway!"* In Isaiah 40:27 Jacob and Israel are upbraided by the prophet for this very thing. *"Why do you say, O Jacob, and speak, O Israel; 'my way is hidden from the Lord, and my just claim is passed over by my God'"?* This complaint is challenged with the knowledge that the God being discussed is the One who created all the stars and calls them each by name. *"By the greatness of His might and the strength of His power; not one is missing."* (Isaiah 40:26) Do you suppose, that if He knows the names of the stars and He knows if they are missing in the night sky, that He does not know or care about your concerns? 2 Timothy 3:12 – Paul declares to the young Timothy: *"...everyone who wants to live a godly life in Christ Jesus will be persecuted."* You can't wiggle out of the word "everyone". We—you and I—do not escape.

John 15:8-9 – Our Lord declares: *"If the world hates you, keep in mind that it hated Me first. If you belonged to the world, it would love you as its own. As it is, you do not belong to the world, but I have chosen you out of the world. That is why the world hates you."* We have been chosen to be His ambassadors in this world at this time. If we align with Him and not reject Him, the world will hate us. We are seeing it more and more each day.

John 16:33 – *"In the world you will have trouble, but take heart, I have overcome the world."* Only Jesus could make that statement.

Psalm 90:10 – Moses——the one who lived 120 years and was labeled as *"very humble, more than any man who was on the face of the earth"* (Numbers 12:3)——wrote this psalm. The truth contained in verse ten is sobering. In NASB it states: *"As for the days of our lives, they contain seventy years, or if due to strength, eighty years, yet their pride is but labor and sorrow, for soon it is gone and we fly away."* Really? All we get out of life on this planet is labor and sorrow? Sounds like a bum deal to me. But when you read further in Moses' Psalm, he is quick to share that when God is in the mix, the labor and sorrow take on meaning, leading to growth. His prayer continues: *"Make us glad according to the days You have afflicted us."* (Psalm 90:15) And, Psalm 90:17 says *"May the favor of the Lord our God be upon us and do confirm for us the work of our hands; yes, confirm the work of our hands."* It reminds me of the words of Brother Lawrence. "Sufferings will be sweet and pleasant to us while we are with Him; and the greatest pleasures will be a cruel punishment to us without Him."[71]

Examples of Cultural Abuse
With Godly and Ungodly Responses

We are living in a culture that thinks with its feelings. Comfort and convenience are paramount. As a result, a selfish entitlement mentality has emerged with a stomping foot and a raised fist. "I deserve better!" I DESERVE MORE!" Complaint has replaced gratefulness. Whining and victimhood are now the norm.

I offer two contrasting pictures of contemporary Jesus-followers. One person has bought into the ways of the world and the idols of the day—comfort and convenience—have replaced worship of the living, merciful, generous God we know as the Most High. Much complaint has issued from this one's mouth—albeit, it has been a difficult year—and the results are visible. Darkness. Vacancy of eyes. Deteriorating health. The casting off of loyal friends. The rejection of wise counsel. And, I do not believe God has been pleased.

Another couple, in their eighties, have also had a challenging year. A flood occurred in their home while they vacationed, destroying much of two floors and costing thousands. Melanoma skin cancer recurred, requiring the now familiar biopsies, surgical procedures and scars. And, the Lord took their best friend Home to Himself. In all of this, they acted appropriately. They cried. They asked for prayer. They cried out to God themselves. And, they led restoration workers on their home into a relationship with Jesus. They were grateful things were not worse and they praised God. (Things can always be worse, you know.) They smashed the idols of comfort and convenience. They couldn't even use their kitchen and laundry room, yet they embraced the difficulties and rejoiced that they would be counted among those who would join Christ in His sufferings. (See 1 Peter 4:13; Colossians 1:24 and 2 Corinthians 1:5.) God smiled and the watching world was encouraged.

God's Reminders In Suffering

There are several places in God's Word that offer God's warnings and reminders when we are in the midst of suffering. The following is not an exhaustive list but just a few verses that give us hope in hard times.

Romans 8:28-29(NASB)– *"And we know that God causes all things to work together for the good to those who love God, to those who are called according to His purpose. For those whom He foreknew, He also predestined to become conformed to the image of His Son...."*

Our family has recently seen the truth of this reminder. Our oldest granddaughter, Hannah, is finishing her second of three years in a double Masters program at a prestigious Mid-Atlantic university. The program is through the medical school and is quite costly, so her grandfather and I started praying at the outset that God would provide the necessary resources. In July, just before the beginning of her first semester, Hannah broke her ankle badly, requiring surgery with pins, plates and bone grafts. This was not an advantageous time for such a dire fracture. In a mere few weeks she was obligated to attend orientation lectures and then classes. Adding a boot, crutches and an electric scooter to the scenario was not helpful.

It soon became obvious that she would not physically be able to attend all of orientation. Some requirements were kindly waived but some of the meetings came highly recommended for attendance. One evening meeting was to be led by the chief medical officer at the university. Hannah managed to get to that meeting and was soon fully engaged. Her report? "This was the most motivational talk I have ever heard. I am so pumped to get started!"

She also reported that she decided to respond in a manner that she never succumbs to. She went to thank the speaker after dismissal was announced. She hobbled to the podium and introduced herself, whereupon the physician, who had just spoken, asked about her foot. She explained the sordid details. He then walked from behind the podium revealing a boot on his foot as well. He shared his story and an immediate bond was forged.

Some minutes later it was apparent that all the other students had left, so the speaker offered to walk Hannah to her car. In the intervening minutes from the lecture hall to the parking lot a lively conversation arose with one question after another posed by this gentleman. "Why did you choose this University?" "And, why did you decide on the two disciplines of Public Health and Public

Policy?" "What is your passion?" "And, what do you bring to the table?"

Hannah began answering his questions. "This is the best school for this discipline. My passion is in helping underprivileged people get good health care. I am articulate and I market well."

The physician stopped walking and just stared at her. "What?", Hannah protested. He continued: "This is not a happen-stance meeting. We are starting a pilot project this year in the very area of your passion. I have medical doctors and administrators on board, but I need the help of a grad student. I think YOU are it, and I believe I can get you a stipend if you choose to join us."

WOW! It began with two broken ankles and ended with an answer to prayer. God did say *"in ALL things"* He would work for our good. This was a faith-builder for all of us and once again we witnessed the faithfulness of our God.

Matthew 5:10-12 The Message – These verses remind us that persecution can actually be a conduit of blessing. Who would have thought it could be so? *"You're blessed when your commitment to God provokes persecution. The persecution drives you even deeper into God's kingdom. Not only that——count yourselves blessed every time people put you down or throw you out or speak lies about you to discredit Me. What it means is that the truth is too close for comfort and they are uncomfortable. You can be glad when that happens—give a cheer, even!—for though they don't like it, I do! And all heaven applauds. And know that you are in good company. My prophets and witnesses have always gotten into this kind of trouble."*

In 2 Corinthians 1:8-9 NIV Paul reminds all of us of his sufferings in Asia. His words help us remember that when the tire hits the road, our God is there. *"We do not want you to be uninformed, brothers and sisters, about the troubles we experienced in the province of Asia. We were under great pressure, far beyond our ability to endure, so that we despaired of life itself. Indeed, we felt we had received the sentence of death. But this happened that we might not rely on ourselves but on God, who raises the dead."*

This business of *"not relying on ourselves"* is a big deal. I learned it the hard way; always self-sufficient, always an over-achiever, always sure trying a little harder trumped trusting God. I had a lot to learn. My prayers had included a plea to learn dependence on my God, to surrender everything, but I never thought He would answer it in the way He did.

When our oldest child was eleven, she was diagnosed with Type I diabetes. It changed everything in our lives——where we went and did not go, what we ate, how I cooked, exercise routines, and sports involvement, among other things. I was overwhelmed. I was learning that just because I had mastered management techniques, doses of insulin and right eating habits, it did not guarantee no troubling challenges with high and low blood sugars. When our oldest left home for college, our youngest child was given the same diagnosis. He was only six and he was a brittle diabetic with many daily challenges to maintain stability. When he left for college, his father got diabetes. This was a gift that kept on giving!

In the early years diabetes was an enemy. It quickly became a teacher and eventually became a gift. It was a gift because it was the very thing that transformed this self-sufficient mother into one that had to depend on her God——for answers, for hope and for sanity in the struggle.

Another wonderful reminder comes through the prophet Isaiah. Isaiah 45:3 promises:

"I will give you the treasures of darkness and hidden riches in secret places that you may know that I, the Lord, who calls you by your name, am the God of Israel." Think of it. Darkness can yield treasures! Secret places can yield *"hidden riches."* This God of ours is personal. He knows our names, our personal dark spaces and our secret places. His plan is good even if it is enveloped in darkness and secrecy at times. Blessings can come through hard times.

To round out the list of God's reminders, I draw your attention to yet more scripture verses.

Psalm 34:19 – *"Many are the afflictions of the righteous but the Lord delivers him out of them all."*

Psalm 119:71 NIV – *"It was good for me to be afflicted so that I might learn Your decrees."*

Romans 5:3-4 NASB – *"...we also exult in our tribulations, knowing that tribulation brings about perseverance; and perseverance, proven character; and proven character, hope; and hope does not disappoint, because the love of God has been poured out within our hearts through the Holy Spirit who was given to us."*

Romans 8:18 NIV – *"I consider that our present sufferings are not worth comparing with the glory that will be revealed in us."*

Romans 8:35 – *"Who shall separate us from the love of Christ? Shall trouble or hardship or persecution or famine or nakedness or danger or sword?"*

1 Peter 4:12-13 NIV – *"Dear friends, do not be surprised at the fiery ordeal that has come on you to test you, as though something strange were happening to you. But rejoice inasmuch as you participate in the sufferings of Christ, so that you may be overjoyed when His glory is revealed."*

1 Peter 1:6-7 NIV – *"In all this you greatly rejoice, though now for a little while you may have had to suffer grief in all kinds of trials. These have come so that the proven genuineness of your faith—of greater worth than gold, which perishes even though refined by fire—may result in praise, glory and honor when Jesus Christ is revealed."*

2 Corinthians 4:8-11 NIV – *"We are hard pressed on every side, but not crushed; perplexed, but not in despair; persecuted, but not abandoned; struck down, but not destroyed. We always carry around in our body the death of Jesus, so that the life of Jesus may also be revealed in our body. For we who are alive are always being given over to death for Jesus' sake, so that His life may also be revealed in our mortal body."*

Philippians 1:29 NIV – *"For it has been granted to you on behalf of Christ not only to believe in Him, but also to suffer for Him."*

A Biblical Example

The Bible is full of whiners and complainers, but also has its share of those who stepped up to the plate in the midst of suffering and understood the value of the lessons they were learning and the character that was developing. One comes to mind for our purposes.

The apostles had gone through the horror of passion week in their recent past, watching the intensity of the unthinkable: the arrest, mocking, scourging, crucifixion and resurrection of Jesus. They had been sent out into an unbelieving Roman world full of force and cruelty. The culture around them did not think the way they did. The world hated them. Jesus had told them it would be so.

After the healing of a lame man, thousands came to a saving faith, which further incensed the watching religious crowd. So, the religious authorities arrested Peter and John. Acts 4:16-18 records the conference of the opposition. *"What shall we do with these men? For, indeed, that a notable miracle has been done through them is evident to all who dwell in Jerusalem, and we cannot deny it. But so that it spreads no further among the people, let us severely threaten them that from now on they speak to no man in this name. So they called them and commanded them not to speak at all nor teach in the name of Jesus."*

How did Peter and John respond? First, they declared their allegiance to God. Acts 4:19-20 states: *"Whether it is right in the sight of God to listen to you more than to God, you judge. For we cannot but speak the things which we have seen and heard."* Furthermore, they called a prayer meeting and asked God to *"look on the threats"* (of the authorities) and that *"with all boldness"* they would *"speak His Word."* (Acts 4:29) They were willing to suffer.

Once again, they were jailed and an angel of the Lord released them. They went out teaching in the name of Jesus in the temple courts which found them back in the Sanhedrin answering the questions of the high priest. Because of the speech of an honorable

Pharisee, named Gamaliel, they were released; but only after a flogging and yet another warning NOT to speak in the name of Jesus. (See Acts 5:40) Their response was astounding. *"So they departed from the presence of the council, rejoicing that that were counted worthy to suffer shame for His name. And daily in the temple, and in every house, they did not cease teaching and preaching Jesus as the Christ."* (Acts 5:41-42 NKJV)

Why Suffering Occurs

The following are ten reasons why God allows suffering. Surely there are more, but this should help us understand the redemptive intentions of our God.

1. <u>Suffering helps correct disobedient life patterns.</u> Jonah is a good example. God loves to give second, third, even 100th, chances to get things right. It was said earlier in this chapter that Jonah was in an uncomfortable situation. He was asked to go as God's prophet to the Ninevites with a message of reconciliation. But, the Ninevites were vicious, evil people and Jonah apparently did not think they deserved a touch from a merciful God. So, he disobeyed. In fact, he went the opposite direction. And, he did it "politely." He bought a ticket on the ship that carried him away from God's plan.

A quick outline of the book of Jonah goes something like this. God told Jonah to GO. He said "NO!" And, there was woe. God told Jonah to Go a second time. He said "Yes". And, God blessed.

GO—NO—WOE

GO—YES—BLESSED

But, Jonah did not see it as a blessing. His disobedience caused trouble. The result was a violent storm, a raging sea, a hungry whale, a strange "prayer closet," a spitting up, a vine for shade and a worm that caused more discomfort. All of these things were appointed by God to touch the angry attitude of a wayward prophet and give him a HUGE nudge to think the way the Almighty was thinking. But, even God could not convince Jonah.

2. Suffering for one may be used by God to prevent future problems for many. Joseph provides this example. Hated by his brothers, he was left for dead in a cistern and eventually sold into slavery and taken to Egypt. His story doesn't get any better there when he was seduced by his boss's wife, framed and unjustly thrown into prison. The darkness continued as he was forgotten in the depths of his cell. Eventually Joseph was exonerated, elevated to high status in this foreign land and saved multitudes of Egyptians and Israelites in the midst of a severe famine.

God will place us where He needs us to accomplish His purposes, and our suffering in the interim does not go unnoticed. Joseph declared the following to his brothers in Genesis 50:20. *"You meant evil against me; but God meant it for good, in order to bring it about as it is this day, to save many people alive."*

3. Suffering is used by God to lead a person to His heart. Job is Exhibit A in this scenario. When we are introduced to Job, we find some defining adjectives that tell us about his character. He is labeled as "blameless" and "upright". But, as his story unfolds we begin to see a man not surrendered to the heart of God. He seemed to have God all figured out. He did a lot of talking; more like spouting, even. He demanded that God answer his questions. He was familiar with God, instructing others in His majesty; proud of the help he offered. He stood up for his personal rights. He learned to out-talk his hot-air friends. He had only heard of God and he seemed big and puffed up.

Everything had fallen apart. God allowed losses of life and resources and health. But, in the end, a surrendered man emerged.

He started bowing to the mystery. He became a listener. He humbly answered God's questions. He traded familiarity for intimacy with God. He was in awe of His majesty. He was repentant and instead of out-talking his friends and his God, he put a hand over his mouth. Now it wasn't just secondhand knowledge of God. His eyes saw Him. Instead of big and puffed up, he knew himself to be small and lifted up. Oh, the wonders of suffering. Treasures in darkness, indeed.

4. Suffering helps us see Him. Shadrach, Meshach and Abednego are apt examples for this truth. They were nice Hebrew boys. The cream of the crop. The king, Nebuchadnezzar, had made an idol and everyone in the land was expected to bow down to it. Everyone! Some of the other Jews caved in. But, these three would not.

The punishment for such defiance was a fiery furnace, and because the king was so enraged, he had it cranked up to seven times the original heat. The confident words of the three young men were as follows. *"Our God whom we serve is able to deliver us from your hand, O king. But if not, let it be known to you, O king, that we do not serve your gods, nor will we worship the gold image which you have set up."* (Daniel 3:17-18)

There was no bowing to the idols of comfort and convenience in this scenario. Suffering was embraced, and, oh, what a reward. As the three were bound and thrown into the flames, the pagan king exclaimed this astounding truth. *"Look! I see four men loose, walking in the midst of the fire; and they are not hurt and the form of the fourth is like the Son of God."* (Daniel 3:25)

We shouldn't be surprised. The prophet Isaiah made it clear before this event in history. In Isaiah 43:1-3 he says: *"Fear not, for I have redeemed you. I have called you by your name. You are Mine. When you pass through the waters, I will be with you; and through the rivers, they shall not overflow you. When you walk through the fire, you shall not be burned. Nor shall the flame scorch you. For I am the Lord you God, the Holy One of Israel, your Savior."* The record is clear.

Shadrach, Meshach and Abednego were not burned. They didn't even smell like smoke. God wants us to see Him, and He will do whatever it takes to open our eyes.

5. Suffering helps us guard against pride. In 2 Corinthians 12:7 Paul confesses: *"Lest I should be exalted above measure by the abundance of the revelations, a thorn in the flesh was given to me, a messenger of Satan to buffet me, lest I be exalted above measure."* Some scholars believe that this "thorn" was a physical problem affecting either Paul's eyes or his writing hand. Their text proof comes from Galatians 6:11. *"See with what large letters I have written to you with my own hand!"*

Whatever specific form of suffering Paul was experiencing, we are told in 2 Corinthians 12:8 that he begged God three times to remove it. God's response comes in 2 Corinthians 12:9a. *"My grace is sufficient for you, for My strength is made perfect in weakness."* Paul responds to this uncomfortable, inconvenient problem by immediately getting in step with the Lord's thinking. *"Therefore, most gladly I will rather boast in my infirmities that the power of Christ may rest upon me. Therefore I take pleasure in infirmities, in reproaches, in needs, in persecutions, in distresses, for Christ's sake. For when I am weak, then I am strong."* (2 Corinthians 12:9b-10)

6. Suffering puts God's work on display. The account of the man blind from birth in John 9 shows us this truth. The disciples asked Jesus: *"Rabbi, who sinned, this man or his parents, that he was born blind?"* (John 9:2) Jesus answered. *"Neither this man nor his parents sinned, but that the works of God should be revealed in him."* (John 9:3)

This whole account created a flurry of combative interchanges between the Pharisees and the healed man, the Pharisees and the man's parents, and the Pharisees and Jesus. It was a perfect opportunity for Jesus to draw attention to their spiritual blindness. In John 9:39 He said: *"For judgment I have come into this world, that those who do not see may see, and that those who see may be made blind."*

7. Suffering happens in our lives so we can learn to comfort others. 2 Corinthians 1:3-5 NIV states: *"Praise be to the God and Father of our Lord Jesus Christ, the Father of compassion and the God of all comfort, who comforts us in all our troubles, so that we can comfort those in any trouble with the comfort we ourselves receive from God. For just as we share abundantly in the sufferings of Christ, so also our comfort abounds through Christ."*

8. Suffering helps us know we truly are God's sons and daughters and heirs.

Romans 8:16-17 – *"The Spirit Himself testifies with our spirit that we are God's children. Now if we are children, then we are heirs—heirs, and co-heirs with Christ, if indeed we share in His sufferings in order that we may also share in His glory."*

Hebrews 12:5-6 – (cf. Proverbs 3:11-12) -*" My son, do not despise the chastening of the Lord, nor be discouraged when you are rebuked by Him; for whom the Lord loves He chastens, and scourges every son He receives."*

9. Suffering offers us the "Crown of Life." Revelation 2:10 states: *"Do not be afraid of what you are about to suffer. I tell you, the devil will put some of you in prison to test you, and you will suffer persecution. Be faithful, even to the point of death, and I will give you life as your victor's crown."* These crowns are important; crowns of life and glory and rejoicing and righteousness and honor. We may receive them all because our Savior wore a crown of thorns; and, all for the purpose of laying them at His feet in worship at The Throne. Our proclamation in so doing would be to say: *"You are worthy, O Lord, to receive glory and honor and power." (See Revelation 4:10-11.)*

10. Suffering produces completeness of character in us; lacking

nothing. Romans 5:3-5 NKJV – *"… we also glory in tribulations, knowing that tribulation produces perseverance; and perseverance, character; and character, hope. Now hope does not disappoint, because the love of God has been poured out in our hearts by the Holy Spirit who was given to us."* This truth is echoed in James 1:2-4 NKJV – *"My brethren, count it all joy when you fall into various trials, knowing that the testing of your faith produces patience. But let patience have its perfect work, that you may be perfect and complete, lacking nothing."*

The bottom line is that our suffering can bring praise to the Most High God. It can also highlight complaint and a host of other negative assertions. I don't know about you, but I choose praise. The way we live our lives will either declare or deny that Jesus is enough and worthy of all praise. 1 Peter 1:6-7 NKJV declares: *"In this you greatly rejoice, though now for a little while, if need be, you have been grieved by various trials, that the genuineness of your faith, being much more precious than gold that perishes, though it is tested by fire, may be found to praise, honor, and glory at the revelation of Jesus Christ."*

Pastor Adrian Rogers clarifies things for us with the following words. "If we pray to escape our pain, then we see pain as our enemy. If we pray to endure our pain, then pain is seen as a master. But if we pray to enlist our pain, we see it as our servant. We are able to find God's grace to glory in our infirmities, that the power of God may be manifest in our lives.[72] Circle the words "escape", "endure" and "enlist" in that quote. You and I have three choices. If we endeavor to escape, then the pain is seen as our enemy. If we buck up and endure only, the pain is mastering us. But, if we can enlist it for God's glory and our sanctification, then it becomes our servant.

How We Can Intentionally Embrace Suffering

So far in this chapter, you may be agreeing with me, but a big question arises. HOW? Following are eight suggestions along with verses to cement their truths. Some of these verses we have already visited. I repeat them for emphasis now.

1. Follow Christ's Example.

1 Peter 2:19-21 NIV – *"For it is commendable if someone bears up under the pain of unjust suffering because they are conscious of God. But how is it to your credit if you receive a beating for doing wrong and endure it? But if you suffer for doing good and you endure it, this is commendable before God. To this you were called, because Christ suffered for you, leaving you an example, that you should follow in his steps."*

1 Peter 4:1-2 NIV – *"Therefore, since Christ suffered in his body, arm yourselves also with the same attitude, because whoever suffers in the body is done with sin. As a result, they do not live the rest of their earthly lives for evil human desires, but rather for the will of God."*

2. Count on His Presence With You.

Isaiah 43:2-3 NIV – *"When you pass through the waters, I will be with you; and when you pass through the rivers, they will not sweep over you. When you walk through the fire, you will not be burned; the flames will not set you ablaze. For I am the Lord your God, the Holy One of Israel, your Savior; I give Egypt for your ransom, Cush and Seba in your stead."*

3. Commit Yourself to God.

1 Peter 4:19 NIV – *"So then, those who suffer according to God's will should commit themselves to their faithful Creator and continue to do good."*

4. Maintain An Eternal Perspective.

2 Corinthians 4:16-18 – *"Therefore we do not lose heart. Though outwardly we are wasting away, yet inwardly we are being renewed day by day. For our light and momentary troubles are achieving for us an eternal glory that far outweighs them all. So we fix our eyes not on what is seen, but on what is unseen, since what is seen is temporary, but what is unseen is eternal."*

1 Peter 1:3, 23 NIV – 3. *"Praise be to the God and Father of our Lord Jesus Christ! In his great mercy he has given us new birth into a living hope through the resurrection of Jesus Christ from the dead."* 23. *"For you have been born again, not of perishable seed, but of imperishable, through the living and enduring word of God."*

1 Peter 2:4-5 NIV – *"As you come to him—the living Stone—rejected by humans but chosen by God and precious to him—you also, like living stones, are being built into a spiritual house to be a hold priesthood, offering spiritual sacrifices acceptable to God through Jesus Christ."*

We get help from three living, eternal sources: God Himself, God's Word and God's people.

5. Help Others in Their Suffering.

2 Corinthians 1:3-4 NIV – *"Praise be to the God and Father of our Lord Jesus Christ, the Father of compassion and the God of all comfort, who comforts us in all our troubles, so that we can comfort those in any trouble with the comfort we ourselves receive from God."*

Galatians 6:2 NIV – *"Carry each other's burdens, and in this way you will fulfill the law of Christ."*

Hebrews 13:1-3 NIV – *"Keep on loving one another as brothers and sisters. Do not forget to show hospitality to strangers, for by so doing some people have shown hospitality to angels without knowing it. Continue to remember those in prison as if you were together with them in prison, and those who are mistreated as if you yourselves were suffering."*

6. Rely On God's Grace.

2 Corinthians 9:8 NASB – *"And God is able to make all grace abound*

to you, so that always having all sufficiency in everything, you may have an abundance for every good deed."

2 Corinthians 12:9-10 NIV – *"But he said to me, 'My grace is sufficient for you, for my power is made perfect in weakness.' Therefore I will boast all the more gladly about my weaknesses, so that Christ's power may rest on me. That is why, for Christ's sake, I delight in weaknesses, in insults, in hardships, in persecutions, in difficulties. For when I am weak, then I am strong."*

7. Purpose to Bring Glory to God with a Joyful Attitude.

James 1:2-4 The Message – *"Consider it a sheer gift, friends, when tests and challenges come at you from all sides. You know that under pressure, your faith-life is forced into the open and shows its true colors. So don't try to get out of anything prematurely. Let it do its work so you become mature and well-developed, not deficient in any way."*

8. Find Joy and Power in the Sharing of His Sufferings and Know Him Better.

Philippians 3:10-14 NIV – *"I want to know Christ—yes, to know the power of his resurrection and participation in his sufferings, becoming like him in his death, and so, somehow, attaining to the resurrection from the dead. Not that I have already obtained all this, or have already arrived at my goal, but I press on to take hold of that for which Christ Jesus took hold of me. Brothers and sisters, I do not consider myself yet to have taken hold of it. But one thing I do: Forgetting what is behind and straining toward what is ahead, I press on toward the goal to win the prize for which God has called me heavenward in Christ Jesus."*

What is "the prize?" JESUS!

Conclusion

I do not know what suffering you are personally facing right now. What I do know is that there is something uncomfortable and inconvenient going on in your life. I know this because you live on the same planet I live on and Jesus called it centuries ago. *"In the world you will have tribulation."* (John 16:33a NKJV)

If we allow Him to finish His sentence and travel to the second half of John 16:33, we will find hope and confidence in Him. His whole statement reads: *"In the world you will have tribulation; but be of good cheer, I have overcome the world."*

Whatever defines your present suffering, you can know with certainty that God sees, He cares, He is speaking a personal word to you and He ever lives to intercede for you. He did it for Hagar in her time of wilderness despair in Genesis 16. He did it for Ruth at the watershed moment of her life when she left Moab with her mother-in-law for Jerusalem, the House of Bread. He did it for David running from the insane jealousy of King Saul and hiding in the caves of Israel. He did it for Mary Magdalene when the tomb was empty and she sorrowed, not knowing where they had taken her Lord—the One who had touched and transformed her life. And, then …… the utterance. "Mary!"

He is doing the same for you. He is speaking your name. Do you hear it? * It's the only way we can embrace suffering, smash the idols of comfort and convenience, be ready for any future persecution, grow in sanctification and bring glory to our Lord and Savior Jesus Christ.

*(NOTE: For your edification, I suggest you access a twelve minute thirty second video on YouTube, filmed in Israel and produced by Kathie Lee Gifford called "The God Who Sees." Consider receiving it as God praying over you and your suffering.)

Prayer Points To Consider

1. Ask God to show you treasures in your personal suffering. Linger with Him and listen for His response.

2. Ask God to lead you to one person you could help this week in the midst of their suffering.

3. Ask God to reveal Himself to you in your suffering.

4. Ask God to help you desire a transformed heart more than just relief from the problem.

5. Ask God to give your suffering meaning.

6. As the Holy Spirit leads.

CHAPTER FOURTEEN – STANDING IN THE GAP

God's Intentional Remnant Reverences the Sanctity of Life

> "The world will not be destroyed by those who do evil, but by those who watch them——without doing anything."[73]
> —Albert Einstein—

Some terms, in common use today, were unthinkable years ago. Things like: "Active shooter." "Shelter in place!" "Lockdown drill." "Pandemic." "Social Distancing." Every decade has boasted threats to life. There will always be tornadoes and hurricanes. As a child, when the Russian satellite Sputnik was roaming the skies, I remember being taught to hide under my desk for any incoming threat. I can still visualize the bowels of Gilbert Knapp Elementary School in Racine, Wisconsin, where we were told to run if the Russians attacked. I wondered then, as now, where exactly would I go and what good would it do?

Although there have always been random hazards posed by menacing foes, it seems that the threats of today are more personal. Disgruntled or bullied students kill classmates and teachers and workplace associates snuff out innocent lives to appease personal angst. Then there are those folks who choose everyday vehicles to mow down unsuspecting pedestrians.

The statistics are staggering. Although some dips occur, most successive years indicate a rise in numbers. The loss of life has occurred at schools, military posts, restaurants, media outlets, movie theaters, places of worship and job sites. Records were begun in the early 1970's and continue until today. It is as God spoke to the prophet Ezekiel. *"The land is full of bloodshed and the city full of perversity."* (Ezekiel 9:9 NKJV)

We should not be surprised that such a lawless, reckless loss of life has occurred. In the 1960's and 70's the theologian Francis Schaeffer prophesied that we would see a rise in deaths if abortion would be the law of the land, as was realized in Roe v. Wade in 1973. The National Right To Life organization reports that 61,628,584 abortions have occurred since 1973.[74] The numbers most certainly exceed that report due to specific states, like California, Oregon, Hawaii and North Carolina, legalizing the procedure before Roe v. Wade was decided upon. It has also been determined that Planned Parenthood provided one-third to one-half of that number.

Some call it "Choice." Others call it "A Woman's Right to Her Own Body." The biggest provider has labeled it "A Sacred Blessing." But, make no mistake, God calls it "Murder." It is "Child Sacrifice" of the most sophisticated sort.

Our culture has lost respect for the sanctity of life. In this chapter we will see that this is an abomination to God; a great grief to His heart, because He is all about life. In John 10:10 NIV Jesus declared: *"The thief comes only to steal and kill and destroy; I have come that they may have life, and have it to the full."* And, Albert Einstein was right. "The world will not be destroyed by those who do evil, but by those who watch them——without doing anything." We must stand in the gap!

Through the prophet Ezekiel God spoke His truth plainly. *"So I sought for a man among them who would make a wall, and stand in the gap before Me on behalf of the land, that I should not destroy it; but I found no one."* (Ezekiel 22:30 NKJV) Oh, that God would find someone today; one or more of us who will choose to be His intentional remnant by being His watchman and filling the gap of untruth with True Truth.

Declarations of Truth

About being God's watchmen, again it is the prophet Ezekiel who speaks. His words should make us squirm a bit. *"So you, son of man: I have made you a watchman for the house of Israel; therefore you shall hear a word from My mouth and warn them for Me. When I say to the wicked, 'O wicked man, you shall surely die!' and you do not speak to warn the wicked from his way, that wicked man shall die in his iniquity; but his blood I will require at your hand. Nevertheless, if you warn the wicked to turn from his way, and he does not turn from his way, he shall die in his iniquity; but you have delivered your soul. Therefore you, O son of man, say to the house of Israel: 'Thus you say, 'If our transgressions and our sins lie upon us, and we pine away in them, how can we then live?' Say to them: 'As I live,' says the Lord God, 'I have no pleasure in the death of the wicked, but that the wicked turn from his way and live. Turn, turn from your evil ways! For why should you die, O house of Israel?'"* (Ezekiel 33:7-11 NKJV) God will not be mocked. The offender of what is an abomination to Him will be held accountable, but so will those who see and do not warn. This is serious business!

In the Old Testament strict laws against child sacrifice were put into place. These were pagan practices and God was highly displeased with it all. Leviticus 18:21 NKJV testifies: *"You shall not let any of your descendants pass through the fire to Molech,, nor shall you profane the name of your God; I am the Lord."* Molech is the biblical name of a Canaanite god associated with child sacrifice. Notice that this sin was on par with one listed in the Ten Commandments—taking the name of the Lord in vain. Leviticus 20:2-5 NKJV goes on to explain what God will do to anyone engaging in child sacrifice or anyone who sees it and does nothing. [2] *"Again, you shall say to the children of Israel: 'Whoever of the children of Israel, or of the strangers who dwell in Israel, who gives any of his descendants to Molech, he shall surely be put to death. The people of the land shall stone him with stones.* [3] *I will set My face against that man, and will cut him off from his people, because he has given some of his descendants to Molech, to defile My sanctuary and profane My holy name. ⁴ And if the people of the land should in any way hide their eyes from the man, when he gives some of his descendants to Molech, and they do not kill him, ⁵ then I will set My face against that man and against his family; and I will cut him off from his people, and all who prostitute themselves with him to commit harlotry with Molech."*

In Deuteronomy 12:29-32 NKJV God gives stiff warnings about following the practices of those who worship false gods. *"When the Lord your God cuts off from before you the nations which you go to dispossess, and you displace them and dwell in their land, ³⁰ take heed to yourself that you are not ensnared to follow them, after they are destroyed from before you, and that you do not inquire after their gods, saying, 'How did these nations serve their gods? I also will do likewise.' ³¹ You shall not worship the Lord your God in that way; for every abomination to the Lord which He hates they have done to their gods; for they burn even their sons and daughters in the fire to their gods.³² Whatever I command you, be careful to observe it; you shall not add to it nor take away from it."*

In Deuteronomy 18:10-12 NKJV we find that killing our children is to appease some foreign god. Today the demanding foreign god that motivates such action is the god of convenience and comfort. In these verses our God calls the action akin to witchcraft, sorcery, conjuring spells and calling up the dead. *¹⁰ There shall not be found among you anyone who makes his son or his daughter pass through the fire, or one who practices witchcraft, or a soothsayer, or one who interprets omens, or a sorcerer, ¹¹ or one who conjures spells, or a medium, or a spiritist, or one who calls up the dead. ¹² For all who do these things are an abomination to the Lord, and because of these abominations the Lord your God drives them out from before you."*

And, yet, with these strict warnings in place the practice continued. You can see in the following verses that certain kings allowed it during their reigns. Solomon (1 Kings 11:4-11) and Manasseh (2 Kings 21:6) and Ahaz (2 Chronicles 28:1-4) and Herod in the

New Testament (Matthew 2:13-18 prophesied in Jeremiah 31:15) all winked at such action. It is the prophet Isaiah who tells us what God thinks of anyone who sheds innocent blood and the results that will inevitably follow. *"Your iniquities have separated you from your God; and your sins have hidden His face from you, so that He will not hear. ³ For your hands are defiled with blood, and your fingers with iniquity; your lips have spoken lies, your tongue has muttered perversity. ⁴ No one calls for justice, nor does any plead for truth. They trust in empty words and speak lies; They conceive evil and bring forth iniquity. 5.they hatch vipers' eggs and weave the spider's web; he who eats of their eggs dies, and from that which is crushed a viper breaks out. ⁶ Their webs will not become garments, nor will they cover themselves with their works; their works are works of iniquity, and the act of violence is in their hands. 7.And they make haste to shed innocent blood; their thoughts are thoughts of iniquity; wasting and destruction are in their paths. ⁸ The way of peace they have not known, and there is no justice in their ways; they have made themselves crooked paths; whoever takes that way shall not know peace."* (Isaiah 59:2-8 NKJV) The results are unmistakable. Separation from God. God turning a deaf ear. Wasting. Destruction. Death. No peace.

In Proverbs 6:16-19 NKJV God tells us six things that He hates, seven that are an abomination to Him. *"These six things the Lord hates, yes, seven are an abomination to Him: ¹⁷ A proud look, a lying tongue, <u>hands that shed innocent blood</u>, ¹⁸ a heart that devises wicked plans, feet that are swift in running to evil, ¹⁹ a false witness who speaks lies, and one who sows discord among brethren."* There is no more innocent blood than an unborn child.

Possibly there is someone reading these words that has had an abortion. To them, the previous truths are horrifying. BUT GOD! Our God has a favorite word. It is "Come!" Anyone who has gone down this road need only to turn to the living God who offers a smile, open arms and forgiveness. Paul David Tripp says: "God's grace will expose what you want to hide, not to shame you, but to forgive and deliver you."[75] He goes on to say: "We cannot grieve what we do not see. We cannot confess what we have not grieved. And, we cannot turn from what we haven't confessed."[76] When we confess a wrong doing we are agreeing with God that the action was against His will. God will shine His light on our darkness to bring us into the light of His Son. We SEE it. We GRIEVE over it. We CONFESS it. And, we get to REPENT of it. With the truth set out plainly before you, I beg you not to leave this page until you have told God your heart and asked for His forgiveness. No more hiding, cover-up, lying, excuses, shifting blame, rationalization, defensiveness, and denial. Allow Him to work. He wants to set you free. The love of the Father, the blood of the Son and the enabling power of the Holy Spirit make forgiveness and liberty a possibility.

Examples of Cultural Abuse

The shedding of innocent blood in our nation has come through many doors. Abortion is by far the largest culprit. Shootings at many different venues, including schools, churches, restaurants, places of work and random street corners are becoming alarmingly common. In an article by Melissa Chan, she states that "Amnesty International, the human rights group, warned travelers to 'exercise caution' when visiting the U.S. due to its gun violence problem." It was also noted that "in 2017, firearms killed 39,773 people and traffic deaths killed 38,659."[77]

The Rockefeller Institute of Government published a Mass Shooting Factsheet in 2017. They state that there have been "340 mass shooting in the United States between 1966 and 2016. They have resulted in 1,141 deaths and 2,526 total victims both injured and killed. Mass shootings have been increasing in frequency since 1966. 1966-1975 revealed twelve mass shootings. 2006-16 boasted 183 mass shootings."[78] The Institute's definition of a mass shooting, developed by Jaclyn Schildkraut and H. Jaymi Elsass is as follows. "A mass shooting in an incident of targeted violence carried out by one or more shooter at one or more public or populated locations.

Multiple victims (both injuries and fatalities) are associated with the attack, and both the victims and location(s) are chosen either at random or for their symbolic value. The event occurs within a single 24-hour period, though most attacks typically last only a few minutes. The motivation of the shooting must not correlate with gang violence or targeted militant or terroristic activity."[79]

Also the rise of terrorism must be on the list of violent activity that plagues the modern culture of today. The "War Against Terrorism" has become synonymous with American foreign policy. Many Americans have lost their lives on native and foreign soil. Since that fateful day in September of 2001, Americans are aware of terrorist activity and the deadly results it leaves. Statista Research Department released the following statistics on January 28, 2020. "There were 32,836 fatalities from terrorism in 2018 globally. The number of terror attacks in Iraq in 2018 was 765. And, number one on the global terrorism index is the country of Afghanistan. There were 60 terrorist attacks in the United States in 1995. The number dipped to six in 2007. In 2017 we were back up to 66 attacks."[80] Truly today is a microcosm of what Ezekiel saw in his vision that *the land is full of bloodshed."* (Ezekiel 9:9 NKJV) Life is not valued.

God's Reminders To Us

There are two scriptures that speak of God's heart concerning life that are especially important. The first is in the New Testament in John 10:10 NKJV. *"The thief does not come except to steal, and to kill and to destroy. I have come that they may have life, and that they may have it more abundantly."* God is talking about over-the-top, skip-in-your-step, song-in-your-heart kind of life. What the enemy offers is the antithesis of God's intention. In the original Greek the word "steal" is a word that sounds like something you have heard of before. The word is "klepto." The word we recognize is kleptomaniac. A kleptomaniac is someone who cannot help but steal. That is the character of our enemy. The original meaning for the word "kill" is "to butcher." The devil desires to cut us up into little pieces and place us on the altar of darkness. And the meaning of "destroy" is "to destroy utterly." Crushed. In despair. Forsaken. DESTROYED! Listen to the apostle Paul's testimony as encouragement for your own heart. *"We are hard-pressed on every side yet not crushed; we are perplexed, but not in despair; persecuted, but not forsaken; struck down, but not destroyed."* (2 Corinthians 4:8-9 NKJV) *"We are more than conquerors through Him who loved us."* (Romans 8:37 NKJV) God came to bring us life; full life, abundant life. Plentiful life. Bountiful life. Lavish life. Rich life.

The other scripture that comes to mind is in the Old Testament. Deuteronomy 30:19-20 NKJV states: *19" I call heaven and earth as witnesses today against you, that I have set before you life and death, blessing and cursing; therefore choose life, that both you and your descendants may live; 20 that you may love the Lord your God, that you may obey His voice, and that you may cling to Him, for He is your life and the length of your days; and that you may dwell in the land which the Lord swore to your fathers, to Abraham, Isaac, and Jacob, to give them."* God gives us a choice: life or death, blessings or curses. What we choose will effect not only us but the generations following. How do we choose life? We realize that the Lord is our life and we follow His three commands. 1. Love Him. 2. Listen and obey His voice. And, 3. Cling to Him. Hold fast and don't let go.

Some of you may remember the movie Titanic in the 90's. There is one scene near the end of the movie that depicts these verses quite well. The ship has gone down and Rose is floating in the cold Atlantic on a door. Her lover, Jack, is in the water clutching to the side of the door. He is already dead; frozen in the frigid waters that engulf him. Rose pries his fingers off of the door and he sinks to the bottom. One lone rowboat goes back to search for survivors. The call goes out. "Is anyone out there?" The silence is deafening. Rose hears the cry of the rescuer. She lifts her head and then puts it down again in resignation. She says nothing in response. And then …… in one moment of choice … her raspy, barely audible voice quivers with these words. "Come back. Come back!" She gets off of the door, slips into the cold Atlantic waters, and dogpaddles to a corpse near her. She pulls the whistle out of the man's mouth and sounds the alarm. Her words and actions say "I want to live."

We have a lone rescuer too. His name is Jesus and He offers full life. He waits to hear a response to His call. *"Is anyone out there?"* It matters not how weak our words come out. His ears are tuned to those who need rescue. We, too, must let go of whatever is dead in our lives to fully enjoy the rescue being offered. And we, too, may have to endure discomfort before we are rescued; a go-through before a break-through. The choice is ours. And the choice is not only for us but for those who follow us.

A Biblical Example

Solomon, David's son, was quite a king. In 1 Kings 3:16-28 we are told of a wisdom test that was set before him. Remember in 1 Kings 2:9, in a meeting with God, Solomon's one request was that he receive understanding and wisdom so he would discern good and evil and be able to bring God's justice to the people. The test came when two harlots stood before him. They had both given birth to babies. They both lived in the same house. One of the women accidently laid on her baby in the night and he died, so, she exchanged babies, placing the dead child with the sleeping mother and keeping the live child for herself. Of course, the other mother noticed the switch and bitterly complained. King Solomon settled the dispute with these words. *"Bring me a sword." "Divide the living child in two, and give half to the one, and half to the other."* (1 Kings 3:24-25 NKJV) The mother of the living child screeched. *"Give her the living child, and by no means kill him!"* The other woman, whose child had already died, said *"Let him be neither mine nor yours, but divide him."* (1 Kings 3:26 NKJV) Because of the responses of these women, Solomon knew who was the mother of the living child. The real mother would rather give him away than see him die. The woman showed respect for the sanctity of life and Solomon agreed.

However, there are many statements made in the accounts of King Solomon that show us he was only half-hearted in his desire to follow his God. 1 Kings 3:3 says *"Solomon loved the Lord, walking in the statutes of his father David, EXCEPT that he sacrificed and burned incense at the high places."* And, further, in 1 Kings 11:2 it is said *"The Lord had said to the children of Israel, 'You shall not intermarry* (with the foreign women), *nor they with you. Surely they will turn away your hearts after their gods. SOLOMON CLUNG TO THESE IN LOVE."* As was stated earlier in this chapter, Solomon was involved in child sacrifice. After his heart was turned by foreign women—700 wives and 300 concubines—he built an altar to Molech. 1 Kings 11:6 NKJV states: *"Solomon did evil in the sight of the Lord, and did not fully follow the Lord, as did his father David."*

God Gives Life

There are many places in the Bible that tell us that God is all about life. The warning in Deuteronomy 30:19-20 appears in The Law through God's messenger, Moses. His message was that life is a choice and the secret is that the Lord is your life. In the prophets, the messenger, Ezekiel, talks to us of dry bones coming alive and the message is that God is capable of opening even our graves. (Ezekiel 37:1-14) The Psalms, too, are full of messages of life. Just a few of the specific scriptures are Psalm 16:11; 27:1; 36:9; 103:4; and 119:50. The messenger is David and his word to us is that the Lord gives life, redeems life and sustains life. In the Gospels, both Dr. Luke and the beloved John speak to us of life. In Luke 8:26-39 we hear of the demoniac and we are told that God can transform life. The choice is ours. Ask Jesus to leave or allow Him to touch. Again in Luke 15:11-32 we learn of the Prodigal. The message is that our God celebrates life. *"My son was dead and is now alive. Let's have a feast and celebrate."* (Luke 15:24 NIV) Abundant life happens when we are near Him, not in the far country. And, John tells us of Jesus' friend, Lazarus, in John 11:1-44. We learn that God wants us out of the grave and He does it with compassion, removing whatever stone is in the way, gratefulness, belief, a personal word and an unbinding. Oh yes. God gives life.

The following scriptures tell us it is so.

- **Job 33:4 NKJV** – *"The Spirit of God has made me, and the breath of the Almighty gives me life."*
- **Acts 17:25 NKJV** – *"He gives to all life, breath, and all things."*
- **John 1:3-4 NKJV** – *"All things were made through Him, and without Him nothing was made that was made. In Him was life, and the life was the light of men.'*
- **JOHN 20:31 NKJV** – *"These are written that you may believe that Jesus is the Christ, the Son of God, and that believing you may have life in His name."*
- **Ezekiel 16:6 NKJV** – *"I said to you in your blood, 'Live!'"*
- **Deuteronomy 32:39 NKJV** – *"Now see that I, even I, am He, and there is no God besides Me; I kill and I make alive; I wound and I heal."*
- **Psalm 36:9 NKJV** – *"For with You is the fountain of life; in Your light we see light."*

God Sustains Life

God not only gives life, He sustains life. The following scriptures testify to this truth.

- **Colossians 1:17 NIV** – *" He is before all things, and in him all things hold together."*

- **1 Corinthians 8:6 NKJV** – *"Yet for us there is one God, the Father of whom are all things, and we for Him; and one Lord Jesus Christ, through whom are all things, and through whom we live."*

- **Acts 17:28 NKJV** – *"For in Him we live and move and have our being."*

- **John 15:5 NKJV** – *"I am the vine, you are the branches; he who abides in Me, and I in him, bears much fruit, for without Me you can do nothing."*

- **Psalm 3:5 NKJV** – *" I lay down and slept; I awoke, for the Lord sustained me."*

- **Isaiah 41:10 NKJV** – *"Fear not, for I am with you; be not dismayed, for I am your God. I will strengthen you, yes, I will help you, I will uphold you with My righteous right hand."*

How We Can Live Intentionally Placing Value on Life

I offer a few reminders of what can be done in your life and mine that makes us people of life, always promoting life wherever we go.

1. **Each day we need to have the attitude of choosing life.** That means that we choose to live as sons and daughters of the King, not as orphans. We opt for the things that pull us toward our God, not away. We choose to be with the people who will motivate us in this quest. We do not give way to orphan emotions like anxiety, fear, unrighteous anger, bitterness, and envy. Our days are lived for the longings of God's heart, not our own. He longs for all of us to know freedom in our spirits, a strong connection with Him, that we are loved by Him, that we have a

purpose in being by building bridges between God and people and people and other people. And, that we would choose holiness as a lifestyle; living His way, set apart for His personal use.

2. **We need to vote pro-life.** It is our duty to understand our legislative system and the men and women who represent us in those forums. We need to know if they support Planned Parenthood and abortion or if they are for life.

3. **We need to fear God.** If we do that we will have the beginning of wisdom and we will understand that if God is for life, we need to be for life too.

4. **We must support Christian Pregnancy Centers and Adoption Agencies.** We can scour our communities for the existence of those agencies that will fight for life. Bethany Christian Services is one such agency and their work is stellar, caring for pregnant mothers and placing children into loving homes.

5. **We must understand how much of LIFE is in God's Word.** And, we must take it to heart. Read those portions over and over. (Deuteronomy 30:19-20; Luke 15:24, 32; Ezekiel 47:9 etc.) Savor the message. Become the message.

6. **Consider joining others in forming "Sanctuary Cities" for the Unborn.** In a short news clip in the AFA Journal Life Site News editors report the following. "Three communities in Texas recently joined five others from the state, declaring themselves 'sanctuary cities for the unborn.' Those eight cities in the Lone Star state have, by vote, voiced disapproval of abortion and their intention to outlaw it once allowed to do so. The measures would also empower families of post-abortive women to sue abortionists for emotional distress."[81]

7. **Teach the next generation the value of life**. Speak of it. Discuss it. Make your home open to those in need— young mothers ready to deliver and new babies waiting for placement. Your children will know that you are adamant about this very serious issue.

Conclusion

Mother Teresa has said the following. "The so-called right to abortion has pitted mothers against their children and women against men. It has sown violence and discord at the heart of the most intimate human relationships. It has aggravated the derogation of the father's role in an increasingly fatherless society. It has portrayed the greatest of gifts——a child——as a competitor, an intrusion and an inconvenience."[82]

We all know stories of children who have been spared abortion by wise, unselfish, brave mothers. Many of those children have grown to be productive members of society; giving much back. Just suppose. One mother chooses to give her baby life. When the child grows, the mother becomes ill and needs an organ transplant. The child is a perfect match. The mother chooses to give her child life and the child chooses to give her mother life. All God's plan. Life sanctified.

John Piper is credited with saying: "Christ died that we might live. This is the opposite of abortion. Abortion kills that someone might live differently."[83] The bloodshed in the land must stop!

Prayer Points To Consider

1. Ask God to make you a humble watchman, willing to speak out on this issue.

2. Ask God to protect the children in our land.

3. Ask God to reveal to you any area of your personal life devoted to death. Ask Him to touch it and show you your marching orders from this time forth.

4. As the Holy Spirit leads.

CHAPTER FIFTEEN – DISAGREEING AGREEABLY

God's Intentional Remnant Seeks Unity

> **"The church should be about multiplication; not division."**
> **—Anonymous—**

We have all heard of wars and rumors of wars, and some are in the church. Some of you readers may have even experienced them for yourselves. People fight over denominational interests; doctrine and the interpretation of it. Worship wars are commonplace. Shall we only sing hymns and limit it to three verses with a key change on the last verse? Or, should we give ourselves solely to contemporary worship? Some think that is a dumbed-down version of *real* worship with repetition of phrases ad nauseum. Some even call it "spiritual whining." Church people fight over the pastor's haircut, the paint selection for the fellowship hall, sprinkling or immersion in baptism, which picture of Jesus to put in the narthex, and even if gluten-free bread should be used for communion or not. Individualism is on the rise in our culture and as a result, many are demanding that it must be their way or the highway. Ravi Zacharias states: "Human beings will always find ways to divide and create hierarchies. Such is the plight of the human heart."[84]

If Jesus' high priestly prayer is to be given credence, then we must learn to maintain the unity which our God attained. Jesus' prayer references the oneness of "Us." Father, Son and Holy Spirit exhibit complete unity. Jesus prayed: *"I do not ask on behalf of these alone, but for those also who believe in Me through their word; that*

*they may all be one; even as You, Father, are in Me and I in You, that
they also may be in Us, so that the world may believe that You sent Me.
The glory which You have given Me I have given to them, that they
may be one, just as We are one; I in them and You in Me, that they may
be perfected in unity, so that the world may know that You sent Me,
and loved them, even as You have loved Me."* (John 17:20-23 NASB)
Jesus' motivation for His request of the Father for unity among all
of us should be ours as well——*"that the world may know"* Jesus
was sent for them and loves them. But, sometimes Christians don't
prepare the way for Jesus. They get in the way of Jesus. Gandhi
once said: "If it weren't for Christians, I'd be a Christian."[85]

Remember the heart cry earlier in this book? The culture will
not change until the church changes, and the church will not
change until individual hearts change. Our culture is full of disunity. You cannot escape deep divisions as you listen to the evening
news, to your neighbors' discussions or to workplace banter. But
we have opportunity to show a watching world that there is indeed
a better way.

The truth of the matter is that unity is not a matter of unifor-
mity. We do not all have to be the same. We can agree to disagree,
and when we disagree, we must do it agreeably. Richard Baxter has
said: "In necessary things, unity; in doubtful things, liberty; in all
things, charity."[86] Our job, then, is to discern the necessary from
the doubtful. That discernment is fostered by attention to God's
Dynamic Duo; the Word and the Holy Spirit. They will inform us
and they will never contradict each other.

Metaphors For the Church

This is not an exhaustive list, but, there are many pictures that the
Word of God draws of the church. They all imply a need for unity.
They are as follows.

1. **A Family.** – 2 Corinthians 6:18 NASB – *"And I will be a father to you, and you shall be sons and daughters to Me,' says the Lord Almighty."* I do not know many families that can escape dysfunctional relating when disunity is present. The church is made up of many unique sorts and it is our job to learn from each and love all.

2. **A Royal Priesthood** – 1 Peter 2:5 NIV – *"...you also, like living stones, are being built into a spiritual house to be a holy priesthood, offering spiritual sacrifices acceptable to God through Jesus Christ."* Not just one stone can build a house. It takes many and they will be of various sizes and shapes and colors. The root word for "priest" in the Latin is "pontus." That means "a bridge." A "pontage" is a toll for crossing a bridge. A pontoon boat is a vessel with two floating devices connected by a bridge. When we take our real place as the priesthood of all believers, we become a bridge between God and man and man and man. Disunity forces us to be people who burn bridges; not folks intent on building bridges.

3. **Sheep in a Flock.** – John 10:16 NIV – *"I have other sheep that are not of this sheep pen. I must bring them also. They too will listen to My voice, and there shall be one flock and one shepherd."* Peter refers to Jesus as the *"Chief Shepherd."* (See 1 Peter 5:4 NIV) John 10:16 is the main reason I say yes to teaching at many Jesus-centered churches. Namely, because my God is looking for One flock and One Shepherd. I can be the under-shepherd that connects all these people who will listen to His voice together. They are not all the same denomination. They do not all worship the same way. But, they all love and serve Jesus as the Center; the Good Shepherd.

4. **The Temple of the Holy Spirit.** – 1 Corinthians 3:16-

17 NIV – *"Don't you know that you yourselves are God's temple and that God's Spirit dwells in your midst? If anyone destroys God's temple, God will destroy that person; for God's temple is sacred, and you together are that temple."* Did you catch that? *"You TOGETHER."* The temple of God was the place where the presence of the living God resided. WE have opportunity to host the presence of God wherever we are. I have learned that the Holy Spirit flourishes where there is unity and fosters unity wherever He is. If you read the book of Acts carefully—the chronicle of the early church—there are thirteen times when the phrase *"of one accord"* or *"all"* is mentioned to signify unity of response. The results of that unity were seen in church growth, effective prayer, wonder and amazement at God's work among them, the sharing of resources, obedience, and the sending out of missionaries. We are all stones in that temple; each one as important as the one next to it. They are meant to be cemented together to build a habitation for God. And, it is supposed to be beautiful.

5. **The Bride of Christ.** – Revelation 21:9 NIV – *"Come, I will show you the bride, the wife of the Lamb."* (cf. Ephesians 5:22-32) The bride and groom are illustrations that we can all identify with. They symbolize love; a coming together. In Ephesians 5:32 Paul clarifies what he is talking about. *"This is a profound mystery—but I am talking about Christ and the church."* We need each other to understand what this love relationship is all about. Ephesians 3:17b-19 NIV states: *"And I pray that you, being rooted and established in love, may have power, together with all the Lord's holy people, to grasp how wide and long and high and deep is the love of Christ, and to know this love that surpasses knowledge—that you may be filled to the measure of all the fullness of God."*

6. **God's Field/God's Fellow-Workers.** – 1 Corinthians 3:6-9 NASB – *"I planted, Apollos watered, but God was causing the growth. So then neither the one who plants nor the one who waters is anything, but God who causes the growth. Now he who plants and he who waters is one; but each will receive his own reward according to his own labor. For we are God's fellow-workers; you are God's field, God's building."* Co-laborers with God. That's quite a label. And, a big responsibility. And, there is no room for one being greater than another. We're in this together.

7. **The Body of Christ.** – 1 Corinthians12:12-27 NKJV – *"For as the body is one and has many members, but all the members of that one body, being many are one body, so also is Christ. For by one Spirit we were all baptized into one body—whether Jews or Greeks, whether slaves or free—and have all been made to drink into one Spirit. For in fact the body is not one member but many. If the foot should say, 'Because I am not a hand, I am not of the body,' is it therefore not of the body? And if the ear should say, 'Because I am not an eye, I am not of the body,' is it therefore not of the body? If the whole body were an eye, where would be the hearing? If the whole were hearing, where would be the smelling? But now God has set the members, each one of them, in the body just as He pleased. And if they were all one member, where would the body be? But now indeed there are many members, yet one body. And the eye cannot say to the hand, 'I have no need of you'; nor again the head to the feet, 'I have no need of you.' No, much rather, those members of the body which seem to be weaker are necessary. And those members of the body which we think to be less honorable, on these we bestow greater honor; and our unpresentable parts have greater modesty, but our presentable parts have no need. But God composed the body, having given greater honor to*

that part which lacks it, that there should be no schism in the body, but that the members should have the same care for one another. And if one member suffers, all the members suffer with it; or if one member is honored, all the members rejoice with it. Now you are the body of Christ, and members individually." There is no need to say more.

A Declaration of Truth

In the Greek language a word is used to describe a stumbling block or an offense. It literally means "bait" for a snare. The word is "skandalon." Peter refers to it in his first letter to the scattered church and identifies the stumbling block as none other than Jesus. From an earlier reference in Isaiah 8:14 Peter references Jesus as *"A stone of stumbling and a rock of offense."* (1 Peter 2:8 NKJV) Sometimes the disunity in our midst arises because the "elephant in the room" is Jesus and a war of spirits ensues. Sometimes it's our own petty opinions and agendas. The following scripture verses highlight some of these divisions.

I Corinthians 11:18 NIV – *"In the first place, I hear that when you come together as a church, there are divisions among you, and to some extent I believe it."*

Jude 1:17-19 NKJV – *"But you, beloved, remember the words which were spoken before by the apostles of our Lord Jesus Christ: how they told you that there would be mockers in the last time who would walk according to their own ungodly lusts. These are sensual persons, who cause divisions, not having the Spirit."*

Luke 12:51-53 NKJV – *"Do you suppose that I came to give peace on earth? I tell you, not at all, but rather division. For from now on five in one house will be divided: three against two, and two against three. Father will be divided against son and son against father, mother*

against daughter and daughter against mother, mother-in-law against her daughter-in-law and daughter-in-law against her mother-in-law."
John 7:40-43 NKJV – *"Therefore many from the crowd, when they heard this saying, said, 'Truly this is the Prophet.' Others said, 'This is the Christ.' But some said, 'Will the Christ come out of Galilee? Has not the Scripture said that the Christ comes from the seed of David and from the town of Bethlehem, where David was?' So there was a division among the people because of Him."*
Luke 11:17 NKJV – *"But He, knowing their thoughts, said to them: 'Every kingdom divided against itself is brought to desolation, and a house divided against a house falls."*

Examples of Cultural and Church Abuse

The American political landscape is ripe with evidence of division. It has been said that "when there is no enemy within, the enemies outside cannot hurt you." The difficulty in the current political climate is that the enemy *is* within and the nation seems to be imploding. Democrats and Republicans cannot agree on anything that will move the country ahead for the good of the people. Instead of legislating, our current Congress is bent on investigating. It's difficult to watch the evening news because the rancor is so great and positions so unyielding. Churches are not much better.

The Baptists cannot abide the practices of the Methodists and evangelical non-denominational churches cannot abide Pentecostals. Presbyterians are of wide variety with main-streamers ordaining homosexuals and reformed thinkers espousing Calvinism unable or unwilling to embrace anything Arminian.

God's Reminders To Us

God's Word is full of admonitions motivating unity. Consider just a few.

Psalm 133:1 NKJV – *"Behold, how good and how pleasant it is for brethren to dwell together in unity!"*

Philippians 2:1-2 NKJV – *"Therefore if there is any consolation in Christ, if any comfort of love, if any fellowship of the Spirit, if any affection and mercy, fulfill my joy by being like-minded, having the same love, being of one accord, of one mind."*

Hebrews 10:24-25 NASB – *"…let us consider how to stimulate one another to love and good deeds, not forsaking our own assembling together, as is the habit of some, but encouraging one another; and all the more as you see the day drawing near."*

1 Corinthians 1:10 NIV – *"I appeal to you, brothers and sisters, in the name of our Lord Jesus Christ, that all of you agree with one another in what you say and that there be no divisions among you, but that you be perfectly united in mind and thought."*

1 Corinthians 12:25 NIV – *"…that there should be no division in the body, but that its parts should have equal concern for each other."*

Romans 12:16 NIV – *"Live in harmony with one another."*

Galatians 3:26-28 NIV – *"So in Christ Jesus you are all children of God through faith, for all of you who were baptized into Christ have clothed yourselves with Christ. There is neither Jew nor Gentile, neither slave nor free, nor is there male and female, for you are all one in Christ Jesus."*

Matthew 12:30 NASB – *"He who is not with Me is against Me; and he who does not gather with Me scatters."*

Acts 2:1 NKJV – *"When the Day of Pentecost had fully come, they were all with one accord in one place."*

What is most noticeable in this list is that the call for unity went out wherever the church was gathered: Rome, Galatia, Corinth and Philippi. It was a universal plea from the very heart of God through His apostles to His people. And, our God makes the same call today ...... wherever the true Church is gathered.

Biblical Examples

In the third and fourth chapters of Nehemiah we are witness to an extraordinary leader bent on unity. Today we call them building contractors. That was the role Nehemiah assumed for the people of Israel returning from exile in Babylon and commissioned to rebuild the wall in Jerusalem. Monumental tasks require colossal cooperation. The work load alone was daunting, but opposition arose from the Arabs, the Ammonites and the Ashdodites, all led by two men named Sanballat and Tobiah. The record says that the opposition was "furious", "indignant", and "very angry." Their ploys? They engaged in name-calling, the mocking of time needed to rebuild and the resources at hand, confusion and even plots to come against the workers in night-time, surprise attacks.

Nehemiah, chapter three, tells of how the work was divided by sections. Each family would work one parcel and another family would carry on the work in the adjoining section. Family by family, artisans and merchants, priests and Levites, fathers and sons joined together all working for a common goal: the rebuilding of the wall.

Nehemiah, chapter four, records the specifics of the plan of operation. There were prayers. In The Message Nehemiah's prayer rings with clarity. *"Oh listen to us, dear God. We're so despised: Boomerang their ridicule on their heads; have their enemies cart them off as war trophies to a land of no return; don't forgive their iniquity, don't wipe away their sin—they've insulted the builders!"* (Nehemiah 4:4) Watches were set up. Words of encouragement were offered. In Nehemiah 4:14 NKJV it was said: *"Remember the Lord, great and awesome, and fight for your brethren, your sons, your daughters, your wives, and your houses."* The men slept in their clothes as they worked around the clock to complete their mission. Nehemiah 4:17 records: *"Those who built on the wall, and those who carried burdens, loaded themselves so that with one hand they worked at construction, and with the other held a weapon."* (NKJV)

Being far apart from each other in the work at hand did not

pose a problem for this unified group. The solution? *"Wherever you hear the sound of the trumpet, rally to us there. Our God will fight for us."* (Nehemiah 4:20 NKJV) If there was a difficulty, a call for help went forth and the committed, unified force answered the call. God did indeed see to it that the wall was rebuilt. *"How good and pleasant it is for brethren to dwell together in unity!"*

Another biblical example should be considered because the picture it paints is not as pretty as what we see with Nehemiah, but its conclusion is noteworthy. This is an illustration of complete disunity among God's people. The account is mentioned in Acts 15:36-41 NKJV. *"Then after some days Paul said to Barnabas, 'Let us now go back and visit our brethren in every city where we have preached the word of the Lord, and see how they are doing.' Now Barnabas was determined to take with them John called Mark. But Paul insisted that they should not take with them the one who had departed from them in Pamphylia, and had not gone with them to the work. Then the contention became so sharp that they parted from one another. And so Barnabas took Mark and sailed to Cyprus, but Paul chose Silas and departed, being commended by the brethren to the grace of God. And he went through Syria and Cilicia, strengthening the churches."*

There you have it. Two men, both fully devoted to the gospel, at such odds over a personnel issue that they had to separate from one another. Apparently, Paul thought John Mark was a wimp; someone not faithful to the cause. But Barnabas, known as *"the Son of encouragement,"* (Acts 4:36 NKJV) had an expectation of hope for this young man. We cannot say who was right in the dispute, although it is interesting that the record notes it was Paul and Silas who were *"commended by the brethren."*

It is not until Paul writes to Timothy that we see any resolution to this disunity. In 2 Timothy 4:11 NKJV we are told of Paul's words. *"Get Mark and bring him with you, for he is useful to me for ministry."* What happened in the intervening time? My supposition is that Barnabas remained with this young one; nurtured him, discipled him and now John Mark was seen as worthy of being on Paul's team. What is interesting is that the gospel of Mark is reported to have been written by this man called John Mark. Two words are mentioned in the translations of his gospel that indicate that John Mark now understood the value of seeing the work as urgent and giving himself wholeheartedly to it. The two words are "Now" and "Immediately."

This biblical example shows us that sometimes disagreements are so deep that the only plausible course of action is separation. Times like that are rare and should only be entered into with reconciliation and restoration always on the horizon. Oh, that God would always call an encourager alongside to help make it happen.

Pictures of the Value of Unity

Aesop wrote a fable about a bundle of sticks. "A certain man had several sons who were always quarreling with one another, and, try as he might, he could not get them to live together in harmony. So he determined to convince them of their folly by the following means. Bidding them to fetch a bundle of sticks, he invited each in turn to break (the bundle) across his knee. All tried and all failed: and then he undid the bundle, and handed them the sticks one by one, when they had no difficulty at all in breaking them. 'There, my boys,' said he, 'united you will be more than a match for your enemies: but if you quarrel and separate, your weakness will put you at the mercy of those who attack you.'"[87]

I submit one more picture for you to consider. As in the drawing to follow, you can notice a triangle with GOD at the top. At the bottom right hand corner of the triad, place your name. At the bottom left, place the name of another person with whom you long for unity. Perhaps it will be a family member, a neighbor, a co-worker, or one you fellowship with at church. If both of you move toward GOD on this triangle, you will inevitably come closer to one another. Let's say *you* move closer to God, but the other person moves away on that dotted line parallel to yours but removed from God. You are now no further apart than you were when you started. The only way you will be miles apart in division is if both of you decide to go your own ways and leave God out of the equation. "W" is for "WRONG!" A perceptive reader may decide that GOD does not have to be at the pinnacle of the triangle. It could be some other unifying thing; like a common interest in sports or politics or work projects. However, after time elapses, most alternative goals fade and you cross over one another into infinity. A wise man by the name of Solomon once said: *"A cord of three strands is not quickly torn apart."* (Ecclesiastes 4:12 NASB)

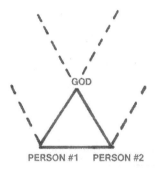

How We Can Intentionally Live in Unity

The following are several suggestions of how we, as God's intentional remnant, can live in unity.

1. **Rely on God.** 2 Chronicles 30:12 NIV – *"Also in Judah the hand of God was on the people to give them unity of mind to carry out what the king and his officials had ordered, following the word of the Lord."*

   Ephesians 2:14 NIV – *"For He Himself is our peace, who has made the two groups one and has destroyed the barrier, the dividing wall of hostility."*

2. **Bear With One Another.** Colossians 3:12-15 NIV – *"Therefore, as God's chosen people, holy and dearly loved, clothe yourselves with compassion, kindness, humility, gentleness and patience. Bear with each other and forgive one another if any of you has a grievance against someone. Forgive as the Lord forgave you. And over all these virtues put on love, which binds them all together in perfect unity. Let the peace of Christ rule in your hearts, since as members of one body you were called to peace. And be thankful."*

Philippians 4:2-3 NIV – *"I plead with Euodia and Syntyche to be of the same mind in the Lord. Yes, and I ask you, my true companion, help these women since they have contended at my side in the cause of the gospel, along with Clement and the rest of my co-workers, whose names are in the book of life."*

3. **Live under the truth that "two are better than one."** We already looked at the fact that with God in the mix, *"a cord of three strands is not quickly torn apart."* The message immediately preceding that truth has much to offer. Ecclesiastes 4:9-12 NASB states: *"Two are better than one because they have a good return for their labor. For if either of them falls, the one will lift up his companion. But woe to the one who falls when there is not another to lift him up. Furthermore, if two lie down together they keep warm, but how can one be warm alone? And if one can overpower him who is alone, two can resist him. A cord of three strands is not quickly torn apart."* Three directions are given to keep the unity. Lift each other up. Keep relationships warm. And, resist the enemy together rather than be easy prey alone. People are rarely the enemy; they are victims of The enemy.

4. **Maintain what God has attained.** Ephesians 4:1-6

NASB – *"Therefore I, the prisoner of the Lord, implore you to walk in a manner worthy of the calling with which you have been called, with all humility and gentleness, with patience, showing tolerance for one another in love, being diligent to preserve the unity of the Spirit in the bond of peace. There is one body and one Spirit, just as also you were called in one hope of your calling; one Lord, one faith, one baptism, one God and Father of all who is over all and through all and in all."*

5. **Grow up!** Ephesians 4:11-16 NASB – *"And He gave some as apostles, and some as prophets, and some as evangelists, and some as pastors and teachers, for the equipping of the saints for the work of service, to the building up of the body of Christ; until we all attain to the unity of the faith, and of the knowledge of the Son of God, to a mature man, to the measure of the stature which belongs to the fulness of Christ. As a result, we are no longer to be children, tossed here and there by waves and carried about by every wind of doctrine, by the trickery of men, by craftiness in deceitful scheming; but speaking the truth in love, we are to grow up in all aspects into Him who is the head, even Christ, from whom the whole body, being fitted and held together by what every joint supplies, according to the proper working of each individual part, causes the growth of the body for the building up of itself in love."*

6. **Warn, and if not heeded, then remove contentious people.** 2 Timothy 2:23-24 NIV *"Don't have anything to do with foolish and stupid arguments, because you know they produce quarrels. And the Lord's servant must not be quarrelsome but must be kind to everyone, able to teach, not resentful."*

Titus 3:10 NKJV – *"Reject a divisive man after the first and second admonition."*

7. **Share affliction with one another.** 2 Corinthians 1:3-7 NIV – *"Praise be to the God and Father of our Lord Jesus Christ, the Father of compassion and the God of all comfort, who comforts us in all our troubles, so that we can comfort those in any trouble with the comfort we ourselves receive from God. For just as we share abundantly in the sufferings of Christ, so also our comfort abounds through Christ. If we are distressed, it is for your comfort and salvation; if we are comforted, it is for your comfort, which produces in you patient endurance of the same sufferings we suffer. And our hope for you is firm, because we know that just as you share in our sufferings, so also you share in our comfort."* Those who go through trials together stick together in unity through the years in the good and bad of life.

8. **Extract the precious from the worthless.** Jeremiah 15:19 NASB – *"Therefore, thus says the Lord, 'If you return, then I will restore you—before Me you will stand; and if you extract the precious from the worthless, you will become My spokesman. They for their part may turn to you, but as for you, you must not turn to them."* So many times in this world unity is sacrificed because the "worthless" in any situation was extracted rather than the precious. God calls for the reverse to be true of us.

9. **Balance Truth and Grace.** John 1:14 NKJV – *"And the Word became flesh and dwelt among us, and we beheld His glory, the glory as of the only begotten of the Father; full of grace and truth."* In Jesus there is both grace and truth. A wise man once said that truth without grace kills, while grace without truth corrupts. We need both to maintain unity. Ravi Zacharias states the following: "It is theoreti-

cally and practically impossible to build any community apart from love and justice. If only one of these is focused upon, an inevitable extremism and perversion follow."[88]

Conclusion

Unity is not something that just happens. It must be painstakingly maintained. Christian folks are no different than others. Disagreements arise. Common ground is hard to find sometimes. What one of us has not been disappointed by a brother or sister who walks into church with us on a regular basis? I have experienced such disunity, but have learned that there are no "throw-away people." That means that you need to try to work things out. Perhaps separation is needed for a time, but our command is to love each other, so restoration must always be on our hearts and a plan for reconciliation must forever be in our minds.

Paul David Tripp asserts: "The only thing that divides human beings is what or whom they worship."[89] Even in the church not everyone worships the One True God. Sin makes all of us guilty of spiritual adultery. We become idolaters when we give our hearts to anything other than God——ourselves, other people or other things.

A.W. Tozer states: "One hundred pianos all tuned to the same fork are automatically tuned to each other. So, one hundred worshipers meeting together, each one looking away to Christ, are in heart nearer to each other than they could possibly be were they to become unity-conscious and turn their eyes away from God to strive for closer fellowship." "To be in harmony with other believers, we must be in tune with Christ."[90] When we are in tune with Christ we choose to live the "one anothers" of scripture rather than divisiveness. Over one-third of the "one another" directives are about the church getting along with each other.

"Have peace with one another." – Mark 9:50

"Do not speak evil of one another." – James 4:11

"Be like-minded toward one another." – Romans 15:5

"Bear with one another and forgive one another." – Colossians 3:13

"Receive one another." – Romans 15:7

"Do not provoke or envy one another." – Galatians 5:26

"Confess your trespasses to one another, and pray for one another." – James 5:16

"Bear with one another in love." – Ephesians 4:2

"Be kind to one another, tenderhearted, forgiving one another, even as God in Christ forgave you." – Ephesians 4:32

"These things I command you, that you love one another." – **John 15:17**

We must choose unity over division.

Prayer Points To Consider

1. Read Ecclesiastes 4:9-12. Ask God to help you live the truth of these verses. Ask Him to help you lift others up, keep situations warm and not cold, and to resist the enemy together; not try to isolate and be easy prey.

2. Ask God to maintain whatever unity exists in the circles in which you live and have influence.

3. Ask God to help you "bear with one another" and to show you what that means in specific circumstances.

4. As the Holy Spirit leads.

CHAPTER SIXTEEN – "HIMPOSSIBLE"

God's Intentional Remnant Lives Out of His Power

> **"Being religious without knowing the cross and the resurrection is like owning a Mercedes with no motor. Pretty package, but where's the power?"**[91]
> ——**Max Lucado**——

Adverse, so-called impossible circumstances and the feelings they provoke happen to all of us. The circumstances do not so much define our lives as our responses to them can carve a destiny. Our culture is dark and perverse. Dreams die. Our children and grandchildren disappoint us from time to time. Relationships lean toward brokenness. Bodies face challenges involving pain and discomfort. Opportunities pass us by. We sometimes feel hopeless. And, all the while our faith seems …. lacking. *"There must be more than this,"* we cry into the dead space around us.

Those circumstances sometimes serve to make us feel like rejected failures. We feel condemnation, even though the scriptures tell us there is *"no condemnation for us who are in Christ."* (See Romans 8:1) We feel worn out, trapped, unwanted, discontented, overwhelmed, forgotten, worthless, fearful and damaged. And, we think no one knows or cares.

So, how does the average person handle all of this? Usually we find what I call "hide-behinds" to cope with the reality swirling in our midst. We employ blaming others for our uncomfortable situations. We succumb to a spirit of infirmity; chasing one malady after another. We convince ourselves we are insufficient, or, at best, that no one else has it any better. We give in to the idols of comfort and convenience and we numb the pain with busyness or alcohol or drugs; even ministry. We doubt. We run to what is familiar and experience no adventure in life. In short, we are miserable.

But, that is not God's plan for us. He is a Promise-Keeper who assures us with His Word. We are told by Peter that *"His divine power has given us everything we need for a godly life through our knowledge of Him who called us by His own glory and goodness."* (2 Peter 1:3 NIV) EVERYTHING! That's astounding! That truth, coupled with the assurance that God gave Paul and the testimony that follows, leave us with a dilemma. Can we live this? Paul reports to the Corinthian church: *"And He said to me, 'My grace is sufficient for you, for My strength is made perfect in weakness.' Therefore most gladly I will rather boast in my infirmities, that the power of Christ may rest upon me. Therefore I take pleasure in infirmities, in reproaches, in needs, in persecutions, in distresses, for Christ's sake. For when I am weak, then I am strong."* (2 Corinthians 12:9-10 NKJV) Who in their right mind takes pleasure in the horrible things that come against them? Apparently, Paul does. Why? He does it *"for Christ's sake."* Without that phrase in the mix, it would be a silly declaration. But, what delight and comfort to know that our very weakness invites His strength.

Strength in weakness does not come because we are so wonderfully full of faith. An anonymous writer once said: *"Power does not come from having great faith in God. It comes from having faith in a Great God."* The dilemma arises in how we will choose to respond to the harsh reality in our lives. Will we ignore it? Will we doubt God in it? Will we despair in it? Or, will we see the hand of God and face it with Him alongside?

In the 1980's an off-Broadway play surfaced with one female actress playing many parts. It was called "The Search For Signs of Intelligent Life in the Universe." One part highlighted was Trudy, the bag lady. This is how she chose to handle difficult reality. "I made some studies, and reality is the leading cause of stress amongst those in touch with it. I can take it in small doses, but as a lifestyle I found it too confining. It was just too needful; it expected me to be there for it all the time, and with all I have to do——I had to let something go."[92]

Contrast that with the wisdom of Francis Schaeffer; pastor, evangelist and author of the 1970's. "We should want to face reality: the glory of the world God has created and the wonder of being human——yes, and even the awful reality of The Fall and the tragedy of marred men and women; even our own flawed character. We are not to be people of escape. The Christian is to be the realist. To face reality as born again and indwelt by the Holy Spirit is the Christian's calling."[93]

There you have it! Decades ago the truth was proclaimed. God's intentional remnant must live contrary to the whining wimps in the culture around us. How many times have we heard the cry: *"I feel unsafe!"*? As followers of Jesus we have the wonderful privilege—and responsibility—of showing the watching world a better way. There is One whose name is a Strong Tower. We can all run into it and be safe! Even if you feel weak. Maybe especially when you feel weak. (See Proverbs 18:10.)

What Jesus said to the Sadducees of His day could easily be declared today. These learned leaders of the culture were arguing about religious technicalities. The discussion included the lofty question of marriage in the resurrection. The custom dictated that a brother who died would leave his wife in the care of another brother. So their query was: *"Whose wife will she be in the resurrection?"* It was a moot point, because they did not even believe in the resurrection. In Matthew 22:29 NLT Jesus answers them. *"Your mistake is that you don't know the scriptures, and you don't know the power of God."*

Not much has changed in the church today. And, it is an abomination to the heart of God that His own people do not live in the power He makes available to all. Paul warned Timothy of the perilous things that will be true *"in the last days."* One of those things amidst a long list of woes is the fact that there will be those who have *"a form of godliness but deny its power."* (2 Timothy 3:5) Paul's advice? *"From such people turn away!"* (2 Timothy 3:5)

Descriptions of God's Power

Adjectives are wonderful tools to help us understand something. The Bible is full of words that describe what God's power looks like. This is not an exhaustive list, but you will get the flavor of it with the following. I will mention the Bible references that contain these descriptors so you may check them out at your leisure. God's Power is:

Sufficient – 2 Corinthians 12:9-10 – That means it's "enough."
Great – Ephesians 1:19; Exodus 32:11 – Not mediocre; but great.
Majestic – Exodus 15:6 – Not commonplace.
Mighty – Deuteronomy 34:12; Psalm 106:8 – Not puny and impotent.
Awesome – Job 10:16 – Not mundane; although it touches the mundane.
Victorious – Psalm 20:6 – Not benign and ineffective.
Sovereign – Daniel 7:14 – Not lacking control or dominion.
Eternal – Romans 1:20 – Not temporary and fickle.

What God's Power Can Accomplish

The accounts recorded in the Bible are full of God's powerful works among the sons of men. This is a short list but impressive by any measure. Again, the scripture references are included so you can check it out for yourself.

God's power answers prayer. – Psalm 102:12-17
It heals. – 2 Kings 5:1-15
It raises the dead; bringing people out of the grave. – John 11;
   1 Corinthians 15:35-49; Ezekiel 37:1-14
It fights our battles. – 2 Chronicles 18:28-21:3
It transforms lives. – Luke 8:26-39; Acts 9:1-22
It brings salvation. – John 3
It offers deliverance. – Luke 8:26-39
It shields us. – 1 Peter 1:5
It breaks chains and strongholds. – 2 Corinthians 10:4

How can we know that God's power is for real? Phillip Yancey is credited with writing the following. "The resurrection is the epicenter of belief."[94] The resurrection——Jesus coming back to life after the crucifixion——is proof in the pudding. No greater power is known to man. No dynamite, no nuclear weapon can match its effectiveness. Earthquakes occur as tectonic plates far below the earth's crust move. The epicenter of such seismic activity reaches the surface at one focal site and the most amazingly powerful results are visible at that precise point. When an earthquake of any significant measure happens, nothing is ever the same again.

The crucifixion and resurrection of our Lord and Savior, Jesus Christ, occurred in history. It had begun far below the surface as God's magnificent love commenced to manifest itself. The cross and the resurrection are the epicenter; the point where this Love surfaced. And, nothing has ever been the same.

Paul pointed to these monumental events when in 2 Corinthians 1:8-9 NIV he shared with others about the hardships they had suffered. He said: *"We were under great pressure, far beyond our ability to endure, so that we despaired even of life. Indeed, in our hearts we felt the sentence of death. But this happened that we might not rely on ourselves but on God who raises the dead."* This power above all powers is able to bring life out of death. This is the One who offers His power to us; for the living of everyday life, and for the stepping up to the plate and willingly signing on to be part of God's Intentional Remnant. We cannot, we must not, rely on ourselves. He is the only One who is *"able to do immeasurably more than all we ask or imagine, according to his power that is at work within us."* (Ephesians 3:20 NIV)

How God's Resurrection Power Is Seen

God's power seems to be concentrated in five things that we can easily observe and employ in our own weaknesses.

1. **HIS LOVE.** – God's power is not on display by forceful measures, but in Love. The sacrificial love of our Savior was written of in a hymn by Samuel Trevor Francis, titled "O the Deep, Deep Love of Jesus." In it the hymn-writer describes this Love as "vast, unmeasured, boundless, free, rolling as a mighty ocean over me." "Underneath me, all around me, is the current of Thy love, leading onward, leading homeward."[95]

2. **HIS BLOOD.** – God's power is not seen in the shedding of other peoples' blood, as is true of some other religions. It is His own blood that flows. We are justified by His blood. (Romans 5:9) We find forgiveness in His blood. (Ephesians 1:7) We are healed by His blood. (1 Peter 2:24) We are given life through His blood. (John 6:53) His blood cleanses us. (1 John 1:7) We are redeemed through His blood. (Ephesians 1:7) We have been brought near by the blood of Christ. (Ephesians 2:13) We can draw near to God because of His blood. (Hebrews 10:22) Victory is ours in the blood of Jesus. (Revelation 12:11)

   The old hymn by Lewis E. Jones, "There's Power in the Blood" is a true description of His amazing work on our behalf. Jones declares Jesus' blood as "wonder-working power" and labels it "precious." Why? Jones' declares the following: The blood "frees you from the burden of sin", assures "o'er evil a victory is won", it frees you from "your passion and pride", "Calvary's tide cleanses", "it makes you whiter than snow, and sin-stains are lost in its life-giving flow."[96] Jones even declares that it is Jesus' blood that gives us power for service and praise to Him. Power indeed!

3. **HIS NAME.** – God's power is not manifested in the denigrating of other names but in the truth that His name is the name that is above all names. There is no other name that brings salvation and healing. Paul declared it to those who had watched the healing of the lame man at the Temple. In his defense before the Sanhedrin, he uttered these words. *"If we this day are judged for a good deed done to a helpless man, by what means he has been made well, let it be known to you all, and to all the people of Israel, that by the name of Jesus Christ of Nazareth, whom you crucified, whom God raised from the dead, by Him this man stands here before you whole. This is the stone which was rejected by you builders, which has become the chief cornerstone. Nor is there salvation in any other, for there is no other name under heaven given among men by which we must be saved."* (Acts 4:9-12 NKJV) Phillips, Craig and Dean proclaimed truth in their song "Great I Am." The worthy, almighty One is the great I Am who makes "the mountains shake and the demons run in fear. No power can stand against this name."[97]

4. **HIS SERVANT'S HEART.** – God's power is not observed in His "lording it over" others, but in stooping and serving. A woman caught in adultery and paraded before religious leaders in the Temple witnessed this first-hand.

Instead of towering over her with a shame-filled pointing finger, Jesus stooped. The God of the Universe stooped! His eyes met hers. He challenged her accusers to throw the first stone, if indeed they had no sin. When people left, fearful of casting the fateful stone, He said: *"Neither do I condemn you; go and sin no more."* (John 8:11 NKJV) "More Like Jesus" is a song written by Passion. In it, the marvels of Jesus' servant-heart are shown with motivation for a like response from us. "You came to the world You created trading your crown for a cross. You willingly died, Your innocent life paid the cost. Counting Your status as nothing, the King of all kings came to serve; washing my feet, covering me with Your love. If more of You means less of me, take everything. Yes, all of You is all I need. Take everything."[98]

5. **HIS PROMISES.** – 2 Corinthians 1:20 tells us an astounding truth. " *For no matter how many promises God has made, they are "Yes" in Christ. And so through him the "Amen" is spoken by us to the glory of God."* The popular contemporary Christian worship song by Chris Tomlin declares "All Your promises are yes and amen." Peter proclaims God's promises as *"very great"* and *"precious."* (See 2 Peter 1:4 NIV) Of course these promises would not be anything special if the author of them was not faithful. But, our God is a promise-keeper. Therefore, we can be assured and stand on the stability of His word to us. Deuteronomy 7:9 NKJV declares*: "Therefore know that the Lord your God, He is God, the faithful God who keeps covenant and mercy for a thousand generations with those who love Him and keep His commandments."* Numbers 23:19 NIV confirms this truth. *"God is not human, that he should lie, not a human being, that he should change his mind. Does he speak and then not act? Does he promise and*

not fulfill?" It is as the second stanza of a hymn written in 1886 by Russell Kelso Carter affirms. "Standing on the promises, I cannot fail. Listening every moment to the Spirit's call. Resting in my Savior as my all in all. Standing on the promises of God."[99]

Reminders in God's Word

Several passages of scripture help us understand that God's power is for real and that it accomplishes much.

<u>Isaiah 40:31 NKJV</u> – *"But those who wait on the Lord shall renew their strength; they mount up with wings like eagles, they shall run and not be weary, they shall walk and not faint."*

I am told that there are four kinds of birds. There are those that soar, those that flit and flap furiously, those that fly awkwardly and those that do not get air-born at all. Eagles soar. Little birds flit and flap. Chickens fly awkwardly; hopping into the air just a few feet only to fall to the earth before blundering again. Steamboat ducks, penguins and ostriches do not fly at all. All of them were created with wings. All of them are gifted in different ways. For instance, the steamboat duck has the ability to make his webbed feet whirl like a paddle-boat so swiftly that this critter can move astoundingly fast in the water. But, though a bird, though equipped with wings; he cannot fly. Eagles soar because they catch the current and go with it. The greatest of the currents come with adverse conditions. Dangerous updrafts. Contrary winds. But the eagles wait. They catch the current, and upward they soar.

Most of us fuss with adverse winds, but if we would wait on our God and catch the current of the Holy Spirit in their midst, we, too, could soar. Unfortunately, the vast majority of Christians I come in contact with flit and flap. They strive. They try to fix things themselves. They do not wait. So, either they continue to work hard or they try to fly with awkward results or they do not try at all.

The psalmist gave great direction in Psalm 27:14 NKJV when he said: *"Wait on the Lord; be of good courage, and He will strengthen your heart. Wait, I say, on the Lord."*

2 Corinthians 9:8 NIV – *"And God is able to bless you abundantly, so that in all things at all times, having all that you need, you will abound in every good work."*

All, All, ALL, EVERY!!! Not just a little bit. Not even merely some. But, ALL!

2 Timothy 1:7 NKJV – *"For God has not given us a spirit of fear, but of power and of love and of a sound mind."*

If God has NOT given a spirit of fear, we can be sure of its source. The powers of darkness hold this destructive emotion over our heads. The enemy seeks to destroy and devour, but our God gives us three things to counteract this spirit of fear. 1. Power 2. Love And, 3. A Sound Mind.

C.S. Lewis is credited with saying "There is no neutral ground in the universe. Every square inch, every split second is claimed by God, and counterclaimed by Satan."[100] But, you can be sure of this. God will have the victory.

Romans 8:28-29 NIV – *"And we know that in all things God works for the good of those who love him, who have been called according to his purpose. For those God foreknew he also predestined to be conformed to the image of his Son, that he might be the firstborn among many brothers and sisters."*

As a young married couple with two small children at the time, my husband and I set out for a state distant from family and friends in search of the perfect job following my husband's completion of his graduate program in Space Science and Engineering. He landed a perfect job in Maryland, far from our roots in Wisconsin. The employment lasted exactly one year when the entire department he worked in was placed on furlough. Because a company further from home had enjoyed his consulting/contract work while he was employed at the mother company, they invited him to come there for the interim of finding a new job. It wasn't long before he got new employment in another high-tech firm, but it was not in his love of aerospace. While at the interim company he met three gentlemen who later invited him to join them in starting their own aerospace engineering company. The lay-off from the original company——an adverse, painful, uncertain time——turned into good in many ways. First of all, the aerospace company created out of that time thrived for thirty years creating many good additions to the US space program. And, best of all, the time created a growing-up opportunity for us both and we were indeed more closely *"conformed to the image of his Son."*

So, What's the Problem?

I believe we do not live in the power of the Spirit because we continue to believe the enemy's lies and live out what we *"once were"* instead of what we *"now are"* in Christ. The scriptures report plainly that we once were *"dead,"* but now we are *"alive."* Why is it we still live as if we are in the grave? Jesus came to give us life, and that to the full. (See John 10:10.) We once were *"children of wrath,"* but now we are *"rich in mercy."* And, His mercy is new EVERY day! (See Lamentations 3:22-23.) We once were *"far off"*, but now we have been *"brought near"* through the blood of Jesus. We once were *"in darkness,"* but now we are *"in the light in the Lord."* We once were *"alienated,"* but now we are *"reconciled."* We stand before God's smile and welcoming arms and can be comfortable there. We once were *"foolish, disobedient, deceived, serving lusts and pleasures, living with malice and envy, hateful and hating,"* but now we are *"justified and heirs."* Our inheritance comes from the Father of All. This incorruptible, undefiled inheritance has been kept in heaven for us by God—the Living Hope—and we are kept for it by His power. (See 1 Peter 1:3-5.) Once we were *"not a people"*, **BUT NOW** we are *"the people of God."* We are part of a vast, loving family! Why, why, why would we want to go back to what we were without Him? It looks like the following in chart form.

Once Were	Scripture	Now Are
"Dead"	Ephesians 2:1	"Alive"
"Children of Wrath"	Ephesians 2:3-4	"Rich in Mercy"
"Far Off"	Ephesians 2:13	"Brought Near"
"In Darkness"	Ephesians 5:8	In the "Light in the Lord"
"Alienated"	Colossians 1:21	"Reconciled"
"Foolish Disobedient Deceived Serving Lusts and Pleasures Living with Malice and Envy Hateful and Hating"	Titus 3:3-8	"Justified" And "Heirs"
"Not a People"	1 Peter 2:10	"The People of God'

How We Can Live Intentionally in God's Power

While the culture around us continues to play the victim, while there are those who cry foul when anyone disagrees with them or they shout "UNSAFE!", we, as God's Intentional Remnant can display a better way to the watching world. I offer four practical suggestions for living as Ephesians 6:10 directs. *"Be strong in the Lord and in the power of HIS might."*

1. Live Out Ephesians 3:20-21 NIV. *"Now to Him who is able to do immeasurably more than all we ask or imagine, according to His power that works within us, to Him be glory in the church and in Christ Jesus through all generations forever and ever. Amen!"* The "Amen" means "SO BE IT!"

I will illustrate what I mean with a true story. A few years back I led a retreat where I met a woman I had never seen before. She came to pray with me before the sessions began; a most welcome gesture. I did not notice something significant about her in that initial meeting. Before the Saturday evening session there was a time of worship. It turned out to be a magnificent event with the presence of the Lord manifested. The young woman who had prayed with me seemed in the center of the group, framed by all the other women. She was exhibiting uninhibited worship; hands raised, eyes closed, tears falling. It was then that I noticed something significant about her. Her hands were grotesquely deformed. Some fingers were missing. There were many scars, indicating previous surgeries. The fingers that remained were gnarled and twisted. But, there she was. Worshiping our worthy God with abandon. When the worship time ended, before the speaking session was to begin, I went to her to tell her how her sincere exaltation of our Lord encouraged my heart. The young woman began to weep, getting red from her toes up. I thought, "Oh my. I have crossed a line I have no business intruding upon." But the woman held my arms and looked intensely into my eyes, saying: "Thank you. This is new for me. For many years I have been hiding my hands under anything available; books, sweaters, notebooks. But, you have been telling us all weekend about the many ways that our Savior gave His ALL. So, I decided it was time to give Him my all, in worship. Many times I have asked Him: 'How could you love me with these deformed hands?' I even imagined that perhaps one morning I would wake up and fingers would just pop out. He can heal me. I know He can! But, this weekend, He did not heal my hands. He healed my heart.'"

As the weekend went on, there were many door prizes for the event. This young woman received one of the envelopes. It was a gift certificate for a ...... manicure. My face fell as she opened it. Once again, she put her hands on my arms and looked at me with intensity. "You really don't get this, do you? God took my shame this weekend. I cannot use the gift card, but I can give it away to someone who can use it."

The story doesn't end there. The woman moved to a different state where, after just a few weeks in her new church, she saw a request in the bulletin for jobs that needed leadership. One of them was a position she had training for, but she wanted to pray over it before signing on. At present she is signing for the hearing challenged, and they understand what she is saying, even with fewer fingers than most.

Ephesians 3:20 carries five parts to it. 1. What we ask of God. 2. What we imagine He could do with our personal situations. 3. The "more" He does. 4. The "immeasurably more" He does. And, 5. The "immeasurably more than all" He accomplishes. In the woman's case, she had asked: "How can you love deformed me?" She imagined fingers would pop out. But, God did more. He healed her heart. Then, He did immeasurably more. He took her shame. Finally, He did immeasurably more than all. She is now serving Him with the very thing she was hiding from Him and others. That's living in God's power. And, that's not just for her. It's for you and me too. It is HIMPOSSIBLE!

2. Live In God's "Dynamic Duo".

God's Dynamic Duo is none other than His Word and His Holy Spirit. That combination is dynamite. Hebrews 4:12 NIV tells us God's view of His own Word. *"For the word of God is alive and active. Sharper than any double-edged sword, it penetrates even to dividing soul and spirit, joints and marrow; it judges the thoughts and attitudes of the heart."* Now that's some power. This word is alive, not dead. It is active, not passive. It is sharp, not dull. It penetrates. It does not bulldoze. It judges things we can easily hide from others, like thoughts and attitudes. It is not benign. The Word of God is life, it gives life, it sustains life and it transforms life. This Word is active. The Word is sharp and it penetrates. It goes right to the needed place, points to the trouble and offers God's solution. The

Word of God also judges. It can split hairs. Joints and marrow require thin slices. Thoughts and heart attitudes are tricky. But, God's Word discerns all. It's light exposes what needs to change in us. 2 Timothy 3:16-17 NIV says: *"All Scripture is God-breathed and is useful for teaching, rebuking, correcting and training in righteousness, so that the servant of God may be thoroughly equipped for every good work."* It teaches. That means God gives instruction on how to live. It rebukes. That means God shows us when and how we are walking on a dangerous path. It corrects. That means the Lord shows a better way. And, it trains. That means that over and over, with persevering patience, our God and Savior helps us to understand His way.

I learned this in an interesting way. Our family owns a lake home in western Maryland. There are many black bears in the county in which we reside. I walk the roads there with regularity, praying each time that God would protect me from people, cars or critters that might intend harm. One morning I set out praying a prayer I had never prayed before, nor have prayed since. I asked the Lord: *"Help me NOT to even see a bear today."* It was the only time I met a bear on the road. Gulp! Now what should I do. I had been told by the experts not to lock eyes with this animal. The considered advice upon such a meeting was that you dump any food in your pockets, and that you turn slowly and walk at the same pace you were going before the encounter in the opposite direction. Do you know how difficult it is not to run? Or to turn around and check on where that long-toothed, sharp-clawed animal was in proximity to you? As I remembered and followed the expert advice, I heard the voice of God speaking sense to me. It was not an audible voice but clear nonetheless. *"Don't ever ask Me not to show you where danger lies. I will TEACH you where to look for it. I will REBUKE your wrong direction. I will CORRECT you to go a better way. And, I will TRAIN you to know better in the future."* It is HIMPOSSIBLE!

The other part of God's Dynamic Duo is His Holy Spirit.

Ephesians 3:16 NIV states: *"I pray that out of His glorious riches He may strengthen you with power through His Spirit in your inner being, so that Christ may dwell in your hearts through faith."* God's riches are vast and immeasurable. That means you and I cannot count them or stack them if we tried. His desire is to make you and me strong. He does it from the inside out by His Holy Spirit. And His goal is that Christ would dwell in us so that when people see us, they see Him.

The Holy Spirit works powerfully within us all that the scriptures say He is capable of accomplishing. The list is amazing. He gives us freedom. (2 Corinthians 3:17-18) He sanctifies us. (1 Peter 1:2) He convicts us, guides us into truth, and He glorifies Jesus in and through us. (John 16:5-15) He helps us remember what we should recall and not what we should not. He counsels us. He teaches us. He comforts us. And, He comes alongside us. (John 14:1, 18, 26-27) He seals us. (2 Corinthians 1:21-22) He reveals things to us. (Ephesians 1:17) He prays for us. (Romans 8:26; Ephesians 6:18) He regenerates us. (Titus 3:5) He gifts us. (1 Corinthians 12:1-11; Romans 12:6-8) He equips us. (Hebrews 2:4; Ephesians 4:11-13) And, as if that were not enough, He assures us and guides us. (Romans 8:14-16)

In Him it is HIMPOSSIBLE!

3. Make Use of Spiritual Weapons, Not the Weapons of the World. 2 Corinthians 10:3-5 NIV – *"For though we live in the world, we do not wage war as the world does. The weapons we fight with are not the weapons of the world. On the contrary, they have divine power to demolish strongholds. We demolish arguments and every pretension that sets itself up against the knowledge of God, and we take captive every thought to make it obedient to Christ."*

The world employs such weapons as name-calling, anger, a demanding spirit, legalism, the strength of numbers, superior intellect, wealth, threats, deception, distortion, resistance, and slander.

God's arsenal is not as noisy or flashy, but is highly effective none-theless. Spiritual weapons include things like transformed lives, surrender, waiting on God, a servant's heart, humility, forgiveness, love, the Word of God, prayer, praise, a soft answer, a single focus on Jesus, blessing for cursing, sacrifice, truth, freedom, confession, the name of Jesus and the blood of Jesus. With the use of these God-ordained weapons, it is HIMPOSSIBLE!

4. Be Surrendered "Yes, Lord" People. Isaiah 26:8-9a NIV – *"Yes, Lord! Walking in the way of your laws, we wait for you. Your name and renown are the desire of our hearts. My soul yearns for you in the night; in the morning, my spirit longs for you."*

Four pieces of evidence show us to be "Yes, Lord" people. 1. We choose to be obedient. We don't just talk about God's law, we walk God's law. 2. We wait for Him. "We wait; we don't take the bait."[101] 3. We choose humility over pride. Our desire is for HIS name and renown; not our own. And, 4. We are people who are passionate for Him 24/7. In the night and in the morning, and in all the hours in between.

Being surrendered to Him makes all things HIMPOSSIBLE!

Conclusion

Perhaps your life is weighing you down at present. Maybe as you have read these pages you have decided that there is no way you have what it takes to be part of God's Intentional Remnant.

The truth is … … you <u>don't</u> have what it takes! But HE does! By your God you can declare as David did that you *"can leap over a wall."* (Psalm 18:29) In Him you are *"more than a conqueror."* (Romans 8:37) You are *"strong in the power of HIS might."* (Ephesians 6:10) You can soar! (Isaiah 40:31)

I would bet that Joshua thought Jericho was impossible. David was surely concerned about Goliath. Daniel undoubtedly squirmed over the thought of the lion's den. Shadrach, Meshach and Abednego were not relishing the thought of the fiery furnace. Moses wondered about the path blocked by the Red Sea. Gideon gulped when his 300 troops faced the Midianites without number. Elijah probably shook inside about his water-soaked altar in front of the priests of Baal. Joseph undoubtedly thought his pit and prison were impossibilities. And, the impossibilities of the Cross of our Savior, Jesus Christ, looked like certain defeat. Defeat … … until Resurrection Morning. Nothing will ever be the same because of that. It IS the epicenter of God's Power. And, it makes all things HIMPOSSIBLE!

It's time to stand ready. *"Be dressed ready for service and keep your lamps burning, like servants waiting for their master to return from a wedding banquet, so that when he comes and knocks they can immediately open the door for him."* (Luke 12:35-36 NIV) *"Therefore put on the full armor of God, so that when the day of evil comes, you may be able to stand your ground, and after you have done everything, to stand."* (Ephesians 6:13)

In Jeremiah 12:5 NIV we witness a shot in the arm for the young prophet. God spoke a hard, but true word for his ears. *"If you have raced with men on foot and they have worn you out, how can you compete with horses? If you stumble in safe country, how will you manage in the thickets by the Jordan?"* Jeremiah had had it and God knew it. He faced a culture similar to ours and he knew the apathy of those who had traditions of being God followers but not much action to make it credible. It raised questions in his mind. *"Why does the way of the wicked prosper? Why do all the faithless live at ease?" "How long will the land lie parched and the grass in every field be withered?"* (Jeremiah 12:1, 4 NIV) And he made a known assertion. *"You are always on their lips but far from their hearts."* Jeremiah was tired. He did not know if he could go on, and he was a young man. But, the things impossible with men are possible with God. Himpossible!

What is astounding to me is that God tells us plainly what the horse can do. When God makes His case with the impertinence of Job and his questions, He makes these statements. *"Have you given the horse strength? Have you clothed his neck with thunder?* ²⁰ *Can you frighten him like a locust? His majestic snorting strikes terror.* ²¹ *He paws in the valley, and rejoices in his strength; He gallops into the clash of arms.* ²² *He mocks at fear, and is not frightened; nor does he turn back from the sword.* ²³ *The quiver rattles against him, the glittering spear and javelin.* ²⁴ *He devours the distance with fierceness and rage; nor does he come to a halt because the trumpet has sounded.* ²⁵ *At the blast of the trumpet he says, 'Aha!'" He smells the battle from afar, The thunder of captains and shouting.* (Job 39:19-25 NKJV) With those truths before us, what I see is that the horse is a symbol of strength. He confronts challenges head on. He is not frightened. And he perseveres. *"He does not come to a halt."* That's the picture God gives us. We can do this. We CAN be His Intentional Remnant in this culture with His power.

Eugene Peterson writes the following. He is writing as if God were speaking directly to Jeremiah. And, of course, that means ...... directly to us too. "Are you going to live cautiously or courageously? I called you to live at your best, to pursue righteousness, to sustain a drive toward excellence. It is easier, I know, to be neurotic. It is easier to be parasitic. It is easier to relax in the embracing arms of The Average. Easier, but not better. Easier, but not more significant. Easier, but not more fulfilling. I called you to a life of purpose far beyond what you think yourself capable of living and promised you adequate strength to fulfill your destiny. What is it your really want, Jeremiah——and YOU——do you want to shuffle along with this crowd, or run with the horses?"[102]

In God's power the holy seed——God's Intentional Remnant——will rise and grow with life for all those who have eyes to see and ears to hear. God promised. If we will humble ourselves, pray, seek Him, and repent, He WILL hear, forgive and heal. So, we—God's own, who are called by His Name—have a choice. We can either be silent, wimpy, armchair Christians or part of God's vast, alive army. We can either be cautious or courageous. It's time for the Bride of Christ to lace up her combat boots. It's time to run with the horses. It is HIMpossible!

Will you join me?

Prayer Points To Consider

1. Ask God to show you how to live in His Power.

2. Ask God to identify the things you are asking and imagining and to be aware of His more, immeasurably more and immeasurably more than all.

3. Ask God to help you employ His Dynamic Duo—His Word and His Spirit——to help you live in His power.

4. Ask God to help you stay clear of worldly weapons and choose spiritual weapons to help you.

5. Ask God to help you be surrendered as a "Yes, Lord" person.

6. Declare "HIMpossible" over your life and your sphere of influence.

7. As the Holy Spirit leads.

EPILOGUE

"Then they shall know that I am the Lord." Ezekiel 36:38 NKJV

You and I began this book with a vision that the Lord showed the prophet Ezekiel of the man clothed with linen putting a mark on the foreheads of those who sigh and cry over the abominations in the land. Today we will end this book back in the words of Ezekiel. Numerous times in Ezekiel's message he proclaims God's truth: *"Then you shall know that I am the Lord!"* He makes that statement so many times that it prompted this close-to-OCD grandmother the need to count them. At first tally, I came up with sixty-nine. I thought: *"Wouldn't it have been astounding if God had made that statement seventy times?"* Seventy is significant because for this prophet of the exile, it was seventy years that Israel was in captivity; one *"You shall know that I am the Lord"* for every year of bondage. So, I recounted. There were indeed … seventy!

In Ezekiel 36:21 NKJV God reports that He *"had concern for His holy name."* His name had been profaned by Israel, much like it has by His apathetic, rebellious people today. He promised He would act not for our sake, but for the sake of His holy name.

Ezekiel 36:23b NKJV confirms the message that this book carries of the need for God's Intentional Remnant to live His way before the watching world. God says: *"'The nations shall know that I am the Lord,' says the Lord God, 'when I am hallowed in you before their eyes.'"* Did you get that? All nations will know what He proclaims seventy times in Ezekiel's book of prophecy when He is made holy in us before their eyes. The world——all nations—— needs to see Jesus in us BEFORE they will know that He is Lord.

The New Living Translation says it this way. *"And when I reveal my holiness through you before their very eyes, says the Sovereign Lord, then the nations will know that I am the Lord."*

The New International Version states: *"Then the nations will know that I am the Lord, declares the Sovereign Lord, when I am proved holy through you before their eyes."*

The Message echoes: *"The nations will realize who I really am, that I am God, when I show my holiness through you so that they can see it with their own eyes."*

A startling clear message!

To cement this true truth into the hearts of those who would hear Ezekiel's prophecy, God affirms seven "I will" messages in the same chapter for those who have ears to hear. If you have persevered to this point in this book, I believe you have ears to hear. These seven "I will's" are promises to you——the Intentional Remnant——from our holy God. So, though being a Christian today is not popular, though in this world you will have trouble, TAKE HEART. God is at work overcoming the world. (See John 16:33.)

The seven "I Will's" are:

1. ***"I will sanctify My great name which has been profaned among the nations."*** – Ezekiel 36:23a NKJV. To "sanctify" means to "set apart." Paul told the Philippian church——and us——that the name of Jesus is above every name; set apart from the rest. At this name every knee will bow and every tongue will confess that Jesus is Lord to the glory of God the Father. (See Philippians 2:10-11.) No surprise when Ezekiel's prophecy agrees with the apostle's words.

2. ***"I will take you from among the nations … and gather you."*** – Ezekiel 36:24 NKJV Israel was to be gathered; to have their own land. We, too, will be gathered. Isaiah, another exile prophet, proclaimed in Isaiah 40:11 NKJV *"He will feed His flock like a shepherd; He will gather the lambs with His arm, and carry them in His bosom...."* I am comforted by the fact that we are being carried by our great God.

3. *"I will sprinkle clean water on you."* – Ezekiel 36:25 NKJV. No more filth. No more idols; not even comfort and convenience. The cleansing process is His work for His intentional remnant. All He asks for is cooperation.

4. *"I will give you a new heart and put a new spirit within you."* – Ezekiel 36:26 NKJV. No more stone-cold responses. He is giving us pliable hearts that will beat like His.

5. *"I will put My Spirit within you and cause you to walk in My statutes."* – Ezekiel 36:27 NKJV. Paul's letter to the Galatian church contains a great biblical definition of surrender. In Galatians 5:25 NKJV he states: *"If we live in the Spirit, let us also walk in the Spirit."* He even gives us a list of nine character qualities that will overflow into our lives if we keep step with the Spirit and abide in Jesus. Galatians 5:22-23 lists them as love, joy, peace, patience, kindness, goodness, faithfulness, gentleness and self-control.

6. *"I will deliver you from all your uncleanness."* - Ezekiel 36:29 NKJV. Perhaps as you have read these pages God has convicted you of needed confession and repentance. Like Paul in Philippians 1:6 *"I am confident...that He who has begun a good work in you* (and me) *will complete it until the day of Jesus Christ."*

7. *"I will multiply the fruit of your trees.'* – Ezekiel 36:30 NKJV. Our lives will bear fruit for the Kingdom of God as we follow His lead, heed His warnings, and live in godly attitude and action.

God is about the business of rebuilding. Read the rest of Ezekiel 36 to see that it is so. It is no surprise that what follows this chapter is Ezekiel's vision of the dry bones coming to life. (Ezekiel

37) Folks, bones are rattling! God is opening up graves. His Spirit is giving us life. An army is standing ready. It is HIS work. Live it as He raises up His Intentional Remnant!

Endnotes

1 Platt, David, "Radical: Taking Back Your Faith From the American Dream," (Sisters, OR: Multnomah Books, 2010), pp. 169-171.

2 Brogden, Dick, "Live Dead Joy," My Healthy Church, Springfield, MO, 2014.

3 A Kempis, Thomas, "The Imitation of Christ," translated by Ronald Knox and Michael Oakley (New York: Sheed and Ward, 1959), pp. 76-77

4 Brogden, Dick, "Live Dead Joy," My Healthy Church, Springfield, MO, 2014, November 26.

5 Hughes, Selwyn, "Every Day With Jesus," February 24, 2019.

6 Hughes, Selwyn, "Every Day With Jesus," February 23, 2019.

7 Peterson, Eugene, "Leap Over A Wall," HarperOne, NY, NY, 1998, p. 185.

8 Tripp, Paul David, "New Morning Mercies," Crossway, Wheaton, IL, 2014, May 29th entry.

9 Rogers, Adrian, "Love Worth Living," February 13, 2019, online.

10 Chesterton, G.K., Goodreads, online.

11 Cloud, Henry Dr., AZQuotes, online.

12 Lewis, C.S., meetville.com, Pinterest, online.

13 Ball, Jesse, *GQ Magazine*, "Twenty-One Books You Don't Have To Read," April 19, 2018,

14 Ortberg, John, BrainyQuote.com, online.

15 Brogden, Dick, "Live Dead Joy: 365 Days of Living and Dying with Jesus," My Healthy Church, Springfield, MO., 2013.

16 Zacharias, Ravi, *Decision Magazine*, BGEA, January, 2018, page 13.

17 Lewis, C.S., Goodreads, online.

18 Einstein, Albert, Goodreads, online.

19 Tripp, Paul David, "New Morning Mercies," Crossway, Wheaton, IL., 2014, June 22 entry.

[20] Tozer, A.W., Goodreads, online.

[21] Ten, Boom, Corrie, Goodreads online.

[22] Harnick, Sheldon, "Do You Love Me?", *Fiddler on the Roof*, Warner Bros. Publications, Los Angeles, CA., 1993, pages 42-45.

[23] Browning, Elizabeth Barrett, "Aurora Leigh," C.S. Francis & Co., NY, NY, 1857.

[24] Falwell, Jonathan, *Decision Magazine*, January, 2019, pp. 26-27.

[25] Tozer, A.W., "Pathways Into Revival," WordPress.com.

[26] Tripp, David Paul, "New Morning Mercies," Crossway, Wheaton, IL, 2014, April 2nd entry.

[27] Tripp, David Paul, Ibid.

[28] Falwell, Jonathan, Ibid.

[29] Zacharias, Ravi, Source Unknown.

[30] VanPay, John, "Marathon Faith," Regnery Faith, Washington, D.C., 2018, page 43.

[31] Brogden, Dick, "Live Dead Joy: 365 Days of Living and Dying With Jesus," My Healthy Church, Springfield, MO., 2013.

[32] Peterson, Eugene, "Leap Over A Wall," HarperCollins, HarperOne, NY, NY, 1997, page 144.

[33] Ibid., page 150.

[34] Whyte, Alexander, "Bible Characters", Edinburgh: Oliphant, Anderson and Ferrier, 1900, page 172.

[35] Lewis, C.S., "The Lion, the Witch and the Wardrobe," HarperCollins, NY, NY, 2000

[36] Chesterton, Gilbert K., brainyquote.com online

[37] Morin, Amy, *Psychology Today*, "Seven Scientifically Proven Benefits of Gratitude, April 3, 2015.

[38] Churchill, Winston, quotefancy.com online.

[39] Perlman, Itzhak, www.azquotes.com online.

[40] Story first appeared in Kaplan, Janice, "The Gratitude Diaries", Dutton, Imprint of Penguin-Random House LLC, NY, NY, 2015, pages 160-163.

[41] Lewis, C. S., libquotes.com online

[42] Moore, Carolyn Rev., "Good News Magazine," Volume 5, Issue 4, August, 2018.

[43] Cloud, Dr. Henry, "Necessary Endings," HarperCollins Publishers, NY, NY, 2010.

[44] Tripp, Paul David, "New Morning Mercies," Crossway, Wheaton, IL, 2014, February 14.

[45] Brogden, Dick, "Live Dead Joy," My Healthy Church, Springfield, MO, 2014,

[46] Stott, John R. W., Goodreads online.

[47] Luther, Martin, Quotefancy online.

[48] Ball, Jesse, *GQ Magazine*, "21 Books You Don't Have To Read," April 19, 2018.

[49] Barna, George, "The State of the Bible Study," 2017.

[50] Ortberg, John, Quotefancy online

[51] Tiberius, Brainyquote online

[52] Tozer, A.W., "The Counselor: Straight Talk About the Holy Spirit," Wing Spread Publications, Camp Hill, PA, 1993, 2009, pp. 112-113.

[53] Potts, Lauren, BBC News, 7 January, 2016.

[54] Statistics provided by The Fuller Institute, George Barna, Lifeway, Schaeffer Institute of Leadership Development, and Pastoral Care Inc, 2020.

[55] Brogden, Dick, "Live Dead Joy," Ibid.

[56] Greenslade, Philip, Every Day With Jesus Devotional

[57] Rogers, Adrian, "Love Worth Finding," Devotional online, January 19, 2018.

[58] Hughes, Selwyn, "Every Day With Jesus" Devotional

[59] Covenant Eyes, Owosso, MI, info@covenanteyes.com

[60] Hughes, Selwyn, "Everyday With Jesus," February 13, 2019.

[61] Rogers, Adrian, "Love Worth Finding" Devotional, Online.

[62] Zacharias, Ravi, "Is Truth Dead?", Decision Magazine, January, 2018, page 13.

63 Brogden, Dick, "Live Dead Joy: 365 Days of Living and Dying with Jesus," My Healthy Church, Springfield, MO., October 17, 2014.

64 Wilson, Jared C., "Pastor As Shepherd" in "Portraits of A Pastor," Jason Allen, General Editor, Moody Press, Chicago, IL., 2017, page 19.

65 Tozer, A.W., Goodreads, Online.

66 Mohler, R. Albert Jr., Decision Magazine, June, 2019, in an article by Jerry Pierce, "The Lie of Progressive Christianity", pages 10-11.

67 MacDonald, George, azquotes.com online

68 Brogden, Dick, "Live Dead Joy", My Healthy Church, Springfield, MO, 2014, March 27, "Death Gate."

69 Zacharias, Ravi, "Has Christianity Failed You?", Zondervan, Grand Rapids, MI, 2010, page 110.

70 Lewis, C.S., "The Problem of Pain," Collins, HarperCollins, NY, NY, 2012, Chapter Six – "Human Pain."

71 Brother Lawrence, "The Practice of the Presence of God," Baker Publishing Group, Ada , MI, 1989.

72 Rogers, Adrian, "Love Worth Finding" Devotional, Online.

73 Einstein, Albert, Goodreads Online.

74 National Right To Life, nrlc.org, Online

75 Tripp, Paul David, "New Morning Mercies, Crossway, Wheaton, IL, 2014, ," February 14 Devotion.

76 Ibid.

77 Chan, Melissa, *Time Magazine*, August, 2019.

78 The Nelson A. Rockefeller Institute of Government, "Mass Shooting Fact Sheet," Albany, NY, 2017.

79 Ibid.

80 Statista Research Department, Facts online.

81 AFA Journal, April, 2020, "Issues At Hand" Newsbrief, from lifesitenews.com, 1/16/20.

82 Mother Teresa, "What Christians Want To Know," Christian Quotes on Abortion, Online.

83 Piper, John, Ibid.

84 Zacharias, Ravi, "Has Christianity Failed You?", Zondervan, Grand Rapids, MI, 2010, page 31.

85 Gandhi, Mahatma, Source Unknown.

86 Baxter, Richard, Christianquotes.info, Online.

87 Aesop, "The Bundle of Sticks," in "The Book of Virtues," compiled by William J. Bennett, Simon and Schuster, NYT, NY, 1993, page 388.

88 Zacharias, Ravi, Christian Quotes Online.

89 Tripp, Paul David, "New Morning Mercies," Crossway, Wheaton, IL, 2014, June 22 Devotion.

90 Tozer, A.W., "The Pursuit of God," Bethany House, Bloomington, MN, 2013, and Our Daily Bread, July 23, 1999.

91 Lucado, Max, Wisefamousquotes.com, Online.

92 Wagner, Jane, "The Search For Signs of Intelligent Life in the Universe," Thriftbooks.com, Online.

93 Schaeffer, Francis, "No Little People," InterVarsity Press, 1974, Crossway, Wheaton, IL., 2003.

94 Yancey, Phillip, "The Jesus I Never Knew," Zondervan, Grand Rapids, MI, 2002.

95 Francis, Samuel Trevor, altered; adapted by Tom Fettke, The Hymnal For Worship and Celebration, Word Music, Waco, TX, 1986, page 212.

96 Jones, Lewis E., Ibid., page 191.

97 Anderson, Jared, writer. Album: "Breathe In," Integrity Music, David C. Cook, Colorado Springs, CO.

98 Written by Kristin Stanfill, Brett Younker, Brooks, Ligertwood, Scott Ligertwood, Sixsteps Music, Capitol, CMGPublishing.com, 2018.

99 Hymnal.net

100 Lewis, C.S., ZA Quotes, Online.

101 Original source – Rhonda Skipper, Loch Lynn Church of God, Oakland, MD.

[102] Peterson, Eugene, "Run With the Horses," InterVarsity Press, Downers Grove, IL, 1983, page 18.

Made in the USA
Middletown, DE
01 September 2020